I0762145

LOUISE NEVELSON

LOUISE NEVELSON

DIE POESIE DES SUCHENS
THE POETRY OF SEARCHING

Museum
Wiesbaden

HIRMER

INHALT
CONTENTS

VORWORT

Louise Nevelson (1899–1988) gehört zu den wichtigsten Bildhauerinnen der US-amerikanischen Kunstszene des 20. Jahrhunderts. Mit ihren monumentalen Assemblagen prägte sie die Entwicklung des Abstrakten Expressionismus ab Mitte der 1950er-Jahre maßgeblich und gilt als Wegbereiterin der Installationskunst. Durch ihre Teilnahme an der Biennale in Venedig (1962) sowie der Documenta in Kassel (1964 und 1968) fand sie auch international große Anerkennung.

Neben den Assemblagen schuf Nevelson auch ein umfangreiches Œuvre an Collagen. Die ältesten datieren aus dem Jahr 1953, die jüngsten entstanden zwei Jahre vor dem Tod der Künstlerin 1988. Zeitlebens stellte sie nur sehr wenige dieser Arbeiten aus. Bis heute hat dieser Werkkomplex nicht die Beachtung gefunden, die ihm gebührt. Daher rückt die vorliegende Ausstellung die Collagen in den Mittelpunkt.

Ob wandfüllende Reliefs, freistehende Skulpturen oder kleinformatige Collagen: Nevelson verwendete für ihre Werke Fundstücke, die sie auf Streifzügen durch New York aufspürte. Diese für sie grundlegende Arbeitsweise lässt sich aus heutiger Sicht als ein Prozess des Upcyclings beschreiben. Nevelson häufte einen immensen Fundus an *objets trouvés* an. Aus ihnen schuf sie einzigartige Kunstwerke, denen eine Poesie des Suchens innewohnt. Eine zweifache sogar: zum einen diejenige des aufmerksamen Sondierens all des achtlos Weggeworfenen in den Straßen der Metropole. Zum anderen diejenige des gestalterischen Zusammenfügens der Fundstücke zu konkreten Werken. Es lohnt sich, dieser Poesie des Suchens auch heute in Nevelsons Werken nachzuspüren.

Es ist sechs Jahre her, dass mir Nevelsons Collagen eindrücklich auffielen. Die in Mailand ansässige Galerie Gió Marconi zeigte damals einige Arbeiten im Rahmen der Gruppenausstellung *I campi magnetici*. 2022 präsentierte sie dann mit *OUT OF ORDER* eine Einzelausstellung zu den Collagen dieser Künstlerin. Es ist mir eine besondere Freude, dass Valerie Ucke – Kuratorin für Moderne und Gegenwart am Museum Wiesbaden – meine Begeisterung für diese Werkgruppe teilt und sie zum Zentrum ihrer Ausstellung gemacht hat.

Das Museum Wiesbaden ist der richtige Ort für eine Schau zu Louise Nevelson. Diese Künstlerin war 1990 Teil der epochalen Ausstellung *Künstlerinnen des 20. Jahrhunderts* in unserem Haus. Im begleitenden Katalog hieß es: »Louise Nevelson – in den sechziger Jahren ein Star in der New Yorker Szene!« Es ist ein Anliegen von Valerie Ucke, Künstlerinnen jener wegweisenden Ausstellung neu zu entdecken, aus anderen Perspektiven zu betrachten und erneut zu Ehren kommen zu lassen.

PREFACE

Louise Nevelson (1899–1988) is one of the most important American women sculptors of the twentieth century. With her monumental assemblages, she had a decisive influence on the development of Abstract Expressionism from the mid-1950s onward and is considered a pioneer of installation art. Nevelson gained international recognition through her participation in the Venice Biennale (1962) and the documenta in Kassel (1964 and 1968).

In addition to her assemblages, Nevelson created an extensive oeuvre of collages. The oldest date from 1953, and the most recent were made two years before her death in 1988. Throughout her life, she exhibited very few of these works. This body of work has not yet received the attention it deserves. The present exhibition therefore focuses on these collages.

Whether wall-filling reliefs, freestanding sculptures, or small-format collages, Nevelson used found objects that she discovered on her forays through New York City. From today's perspective, this working method can be described as upcycling. Nevelson amassed an immense collection of *objets trouvés*. From these, she created unique works of art imbued with a poetry of searching. A twofold poetry, in fact: on the one hand, of attentively probing all that had been carelessly discarded on the streets of the metropolis, and on the other, of creatively assembling the found objects into concrete works. It is worthwhile to trace this poetry of searching in Nevelson's works today.

Six years have passed since Nevelson's collages first caught my eye. At that time, Gió Marconi Gallery in Milan was showing some of her works as part of the group exhibition *I campi magnetici* (The Magnetic Fields). In 2022, the gallery then presented *OUT OF ORDER*, a solo exhibition of the artist's collages. I am particularly pleased that Valerie Ucke, curator of modern and contemporary art at the Museum Wiesbaden, shares my enthusiasm for this group of works and has chosen them as the focus of her exhibition.

The Museum Wiesbaden is the ideal venue for an exhibition dedicated to Louise Nevelson. This artist was featured in the seminal exhibition *Women Artists of the 20th Century* at our museum in 1990. The accompanying catalogue stated: »Louise Nevelson – a star of the New York scene in the 1960s!« Valerie Ucke is eager to revisit the women artists of that groundbreaking exhibition, view them from new perspectives, and honor them once again.

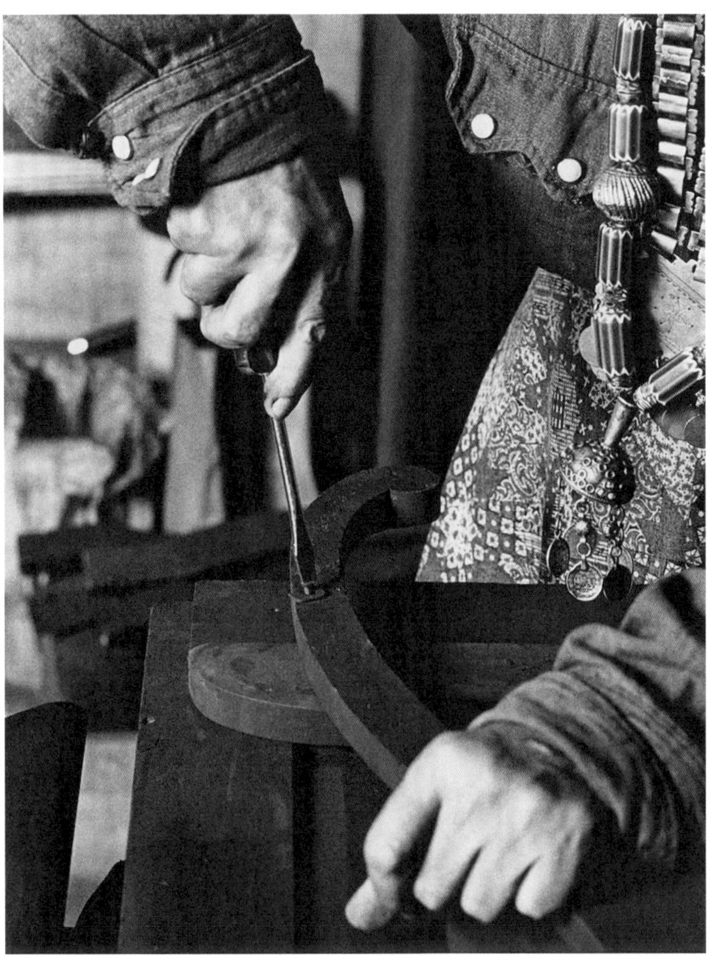

1 Louise Nevelson beim Verschrauben einer Assemblage
Louise Nevelson screwing together an assemblage, Photo: Lewis Brown, Archives of American Art

In fünf Sektionen zeigen wir die Collagen im Dialog mit den großformatigen, skulpturalen Wandreliefs und Skulpturen. Die Werke sind nicht chronologisch angeordnet, sondern anhand ihrer technischen, materiellen und visuellen Merkmale und Ähnlichkeiten gruppiert. Leitend war dabei die Frage danach, welche Bedeutung dem Suchen und Finden im Werkprozess Nevelsons zukommt. Den Ansatz einer Kategorisierung verfolgte bereits der Kunsthistoriker Yuval Etgar in einem großangelegten Forschungsprojekt in Verbindung mit der Mailänder Galerieausstellung zu Nevelsons Collagen. In seinem Essay im vorliegenden Katalog legt er die Kriterien seiner Einteilung ihres Schaffens erneut dar, die eine wichtige Inspirationsquelle für unsere Ausstellung darstellt. Die Kuratorin Anne Horvath vom Centre Pompidou-Metz konnten wir ebenfalls für einen Katalogbeitrag gewinnen. Er behandelt Nevelsons Verhältnis zu Körperlichkeit und Raum. Wir freuen uns, dass ab Januar 2026 parallel zu unserer Ausstellung eine umfangreiche Retrospektive in Metz stattfindet: *Louise Nevelson – Mrs. N's Palace*. Dort wird insbesondere der Frage nachgegangen, welchen Einfluss die performative Kunst auf Nevelsons Arbeit hatte. In einem weiteren Essay begibt sich Valerie Ucke auf die Spur der Poesie des Suchens in Nevelsons Werk. Allen Autorinnen und Autoren sowie dem Hirmer Verlag danke ich für ihr Engagement für den vorliegenden Band, ebenso wie Uta Kopp und Eva-Maria Bolz, in deren Händen die Gestaltung lag.

In five chapters, we present the collages in dialogue with Nevelson's large-format wall reliefs and sculptures. Rather than arranging the works chronologically, we grouped them according to their technical, material, and visual characteristics and similarities. Our guiding theme was the significance of searching and finding in Nevelson's creative process. Art historian Yuval Etgar had already undertaken a major research project to categorize Nevelson's collages, conducted in conjunction with the Milan gallery exhibition. In his essay in this catalogue, Etgar once again sets out the criteria for his classification of Nevelson's work, which is an important source of inspiration for our exhibition. We were also able to secure an essay from Anne Horvath, curator at the Centre Pompidou-Metz, in which she discusses Nevelson's relationship to physicality and space. We are delighted that, starting in January 2026, an extensive retrospective will take place in Metz in parallel with our exhibition: *Louise Nevelson – Mrs. N's Palace*. There, the influence of performance art on Nevelson's work will be a central focus of inquiry. In another essay, Valerie Ucke traces the poetry of searching in Nevelson's work. I would like to thank all the authors, as well as Hirmer Publishers, for their commitment to this volume. Thanks also to Uta Kopp and Eva-Maria Bolz, who were responsible for the design of this publication.

My heartfelt thanks go first and foremost to Valerie Ucke. With this exhibition and catalogue, she offers a new perspective on Louise Nevelson's oeuvre. This update is all the more important given that the last comprehensive exhibition of Nevelson's work in Germany took place half a century ago, in 1974, at the Neue Nationalgalerie in Berlin. With her expertise in modern and contemporary art, Valerie Ucke has created an exhibition that allows us to share in Nevelson's poetry of searching. At the same time, this brilliant show concludes the series of anniversary exhibitions with which the art department is celebrating the 200th anniversary of the Museum Wiesbaden.

This exhibition would not have been possible without generous financial support from various sources. I would like to thank the Art Mentor Foundation Lucerne, in particular its president, Christoph Reinhardt, for their once again truly fundamental support. We are also grateful to the Fondazione Marconi and the Rudolf-August Oetker-Stiftung, as well as the Friends of the Museum Wiesbaden, for their support. I would also like to express my sincere gratitude to Esther Quiroga and Gió Marconi, not least for their collegial provision and mediation of loans. Our thanks also go to the Museum Ludwig in Cologne and to various private lenders. Special thanks go to Maria Nevelson and the Louise Nevelson Foundation for initiating a four-year celebration of the artist's 125th birthday. We would also like to thank *Monopol* and *hr2 Kultur* for their media partnerships. Finally, I would like to thank Adina and Martin Rieckmann, particularly for the joint discovery tours that led us to Louise Nevelson.

2 Die Künstlerin bei der Eröffnung ihrer Ausstellung im Studio Marconi, Mailand 1973
The artist at the opening of her exhibition at Studio Marconi, Milan, 1973, Photo: Enrico Cattaneo, Fondazione Marconi, Milan

Mein herzlicher Dank gilt zuallererst Valerie Ucke. Sie gewährt mit Ausstellung und Katalog einen neuen Blick auf das Œuvre Louise Nevelsons. Diese Aktualisierung ist umso wichtiger, als die letzte umfassende Ausstellung dieser Künstlerin in Deutschland schon ein halbes Jahrhundert zurückliegt: Sie fand 1974 in der Neuen Nationalgalerie in Berlin statt. Valerie Ucke hat mit ihrer Expertise für die Kunst der Moderne und Gegenwart eine Ausstellung geschaffen, in der wir an Nevelsons Poesie des Suchens teilhaben dürfen. Zugleich beschließt sie für die Kunstabteilung mit dieser fulminanten Schau den Reigen der Jubiläumsausstellungen, mit dem wir das 200-jährige Bestehen des Museums Wiesbaden feiern.

Diese Ausstellung wäre nicht möglich geworden ohne die großzügige finanzielle Unterstützung von verschiedenen Seiten. Ich danke der Art Mentor Foundation Lucerne, namentlich ihrem Präsidenten Christoph Reinhardt, für die wieder einmal im wahrsten Sinne des Wortes Grund legende Förderung. Auch der Fondazione Marconi und der Rudolf-August Oetker-Stiftung wissen wir uns sehr dankbar verbunden für die gewährte Unterstützung, ebenso dem Verein der Freunde des Museums Wiesbaden. Darüber hinaus möchte ich Esther Quiroga und Gió Marconi einen herzlichen Dank zurufen, nicht zuletzt für die kollegiale Bereitstellung und Vermittlung von Leihgaben. Ebenso gilt unser Dank dem Museum Ludwig in Köln sowie privaten Leihgeberinnen und Leihgebern. Einen besonderen Dank möchten wir Maria Nevelson und der Louise Nevelson Foundation aussprechen, die zu einer vierjährigen Feier anlässlich des 125. Geburtstags der Künstlerin aufgerufen haben. *Monopol* und *hr2 Kultur* danken wir für die Medienpartnerschaften. Gerne schließe ich in meinen Dank überdies Adina und Martin Rieckmann mit ein für die gemeinsamen Entdeckungstouren, die uns auch zu Louise Nevelson geführt haben.

Selbstverständlich ist es mir ein Bedürfnis, auch allen an Ausstellung und Katalog Beteiligten meinen aufrichtigen Dank ausdrücken, intern und extern. Das ganze Museumsteam – quer durch alle Abteilungen – hat in diesem ohnehin schon vollgepackten Jubiläumsjahr auch diese Ausstellung mit großer Professionalität, Kollegialität und Effizienz gestemmt. Dafür gebührt allen Beteiligten große Anerkennung.

Den Besucherinnen und Besuchern der Ausstellung wünsche ich, auch im Namen der Kuratorin Valerie Ucke, viele Momente der Inspiration beim Nachspüren der Poesie des Suchens. Selbstredend mögen diese auch alle Leserinnen und Lesern des Katalogs erfahren.

Andreas Henning
Direktor

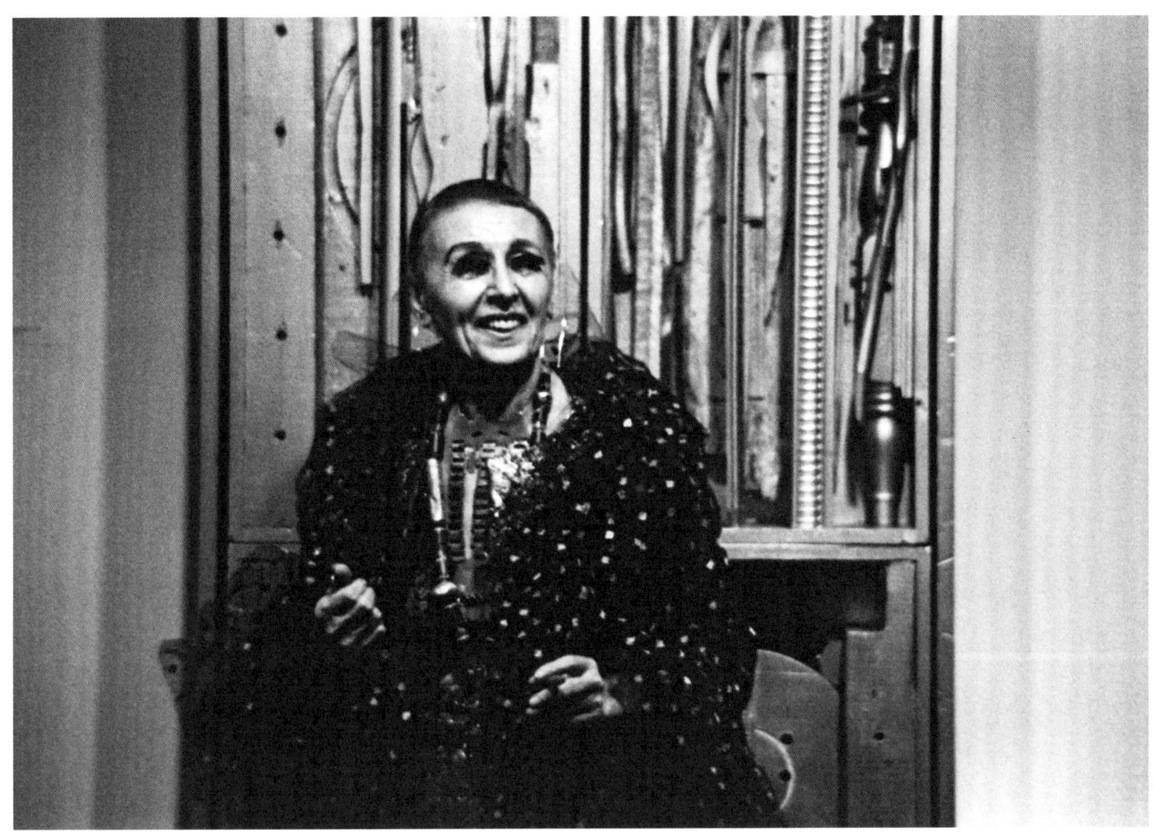

I would of course also like to express my sincere gratitude to everyone involved in the exhibition and catalogue, both internally and externally. The entire museum team – across all departments – has worked with great professionalism, collegiality, and efficiency to make this exhibition a reality in what is already a busy anniversary year. For this, all those involved deserve great recognition.

On behalf of the curator, Valerie Ucke, I wish visitors to the exhibition many moments of inspiration as they explore the poetry of searching. Naturally, I hope that all readers of the catalogue will experience this as well.

Andreas Henning
Director

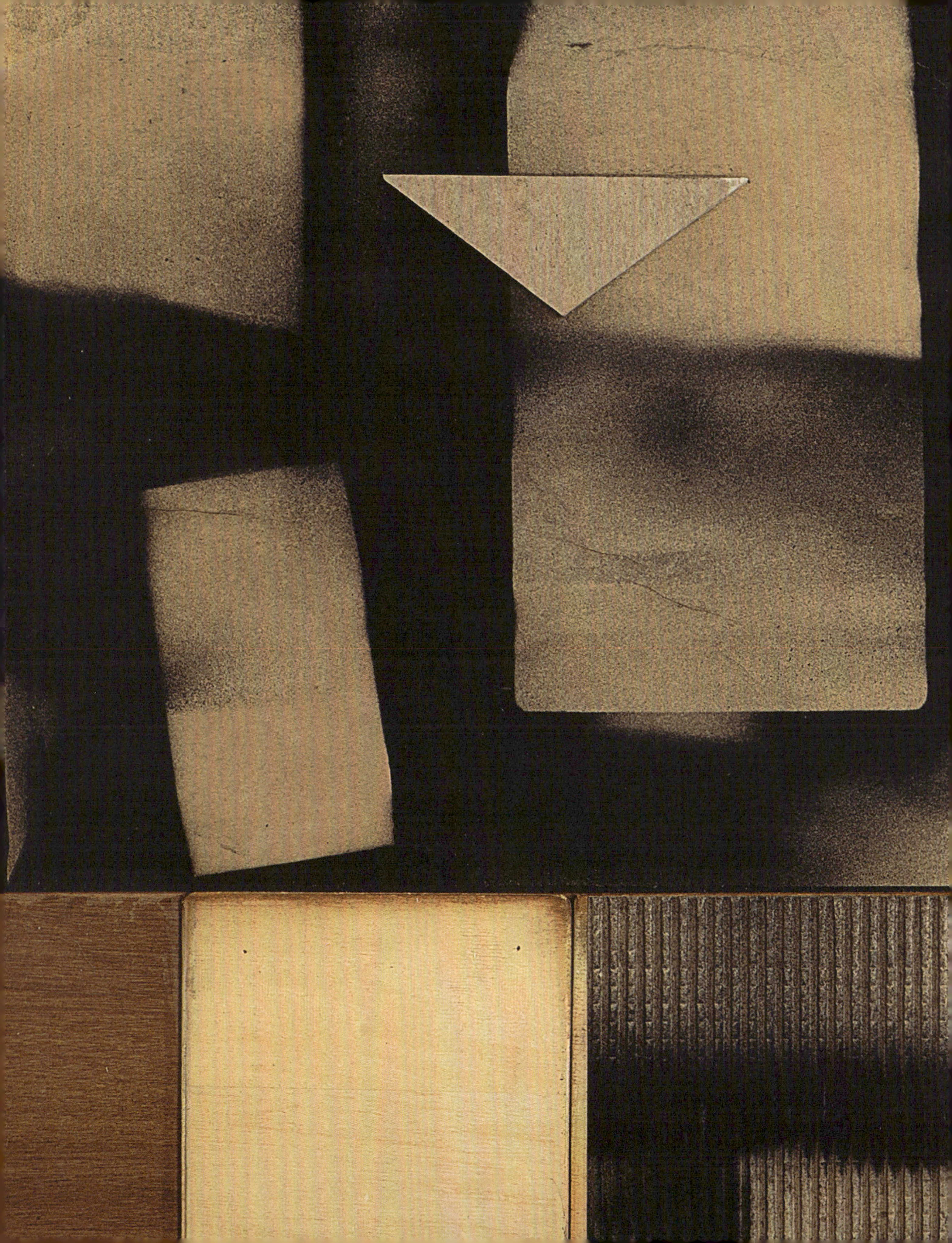

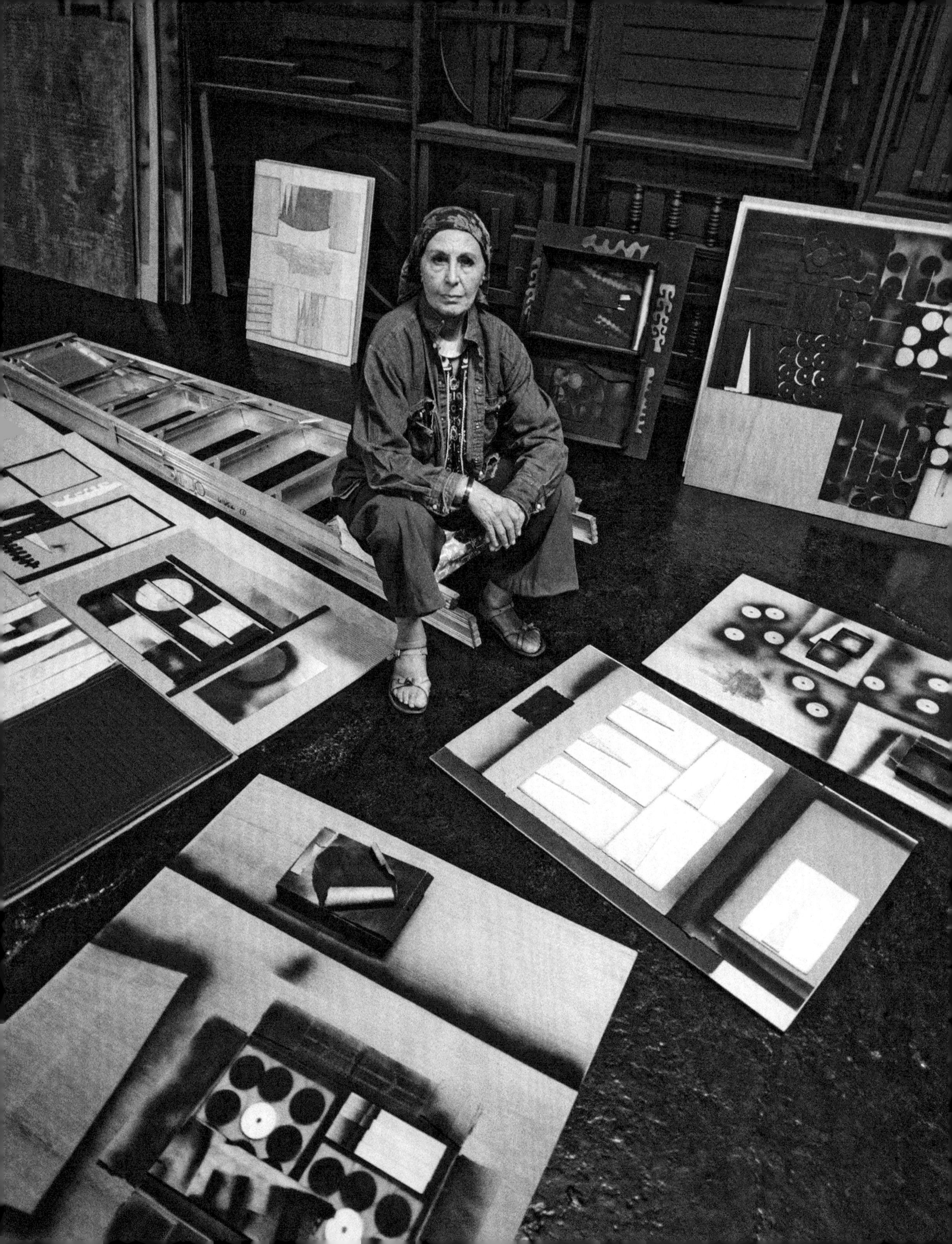

DIE POESIE DES SUCHENS

VALERIE UCKE

THE POETRY OF SEARCHING

»Wenn ich arbeite, bin ich nicht auf der Suche nach Perfektion. Ich suche nach dem Leben.«

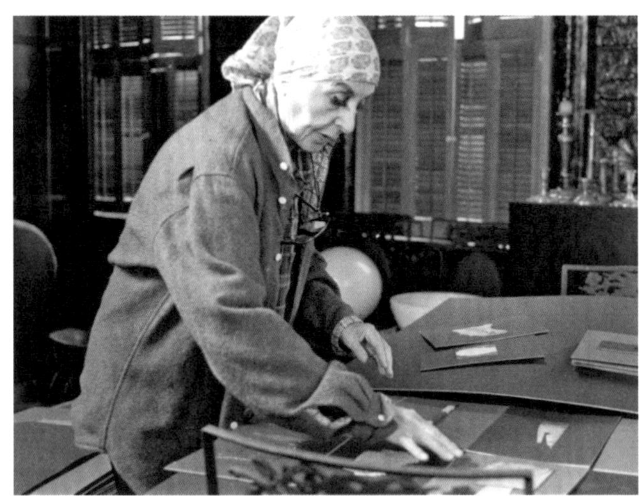

Die Poesie des Suchens

Wir suchen. Immer. So ist es auch in der Kunst: eine ständige Suche nach Formen, nach dem richtigen Material, nach Ausdruck. Louise Nevelsons Collagen sind stille Zeugen einer solchen Suche – einer, die nicht zielgerichtet ist, sondern tastend, lauschend, sammelnd. Ihre Kunst entsteht aus dem Fragment, aus dem, was scheinbar übriggeblieben ist. Holzstücke, Alltagsmaterialien oder Überreste des künstlerischen Prozesses, gefundene Objekte – von der Welt ausrangiert, von Nevelson wiederbelebt.

In der Ausstellung *Die Poesie des Suchens*, die zahlreiche collagierte Arbeiten Nevelsons präsentiert, begegnen wir einer Künstlerin, die mit dem Blick einer Bildhauerin denkt und mit der Sensibilität einer Poetin formt. Die Suche ist in ihrem Werk eine physische und zugleich eine geistige Bewegung: ein Experimentieren mit Struktur, Rhythmus, Material und Kontrast. Es ist das ständige Abwägen zwischen dem, was gewesen ist, und dem, was daraus werden kann.

Nichts scheint zufällig, und doch bleibt vieles offen. Ihre Kompositionen wirken wie gefundene Gedichte, wie Material gewordene Verse, in denen sich Ordnung und Chaos berühren, in denen das Schweigen zwischen den Formen ebenso sprechend ist wie die Formen selbst.

Die Poesie des Suchens weist zum einen auf Nevelsons schöpferische Haltung: eine hohe Aufmerksamkeit für das Unsichtbare im Sichtbaren, für das Potenzial des Vergessenen, für die stille Würde des Materials. Zum anderen deutet der Titel ihr tiefgehendes Interesse am Entdecken und dem daraus hervorgehenden kreativen Prozess an, aus Alltagsmaterialien und künstlerischen Überresten etwas Neues zu schaffen. »Wenn ich arbeite, bin ich nicht auf der Suche nach Perfektion. Ich suche nach dem Leben.«[1] Ihre Arbeiten, sowohl im kleinen wie auch im großen Format, zeugen von einer anhaltenden Suche, die mit dem Sammeln von Dingen beginnt und mit der Formwerdung durch Sortieren, Zusammenstellen, Collagieren vorerst einen Abschluss findet.[2]

Collagen

Als eine der wichtigen Errungenschaften der Avantgarde gilt die Collage. Aber wie ist eine Collage zu definieren, und wie unterscheidet sie sich von der ebenso häufig verwendeten Assemblage? Als künstlerische Technik entstand die Collage Anfang des 20. Jahrhunderts und war eng mit der Entwicklung des Kubismus verbunden. Künstler wie Pablo Picasso und Georges Braque experimentierten um 1912 erstmals damit, Alltagsmaterialien wie Zeitungsausschnitte oder Tapetenreste in ihre Gemälde zu integrieren. Dadurch brachen sie mit der traditionellen Malerei und erweiterten die Vorstellung von Bildgestaltung, Dimension und Wirklichkeit im Kunstwerk.

3 Louise Nevelson bei der Arbeit an ihren Collagen
Louise Nevelson working on her collages, Photo: Pedro E. Guerrero,

»When I work I'm not searching for perfection. I'm searching for life.«

The Poetry of Searching

We search. Always. The same is true in art: a constant search for forms, the right material, and expression. Louise Nevelson's collages are silent witnesses to such a search – one that is not goal-oriented, but rather tentative, listening, collecting. Her art emerges from fragments, from what appears to be left over: pieces of wood, everyday materials, remnants of the artistic process, or found objects – discarded by the world, revived by Nevelson.

In the exhibition *The Poetry of Searching,* which features numerous collaged works by Nevelson, we encounter an artist who thinks with the eye of a sculptor and forms with the sensitivity of a poet. In her work, the search is both a physical and a mental action: an experimentation with structure, rhythm, material, and contrast. It is a constant balancing act between what has been and what can become.

Nothing seems random, yet much remains open. Her compositions seem like found poems – verses that have taken on a physical form, in which order and chaos touch each other, and the silence between the forms is as eloquent as the forms themselves.

On the one hand, *The Poetry of Searching* points to Nevelson's creative attitude: a keen awareness of the invisible in the visible, the potential of the forgotten, the quiet dignity of the material. On the other hand, the title hints at her deep interest in discovery and the creative process that emerges from it, creating something new from everyday materials and artistic remnants.

»When I work, I'm not searching for perfection. I'm searching for life.«[1] Her works, both small and large in format, testify to an ongoing search that begins with the collection of objects and finds its initial conclusion in the creation of form through sorting, assembling, and collaging.[2]

Collages

The collage technique is considered one of the important achievements of the avant-garde. But what is a collage, and how does it differ from the equally frequently used technique of assemblage? The collage emerged in the early twentieth century and was closely linked to the development of Cubism. Around 1912, Pablo Picasso and Georges Braque first experimented with incorporating everyday materials, such as newspaper clippings and wallpaper remnants, into their paintings. In doing so, they broke with traditional painting and expanded the concepts of image design, dimension, and reality in art.

The collage opened up new ways of representing reality, time, and space simultaneously – it became the medium of a modern, fragmented, and multi-perspective perception of the world. The term collage (from the French *coller,* meaning »to glue«, »to stick together«) refers to an artistic technique in which materials such as paper, fabric, photographs, or other flat found objects are glued onto a surface and assembled into a new image. Typically two-dimensional, collages are characterized by the juxtaposition or superimposition of different elements that form new visual or contextual connections. An assemblage, on the other hand, is a three-dimensional composition consisting of *objets trouvés* (found objects) or various materials joined, mounted, or arranged together in some way. In the work of Louise Nevelson and other artists, the boundary between collage and assemblage is fluid.

Collage played a central role in various art movements, including Dada, Surrealism, and Pop Art. Artists such as Hannah Höch, Kurt Schwitters, and Robert Rauschenberg used the technique to reflect on social, political, and cultural issues.

4 Sortieren und Anordnen. Louise Nevelson in ihrem New Yorker Studio, 1979
Ordering and arranging. Louise Nevelson in her New York studio, 1979, Photo: Brownie Harris

Die Collage eröffnete neue Wege, Wirklichkeit, Zeit und Raum simultan darzustellen – sie wurde zum Medium der modernen, fragmentierten und multiperspektivischen Wahrnehmung der Welt. Collage (frz. *coller* = kleben) bezeichnet eine künstlerische Technik, bei der Materialien wie Papier, Stoff, Fotografien oder andere flache Fundstücke auf eine Fläche aufgeklebt und zu einem neuen Bild zusammengesetzt werden. Meist zweidimensional, zeichnet sich die Collage durch das Nebeneinander oder die Überlagerung unterschiedlicher Elemente aus, die eine neue visuelle oder inhaltliche Verbindung eingehen. Eine Assemblage hingegen ist eine dreidimensionale Komposition, die aus gefundenen Objekten, sogenannten *objets trouvés*, oder verschiedenen Materialien besteht, die zusammengefügt, montiert oder auf andere Weise miteinander arrangiert werden. Bei Louise Nevelson und auch anderen Künstler:innen verläuft die Grenze zwischen Collage und Assemblage fließend.

In verschiedenen Kunstströmungen spielte die Collage eine zentrale Rolle, darunter Dada, Surrealismus und Pop-Art. Künstler:innen wie Hannah Höch, Kurt Schwitters oder Robert Rauschenberg nutzten die Technik, um gesellschaftliche, politische und kulturelle Themen zu reflektieren.

»Meine Art zu denken ist eine Collage.«[3] Mit diesem Ausspruch machte Louise Nevelson deutlich, wie wichtig ihr das Collagieren war, also das Auseinandernehmen und Zusammenfügen, das Umdeuten bestehender Strukturen, das Übereinanderlegen verschiedener Schichten, das Miteinander-in-Beziehung-Setzen verschiedenartiger Fragmente, Dinge, Materialien, Oberflächen und Formen. Das Zitat zeigt auch, dass die ihrer Kunst zugrunde liegende Art des Denkens sich nicht ausschließlich auf die Werkgruppe der Collagen bezog, sondern auf alle Bereiche ihres Lebens Einfluss hatte. Die Art, wie sie sich kleidete, das collagenhafte Zusammenstellen ihres Zuhauses,[4] ihre skulpturalen Assemblagen, die großformatigen Environments, aber auch Nevelsons Blick auf ihre Heimatstadt New York belegen dies: »Wenn eine Stadt über die Jahre entsteht, wird sie ein Collage von Zeit und Raum. [...] New York City ist die größte Collage der Welt.«[5]

Die große, wenn auch nicht konkret bezifferbare Menge an Collagen, die zwischen 1953 und ihrem Todesjahr 1988 entstanden sind, geben Anlass, an eine Art meditativen Prozess in der künstlerischen Erarbeitung zu denken. Wir können uns vorstellen, dass sie regelmäßig, vielleicht täglich, an den Collagen gearbeitet hat. Auch wenn sich die Maße der Collagen unterscheiden, so sind sie doch alle in einem handhabbaren Format gedacht und realisiert und so auch für das Arbeiten ohne die Hilfe von Assistent:innen, außerhalb der riesigen Ateliers, in der häuslichen Umgebung geeignet.[6] Diese Größe, die auf der einen Seite das praktische Arbeiten vereinfachte, mag auf der anderen Seite der Grund dafür gewesen sein, dass diese Werkgruppe selbst während Nevelsons erfolgreichster Jahre sehr geringe, wenn überhaupt Beachtung fand. Lediglich auf einigen wenigen Galerieausstellungen, wie zum Beispiel in der New Yorker Pace Gallery, wurden die Collagen noch zu ihren Lebzeiten gezeigt.[7]

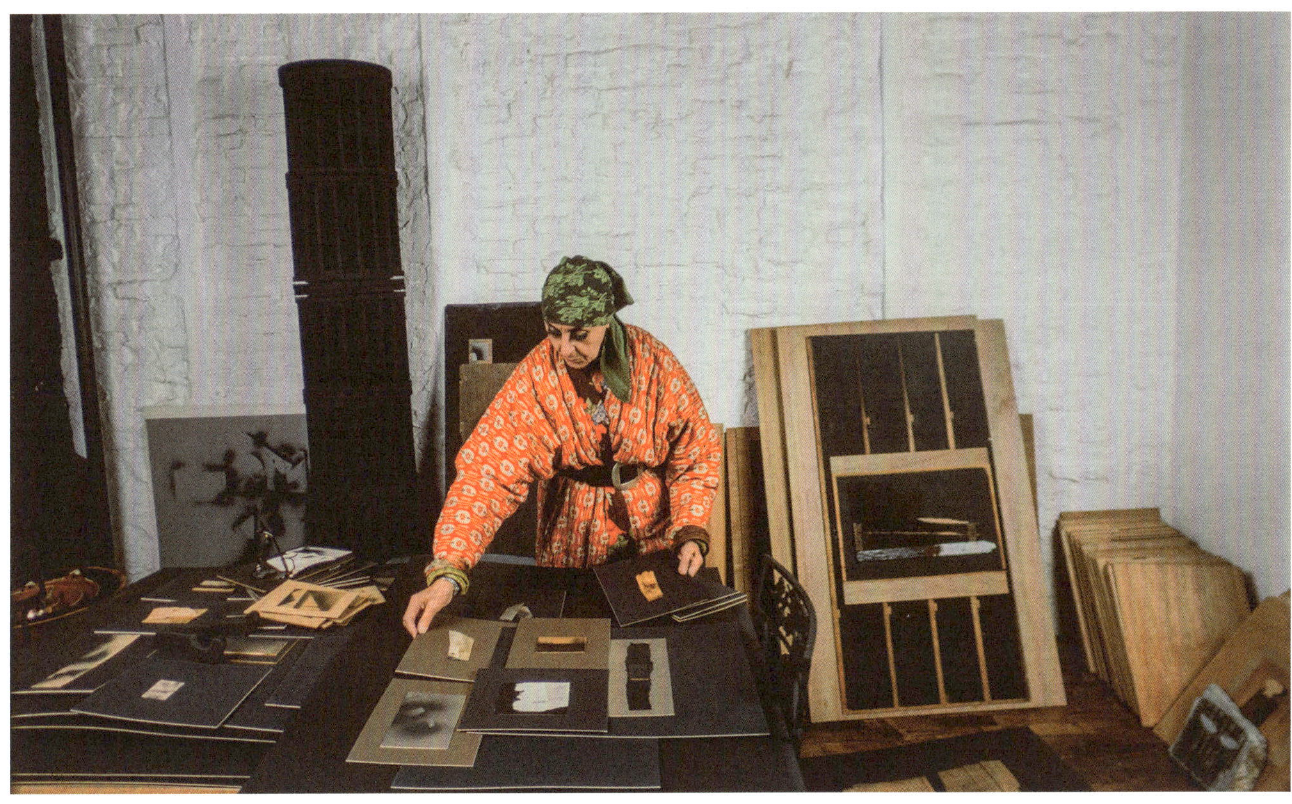

»The way I think is collage.«[3] With this statement, Louise Nevelson made clear how important the act of collaging was to her – taking things apart and putting them back together, reinterpreting existing structures, superimposing different layers, and placing diverse fragments, objects, materials, surfaces, and forms in relation to one another. The quote also shows that the way of thinking underlying her art did not apply exclusively to her collages but influenced all areas of her life. This is evident in the way she dressed, the collage-like arrangement of her home,[4] her sculptural assemblages, her large-scale environments, and Nevelson's view of her hometown, New York: »When a city is built over the years, it becomes a collage in time and space. [...] New York City is the world's greatest collage.«[5]

The large, albeit not precisely quantifiable, number of collages Nevelson created between 1953 and her death in 1988 suggest a kind of meditative process in her artistic development. We can imagine that she worked on the collages regularly, perhaps even daily. Although the collages vary in size, they are all designed and realized in a manageable format, suitable for creation without assistants, outside large studios, and within a domestic environment.[6] This size, which on the one hand simplified practical work, may on the other hand have been the reason why this group of works received very little, if any, attention even during Nevelson's most successful years. Only a few galleries, such as Pace Gallery in New York, exhibited the collages during her lifetime.[7]

Given the trends in the art scene from the 1950s to the 1980s, Nevelson's shift toward large formats seems understandable. Whether we think of Jackson Pollock's action paintings, Barnett Newman's zip paintings, or Frank Stella's striped paintings, Louise Nevelson was surrounded by male artists in the New York art scene who loved and exhibited wall- and room-filling formats and oversized works. She was the only woman to participate in the famous 1959 exhibition *Sixteen Americans* at The Museum of Modern Art in New York, where she presented her first room-sized installation of monochrome white objects ↳ **fig. 5.**

Mit Blick auf die Tendenzen der Kunstszene der 1950er- bis 1980er-Jahre scheint Nevelsons Hinwendung zu Großformaten verständlich. Ganz gleich, ob wir an Jackson Pollocks Action Paintings, Barnett Newmans Zip Paintings oder Frank Stellas Streifenbilder denken: Louise Nevelson war in der New Yorker Kunstszene umgeben von männlichen Künstlern, die das wand- und raumfüllende Format, das Überdimensionierte liebten und ausstellten. Als einzige Frau war Nevelson 1959 an der berühmten Ausstellung *Sixteen Americans* im Museum of Modern Art beteiligt, wo sie erstmals eine gesamte Rauminstallation mit monochrom weißen Objekten präsentierte ↪ **Abb. 5.**

Ob das künstlerische Umfeld und die Tatsache, dass sie als Frau mit den Formaten ihrer männlichen Kollegen mithalten wollte, ausschlaggebend dafür war, die Collagen nicht der Öffentlichkeit zu präsentieren, oder ob sie schlicht nicht gefragt waren, bleibt ungeklärt.

Nevelsons Collagen sind keine Ideenskizzen für die großformatigen Arbeiten. In ihnen fließen verschiedene Aspekte zusammen, die sie deutlich von ihren »großen Schwestern«, den skulpturalen Assemblagen, unterscheiden. Das Gespür für Farbe, Komposition, Stille und Poesie spricht ebenso aus den Collagen wie eine gewisse Rastlosigkeit und der Wunsch zu experimentieren. Und doch geht das Experiment bei den Collagen nicht weiter als der vorgegebene Rahmen – meist die Holzplatte – es erlaubt. Die Suche nach der ausgewogenen Form, der materiellen Begegnung, der interpretierbaren Struktur der einzelnen Elemente erscheint daher immer auch als ein kontrollierter Prozess.

Einige der Werke konzentrieren ihre Formen in der Bildmitte, andere lassen die Materialien bis an die Bildränder vordringen. Häufig ist jedoch der hölzerne Bildgrund nicht bis zum Rand bedeckt und wird somit zum eigenständigen Bildelement. Holz und Sprühfarbe spielen in Nevelsons Arbeiten eine zentrale Rolle – nahezu jedes Werk enthält Elemente dieser Materialien. Besonders in den 1950er-Jahren ist der Einsatz von gesprühter Farbe markant und prägend. Auch Papier findet vielfach Verwendung, oft in unterschiedlichen Zuständen und Bearbeitungsformen. Obwohl sich in zahlreichen Werken farbige Akzente finden – etwa durch die Verwendung von buntem Karton –, dominiert die Farbe Schwarz. Diese bildet einen starken Kontrast zur natürlichen, hellbraunen Oberfläche der Holzplatten, auf denen die Collagen montiert sind. Wiederholt taucht ein kräftiges Orange auf, das als wiederkehrendes Farbzeichen lesbar wird.

Die meisten Arbeiten bleiben innerhalb der Grenzen des Bildträgers, doch in ihrer physischen Tiefe überschreiten sie die Zweidimensionalität. Bei einigen Collagen offenbart ein Blick von der Seite, dass einzelne Elemente aus der Fläche heraustreten und den Betrachtenden entgegenkommen – die *flatness* wird durchbrochen. Trotz dieser räumlichen Wirkung sind die Werke leise, beinahe meditativ. Ihre Kompositionen wirken nicht zufällig, sondern durchdacht und präzise – weniger spontane Skizze als gezieltes Experiment.

Manche Materialien treten in Kontakt miteinander, andere befinden sich nebeneinander, ohne sich zu berühren – ein Wechselspiel zwischen Nähe und Autonomie. Eine vergleichbare Beziehung lässt sich auch zwischen den Collagen und den monochromen Wandarbeiten Nevelsons beobachten, die sich in Formfindung und – trotz ihrer Abstraktheit – Motivik ähneln.

Wie in diesen großformatigen Assemblagen entzieht Nevelson den gefundenen Objekten auch in ihren Collagen ihre ursprüngliche Funktion. Alltagsgegenstände – einst Kochlöffel, Zeitung, Zigarettenverpackung oder Pappkarton – verlieren ihren Kontext und werden zur reinen Form, zum Material der Kunst. Nicht das Einzelteil, sondern das Ganze zählt. Dennoch bleibt der Blick nicht frei von Assoziationen: Bekanntes blitzt auf und fordert zur Interpretation heraus.

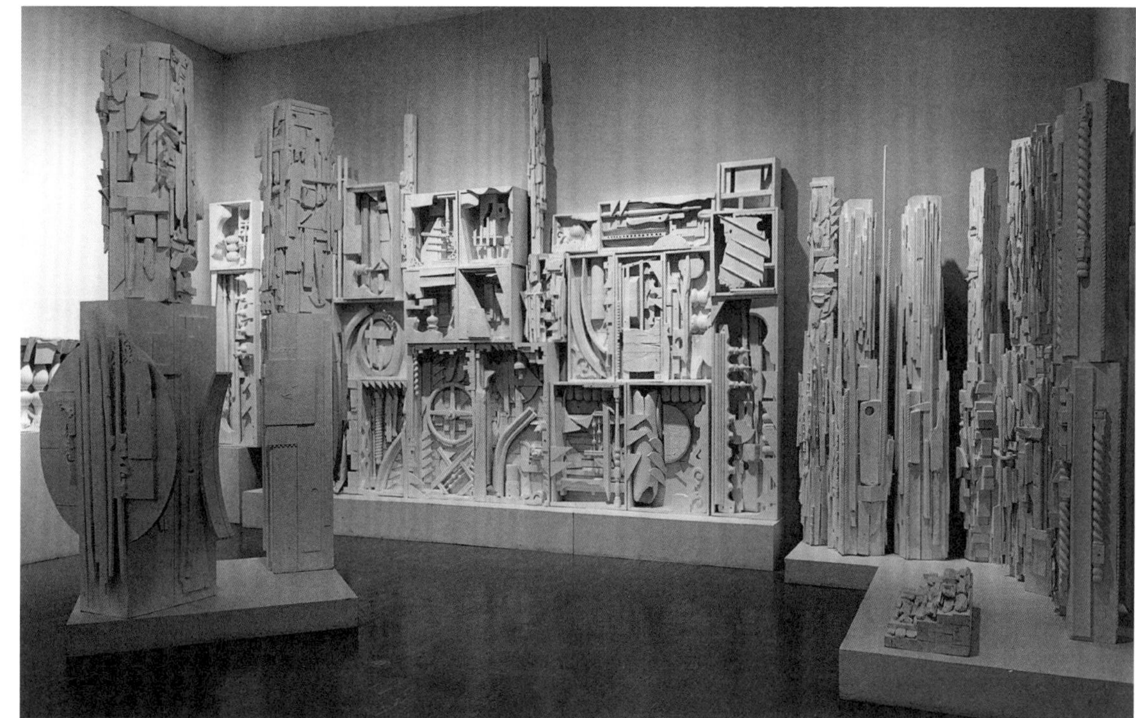

5 Installationsansicht von *Dawn's Wedding Feast* (1959) in der Ausstellung *16 Americans* im Museum of Modern Art, New York, 1959/60
Installation view of Nevelson's work *Dawn's Wedding Feast* (1959) in the exhibition *16 Americans* at the Museum of Modern Art, New York, 1959/60, Photo: Rudy Burckhardt, The Museum of Modern Art, New York/Scala, Florence

It is unclear whether the artistic environment and her desire to compete with her male colleagues using the same formats was the deciding factor in her decision not to present the collages to the public, or if they simply were not in demand.

Nevelson's collages are not conceptual sketches for her large-scale works. They bring together various aspects that clearly distinguish them from their »big sisters«, the sculptural assemblages. The collages reveal the same sensitivity to color, composition, tranquility, and poetry as well as a certain restlessness and desire to experiment. However, experimentation in the collages never goes beyond the given framework, usually a wooden panel. Therefore, the search for balanced form, material juxtapositions, and interpretable structures of the individual elements always appears to be a controlled process.

Some works concentrate their forms in the center of the picture, while others allow the materials to extend to the edges. However, the wooden background is often not covered to the edge, thus becoming an independent pictorial element. Wood and spray paint play central roles in Nevelson's work; almost every piece contains elements of these materials. The use of spray paint is particularly striking and distinctive in the works of the 1950s. Paper is also used extensively, often in different states and forms of processing. While colorful accents can be found in many works – for example, through the use of colorful cardboard – black dominates. This contrasts strongly with the natural, light brown surface of the wooden panels on which the collages are mounted. A strong orange color appears repeatedly, becoming recognizable as a recurring color symbol.

While most of the works remain within the boundaries of the picture support, they transcend two-dimensionality with their physical depth. In some collages, a glance from the side reveals that individual elements emerge from the surface and come toward the viewer – the flatness is broken. Despite this spatial effect, the works are quiet and almost meditative. Their compositions appear well thought out and precise – less spontaneous sketches than deliberate experiments.

Some materials come into contact with each other, while others are placed side by side without touching – an interplay of proximity and autonomy. A similar relationship can be observed between Nevelson's collages and her monochrome wall works, which are similar in their form-finding process and – despite their abstract nature – in their motifs.

»Ich mache Collagen, ich füge die zerbrochene Welt zusammen und schaffe eine neue Harmonie.«

Zur Präsentation im Museum Wiesbaden

Zwei unterschiedliche und doch eng miteinander verbundene Werkgruppen treten in der Ausstellung in einen Dialog: knapp 60 kleinformatige Collagen auf Holz, überwiegend bestückt mit den Materialien Papier, Holz, Sprühfarbe, die in der bisherigen Rezeption ihres Œuvres kaum Beachtung gefunden haben. Demgegenüber sind zwölf mehrheitlich großformatige, überwiegend monochrom besprühte Assemblagen, Reliefs, Skulpturen zu sehen, zusammengesetzt aus unterschiedlichsten zerlegten Möbelstücken, Treibholz und anderen Überresten der Konsumgesellschaft, mit denen Nevelson ab Mitte der 1950er-Jahre große Erfolge feierte.

Obwohl es in den beiden Techniken diverse Gemeinsamkeiten in Materialität und Formfindung gibt, sind die Gegensätze, die Nevelsons Arbeiten eher in die eine oder die andere Kategorie rücken, auf den ersten Blick ersichtlich. Auf der einen Seite die Collagen mit den beschriebenen Besonderheiten. Auf der anderen Seite die Arbeiten in dem größeren Format, der raumeinnehmenden Wirkung, der Dreidimensionalität und der Einheitlichkeit in der Farbe. All das sind Merkmale, die man in diesem Kontext unter dem Begriff der skulpturalen Assemblage zusammenfassen kann. Zusammengesetzt aus einer Vielzahl an gefundenen, zerlegten und recycelten Objekten, meist aus Holz, bilden diese skulpturalen Assemblagen neue Einheiten, in ihrer ursprünglichen Präsentation zum Teil ganze Räume.[8]

Die Ausstellung ist in fünf thematische Sektionen gegliedert, die Nevelsons Collagen in einen dialogischen Zusammenhang mit ihren skulpturalen Assemblagen stellen. Inspiriert von Yuval Etgars Publikation und Ausstellung *Out of Order*, die einen besonderen Fokus auf die materiellen Ausprägungen der Collagen legt, zeigt die Wiesbadener Ausstellung in einem erweiterten Ansatz visuelle, technische und materielle Gemeinsamkeiten sowie Unterschiede zwischen beiden Werkgruppen auf. Dabei wird insbesondere die Bedeutung der Suche – sowohl die physische als auch die gedankliche – für Nevelson und ihre Kunst hervorgehoben, wie oben ausgeführt. Der so entstehende Dialog lädt dazu ein, die Collagen und skulpturalen Assemblagen als eng miteinander verbundene Werkgruppen wahrzunehmen oder neue Bezüge zu entdecken.[9]

1. Gesprühte Poesie

In dieser Sektion wird der Einsatz von Sprühfarbe als künstlerisches Mittel untersucht. Während in den skulpturalen Arbeiten durch monochromes Besprühen der Holzelemente eine Einheitlichkeit erreicht wird und die Individualität der Dinge verschwindet, entfaltet sich dadurch in den Collagen eine expressive Vielfalt. Hier dient das Sprühen als kreativer Akt, der durch Schablonen, freie Bewegungen oder filigrane Formen poetische Ausdrucksformen schafft. Die wiederkehrenden geometrischen Formen wie Kreis und Quadrat wecken kosmische oder alltägliche Assoziationen und finden sich auch in den großformatigen Arbeiten wieder.

2. Die Suche nach dem Alltäglichen – *objet trouvé*

Alltagsgegenstände, die auf der Straße, im eigenen Haushalt oder im 1-Dollar-Shop gefunden wurden, bilden das Fundament dieser Arbeiten. Stuhllehnen, Bilderrahmen oder Stoffreste verlieren ihren ursprünglichen Nutzen und werden in neuen Kontexten zu Formen einer anderen Realität. Die nunmehr dreidimensionalen Collagen ragen in den Raum hinein und werfen bei den Betrachtenden die Frage auf, wo die Grenze zwischen Collage und Assemblage verläuft.

»I make collages, I join the shattered world, creating a new harmony.«

In her collages, as in these large-format assemblages, Nevelson strips found objects of their original function. Everyday items – a wooden spoon, a newspaper, a cigarette packet, or a cardboard box – lose their context and become pure form, the material of art. The individual part is not important, only the whole matters. Nevertheless, the viewer's gaze does not remain free of associations: familiar elements flash up and invite interpretation.

On the Presentation in the Museum Wiesbaden

The exhibition features two different yet closely related groups of works that enter into dialogue with each other. The first group consists of nearly sixty small-format collages on wood – predominantly made with paper, wood, and spray paint – that have received little attention in previous discussions of Nevelson's oeuvre. These are juxtaposed with the second group: twelve mostly large-format, predominantly monochrome spray-painted assemblages, reliefs, and sculptures composed of a wide variety of dismantled furniture, driftwood, and other remnants of consumer society, with which the artist enjoyed great success from the mid-1950s onward.

Though the two techniques have various similarities in terms of materiality and form, the differences that place Nevelson's works in one category or the other are apparent at first glance. On the one hand, there are collages with the aforementioned characteristics. On the other hand, there are larger-format works that have a space-consuming effect, three-dimensionality, and uniform color. These characteristics can be summarized under the term »sculptural assemblage«. Composed of a multitude of found, dismantled, and recycled objects, mostly made of wood, these assemblages form new entities, some of which, in their original presentation, fill entire rooms.[8]

The exhibition is divided into five thematic chapters that present Nevelson's collages in dialogue with her sculptural assemblages. Inspired by Yuval Etgar's publication and exhibition, *Out of Order*, which focuses in particular on the material characteristics of the collages, the exhibition in Wiesbaden takes a broader approach, highlighting the visual, technical, and material similarities and differences between the collages and the sculptural assemblages. In particular, it emphasizes the importance of searching – both physically and mentally – for Nevelson and her art. This dialogue invites viewers to perceive the collages and sculptural assemblages as closely related groups of works or to discover new connections between them.[9]

1. Sprayed Poetry

This chapter explores the use of spray paint as an artistic medium. While the sculptural works achieve uniformity through monochrome spraying, causing the wooden elements to lose their individuality, the collages reveal expressive diversity. Here, spraying serves as a creative act that allows poetic forms of expression to emerge through stencils, free movements, and filigree shapes. Recurring geometric shapes, such as circles and squares, evoke cosmic or everyday associations and are also found in the large-format works.

2. The Search for the Everyday – *Objet Trouvé*

Everyday objects found on the street, in the artist's home, or in a dollar store form the basis of these works. The backs of chairs, picture frames, and fabric remnants lose their original purpose and take on new forms in new contexts, creating a different reality. These three-dimensional collages protrude into the space, raising the question of where the boundary between collage and assemblage lies.

3. Vom Suchen und Finden –
Überreste als künstlerisches Konzept

In diesem Teil der Ausstellung wird die »Resteverwertung« im künstlerischen Prozess thematisiert. Kleine Holzteile, die bei der Arbeit an größeren Skulpturen übriggeblieben sind, finden in den Collagen zu neuem Leben. Dieser nachhaltigen und aus heutiger Sicht umweltbewussten Herangehensweise entspricht auch die Wahl des Materials: Seit den 1940er-Jahren verwendete Nevelson Holz für ihre Installationen und Wandarbeiten. Aus Überresten schuf sie neue Kunst.

4. Das fortwährende Entdecken –
Form, Farbe und Textur

Diese Arbeiten könnten als klassische Collagen verstanden werden. Nevelson kombiniert flache Materialien wie Papier, Pappe, Zeitungsausschnitte und Ausschnitte von Fotografien zu zweidimensionalen Kompositionen. Sie reißt oder schneidet die Papierstücke in die gewünschte Form, schichtet und spielt mit Farbe, Kontrasten und Strukturen der Materialien. Während in anderen Bereichen Schwarz und Braun dominieren, entstehen hier überraschende farbige Begegnungen beispielsweise in Pastelltönen.

5. Die Suche nach Struktur und Ordnung

In dieser Sektion dominieren klare Strukturen und eine setzkastenartige Gliederung der Elemente, eine gewisse Konformität. Wie eine Naturforscherin hat Nevelson in den hier gezeigten Arbeiten einzelne Pappen nebeneinander angeordnet, gesammelt, versammelt und sie auf einem größeren Untergrund bewahrt sowie mit Datum versehen, um eine spätere Zuordnung zu ermöglichen. Doch die strikte Ordnung ist lediglich der äußere Rahmen – im Inneren des Werks zeigt sich im Zusammentreffen der unterschiedlichsten Formen erneut Louise Nevelsons ausgewogener Umgang mit der Komposition der Formen. »Ich mache Collagen, ich füge die zerbrochene Welt zusammen und schaffe eine neue Harmonie«.[10] Zusammenfassend betrachtet, arbeitete Nevelson spätestens ab den frühen 1950er-Jahren stets nach dem Prinzip, die Welt auseinanderzunehmen und sie nach eigenen Maßstäben wieder zusammenzusetzen. Im Bewusstsein dieser Herangehensweise macht die Ausstellung *Louise Nevelson. Die Poesie des Suchens* deutlich: In der stetigen Bewegung zwischen Fundstück und Transformation, Fläche und Raum, Nähe und Distanz entstanden Werke, die nicht nur als Collagen oder Assemblagen funktionieren – sondern als poetische Reflexionen eines aufmerksamen Suchens, das im Bild selbst weiterlebt und dazu einlädt, neue Wahrnehmungsräume zu erkunden.

---

1 Louise Nevelson, zit. in: Jean Lipman, *Nevelson's World*, New York 1983, S. 209.

2 Die Suche endete nur vorerst, da Räume, Environments oder Skulpturen, die sie für Ausstellungen entstehen ließ, anschließend teilweise demontiert und zu neuen Werken weiterentwickelt wurden und somit die Suche von Neuem begann.

3 Vermutlich aus dem Jahr 1975. Zit. nach: Yuval Etgar, *Out of Order: The Collages of Louise Nevelson*, hg. von Yuval Etgar, Fondazione Marconi, Mailand 2022.

4 Siehe auch den Essay von Anne Horvath im vorliegenden Katalog.

5 Zit. in Lipman 1983 (wie Anm. 1), S. 211.

6 »… Nevelson has set aside several large rooms in her house for the creation and storage of her collages«, Jean Lipman in: Ebd., S. 182.

7 Exemplarische Galerieausstellungen: Pace Gallery, New York, 1974; Galleria d'Arte Sagnoli, Florenz, 1975; Galerie de France, Paris, 1981.

8 Siehe auch den Essay von Anne Horvath im vorliegenden Katalog.

9 Siehe den Essay von Yuval Etgar im vorliegenden Katalog für eine ausführliche Materialbeschreibung der von ihm definierten Gruppen.

10 *Louise Nevelson* (Ausst.-Kat. Moderna Museet, Stockholm), Stockholm 2017.

3. Searching and Finding –
Leftovers as an Artistic Concept

This chapter focuses on the »making use of leftovers« in Nevelson's artistic process. Small pieces of wood left over from larger sculptures are given new life in the collages. This sustainable and, from today's perspective, environmentally conscious approach is also reflected in the choice of material: Since the 1940s, Nevelson used wood for her installations and wall works, creating new art from the leftovers.

4. The Ongoing Discovery –
Form, Color, and Texture

The works in this chapter can be understood as classic collages. Nevelson combined two-dimensional materials, such as paper, cardboard, newspaper clippings, and cutouts from photographs, to create compositions. She tore or cut pieces of paper into the desired shapes, layered them, and experimented with colors, contrasts, and textures. While black and brown dominate in other areas, surprising colorful combinations emerge here, such as pastel shades.

5. The Search for Structure and Order

This chapter is characterized by clear structures, a box-like arrangement of elements, and a certain sense of conformity. Like a natural scientist, Nevelson collected, assembled, and arranged individual pieces of cardboard side by side in the works shown here, preserving them on a larger surface and dating them to enable later classification. However, this strict order is merely the outer framework. Within the works themselves, the interplay of diverse forms reveals Nevelson's balanced approach to composition.

»I make collages, I join the shattered world, creating a new harmony.«[10] In summary, from the early 1950s onward, Nevelson consistently worked according to the principle of taking the world apart and reassembling it according to her own standards. Aware of this approach, the exhibition *Louise Nevelson: The Poetry of Searching* makes it clear that in the constant oscillation between found object and transformation, surface and space, proximity and distance, the artist created works that function not only as collages or assemblages, but as poetic reflections of an attentive search that lives on in the image itself and invites viewers to explore new spaces of perception.

---

1 Quoted in: Jean Lipman and Louise Nevelson, *Nevelson's World* (New York: Hudson Hills Press, 1983), p. 209.

2 However, the search ended only temporarily, as the rooms, environments, and sculptures she created for exhibitions were subsequently dismantled and redeveloped into new works, thus beginning the search anew.

3 This quote is probably from 1975. Quoted in: *Out of Order: The Collages of Louise Nevelson*, ed. Yuval Etgar, exh. cat. Fondazione Marconi, Milan 2022.

4 See also the essay by Anne Horvath in this volume.

5 Quoted in: Lipman/Nevelson 1983 (see note 1), p. 211.

6 »Nevelson has set aside several large rooms in her house for the creation and storage of her collages.« Jean Lipman, in: ibid., p. 182.

7 Examples of such exhibitions include Pace Gallery, New York (1974), Galleria d'Arte Sagnoli, Florence (1975), and Galerie de France, Paris (1981).

8 See also the essay by Anne Horvath in this volume.

9 For a detailed description of the groups defined by Yuval Etgar, see his essay in this volume.

10 Quoted in: *Louise Nevelson*, exh. cat. Moderna Museet, Stockholm 2017.

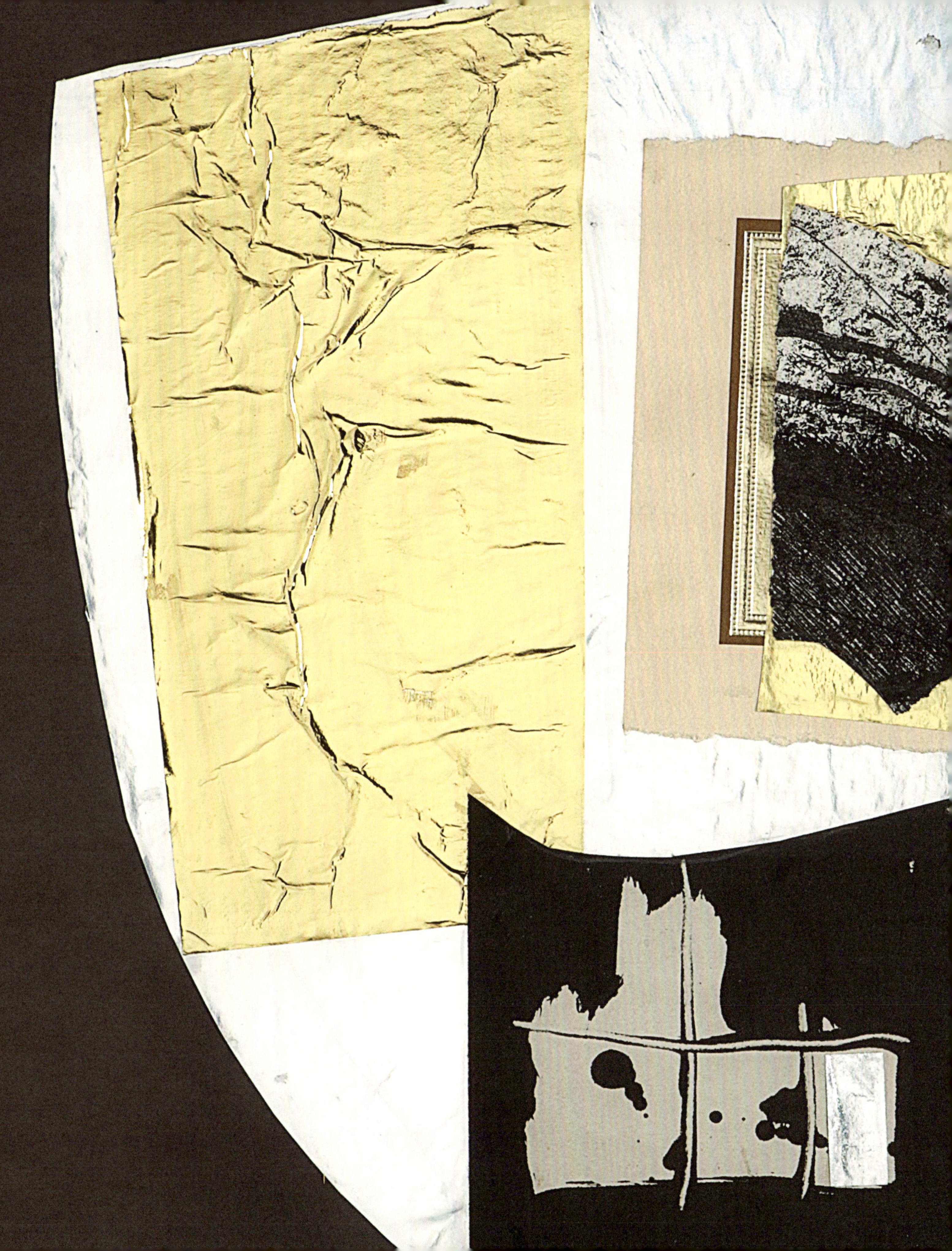

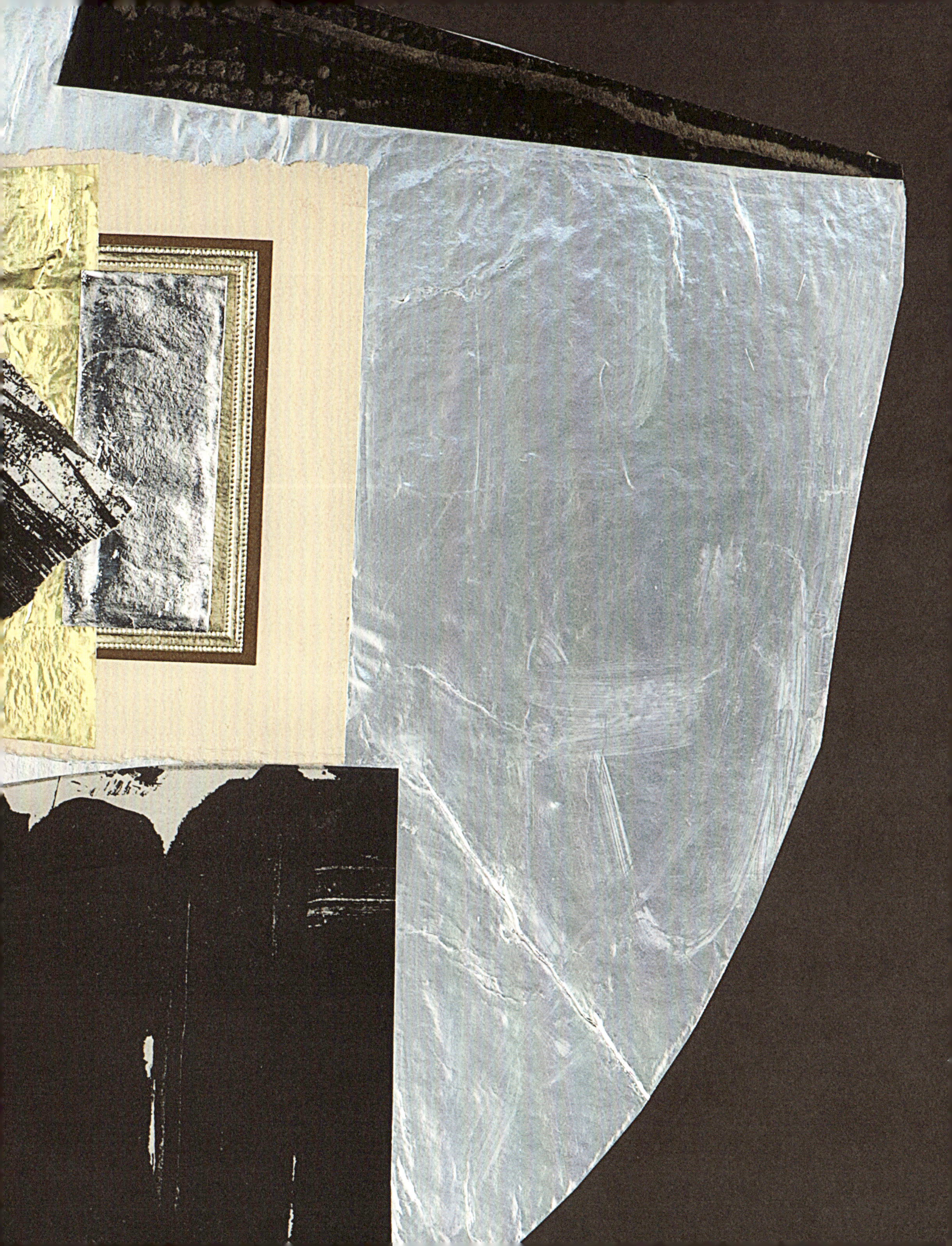

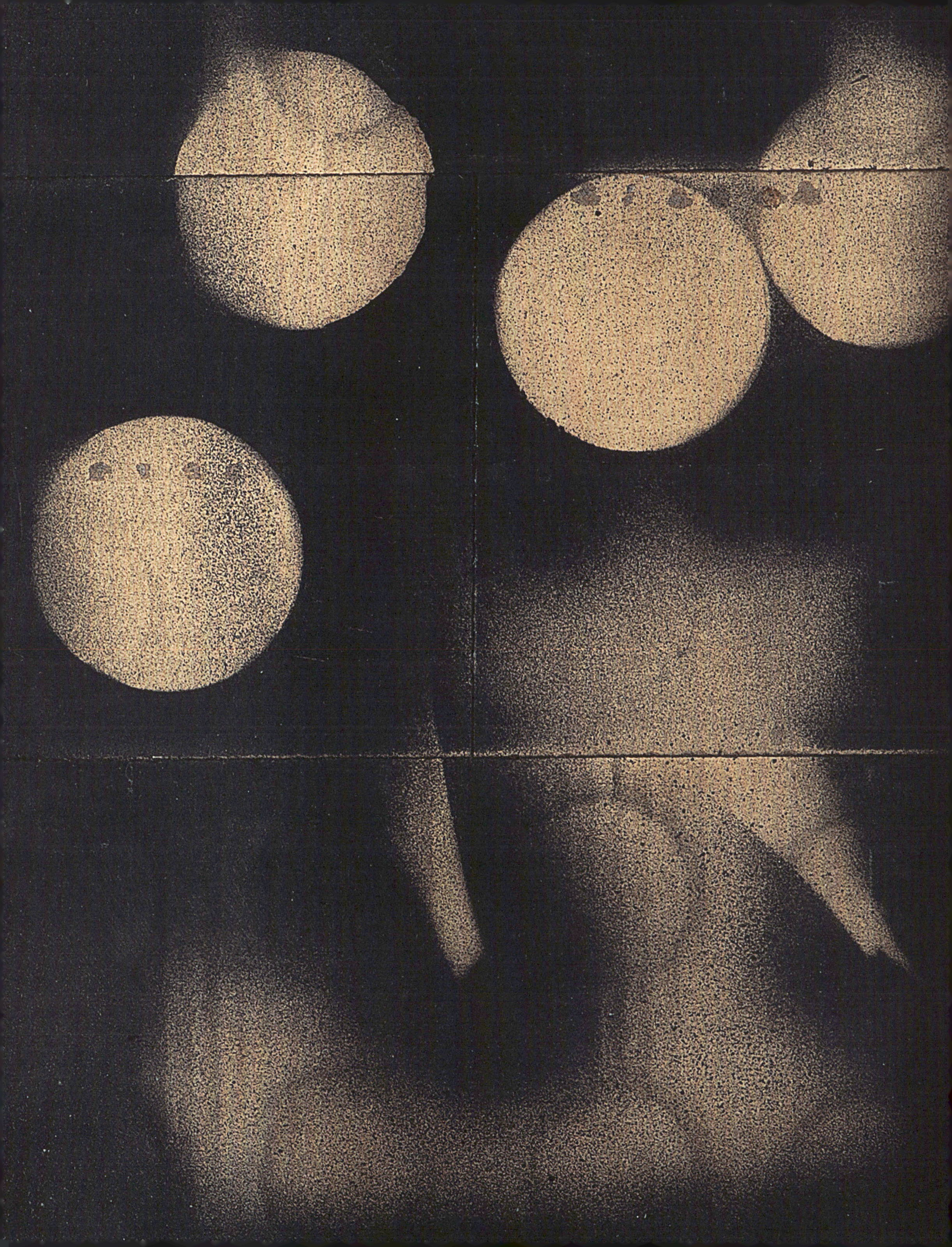

GESPRÜHTE POESIE SPRAYED POETRY

NO 1

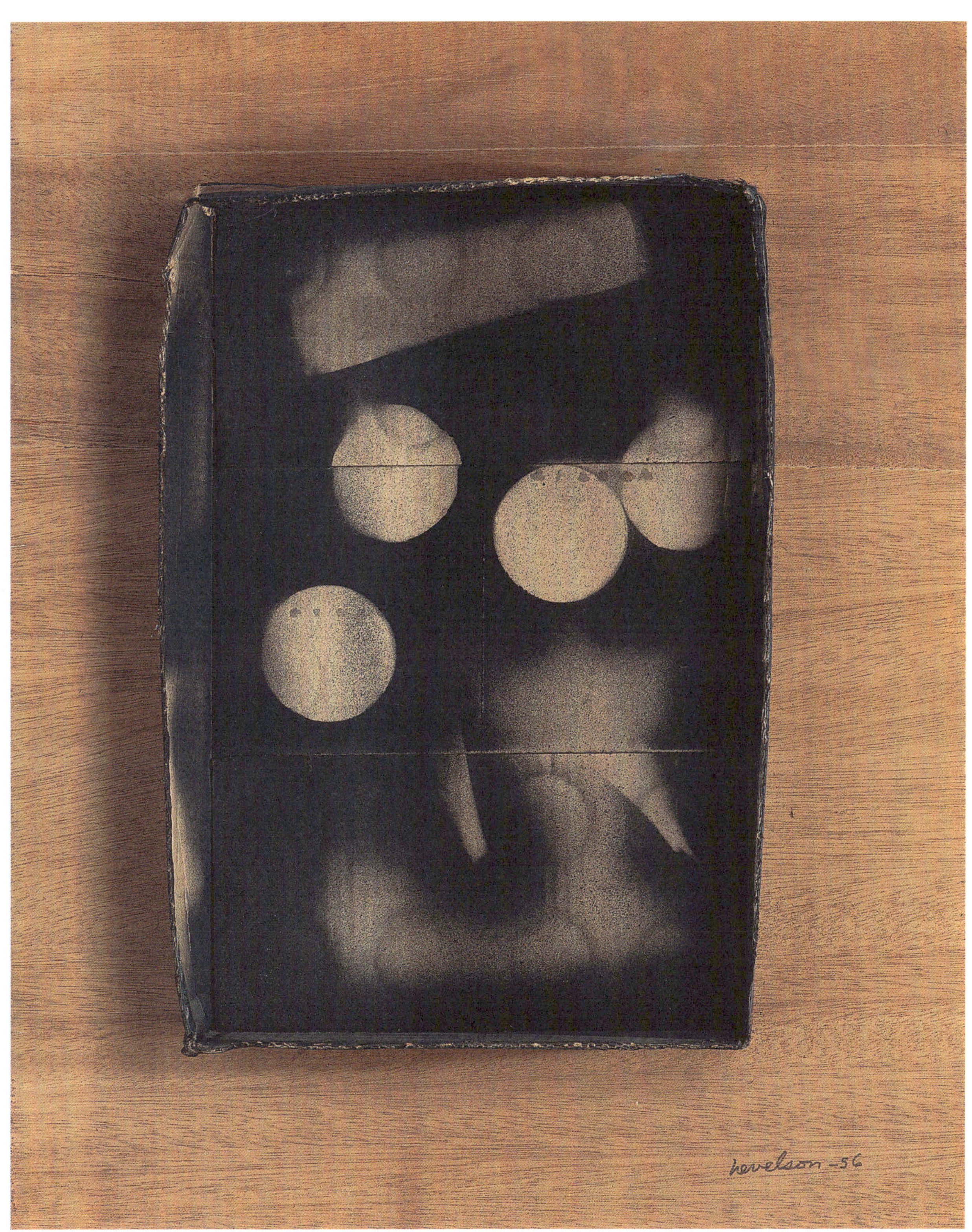

1.1 Untitled 1956, cardboard and spray paint on board, 56 × 46 cm

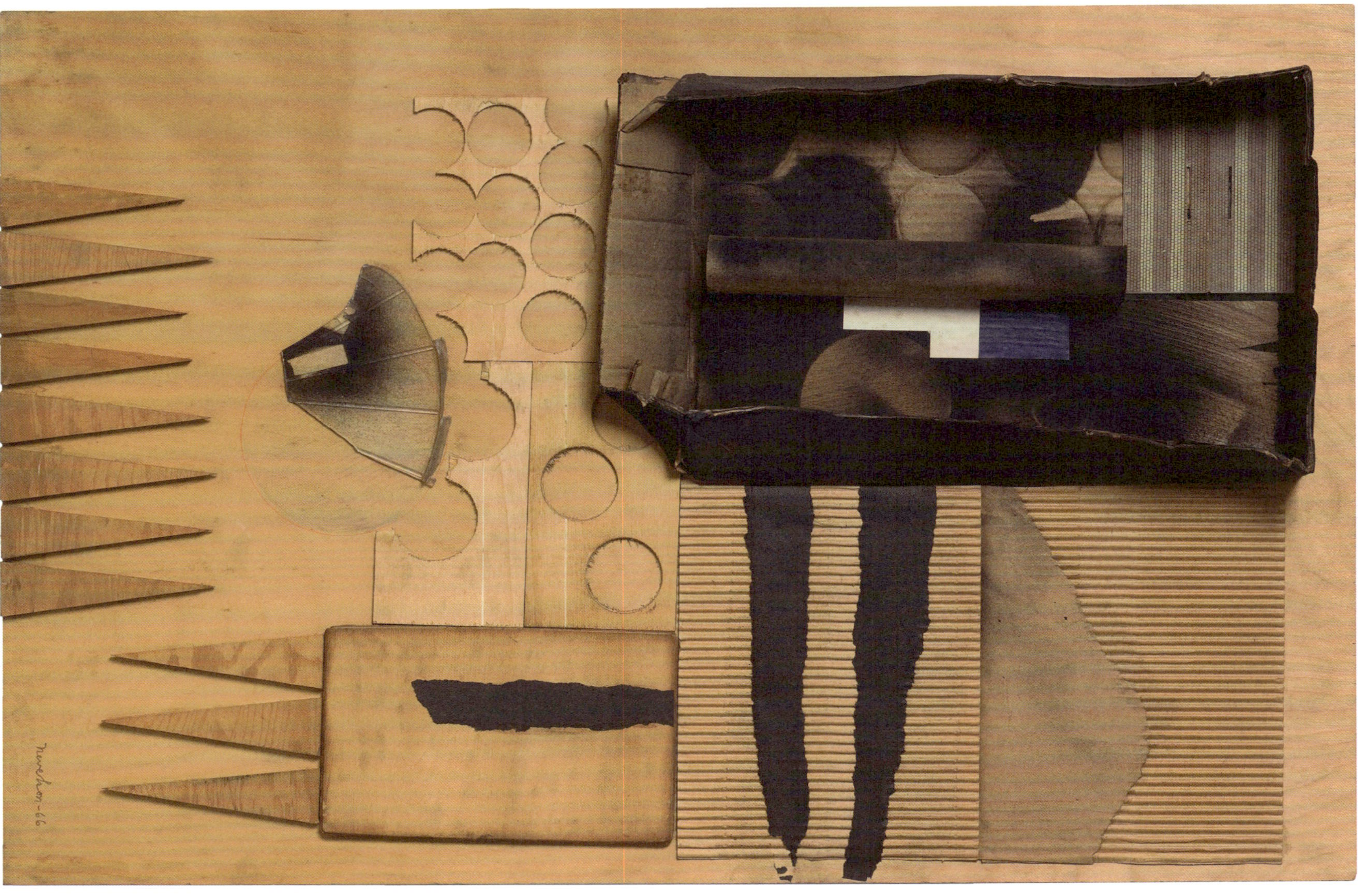

1.2 Untitled 1966, cardboard, spray paint and wood on, 90 × 60 × 9 cm

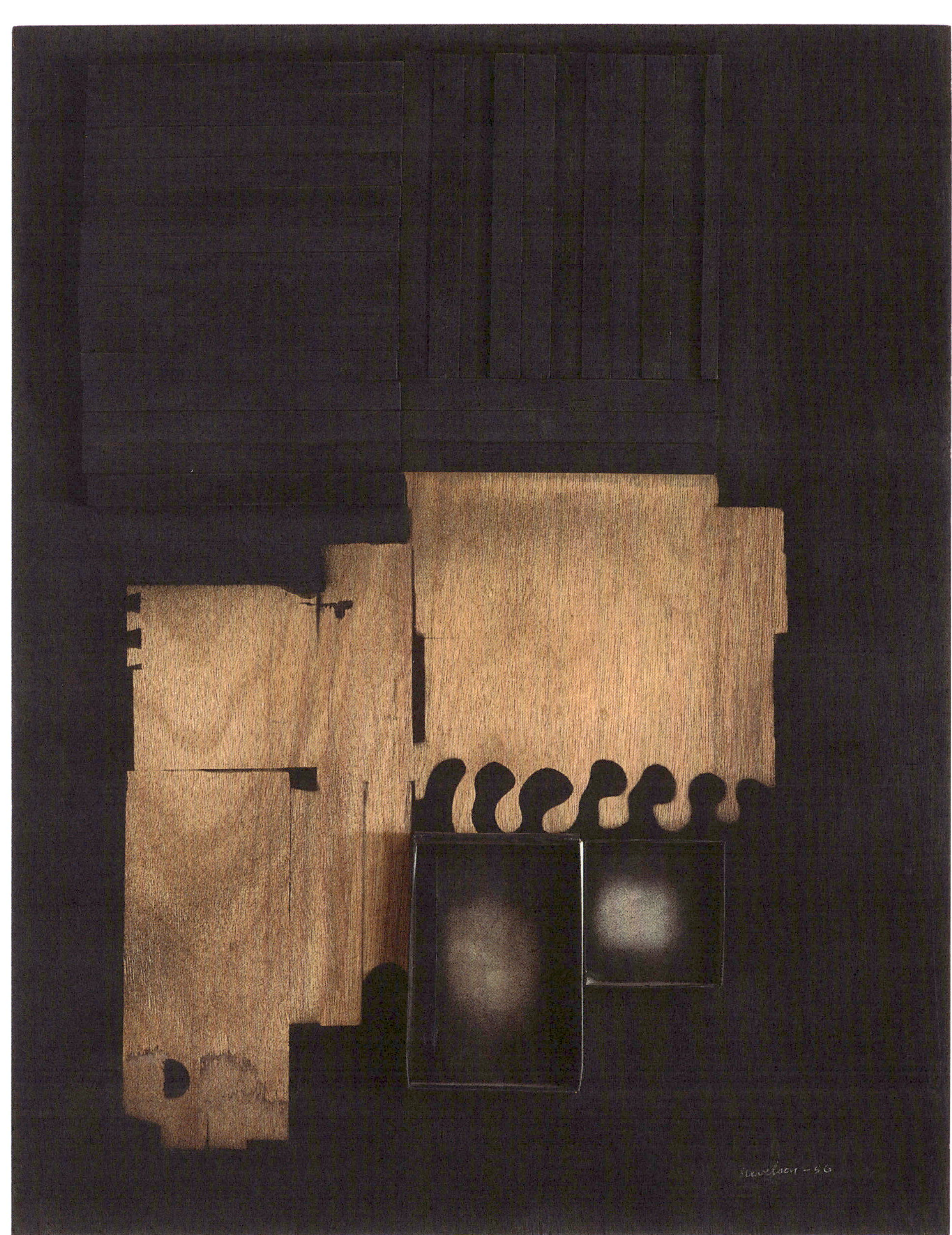

1.3 Untitled 1956, cardboard, spray paint, paint and wood on board, 76 × 61 cm

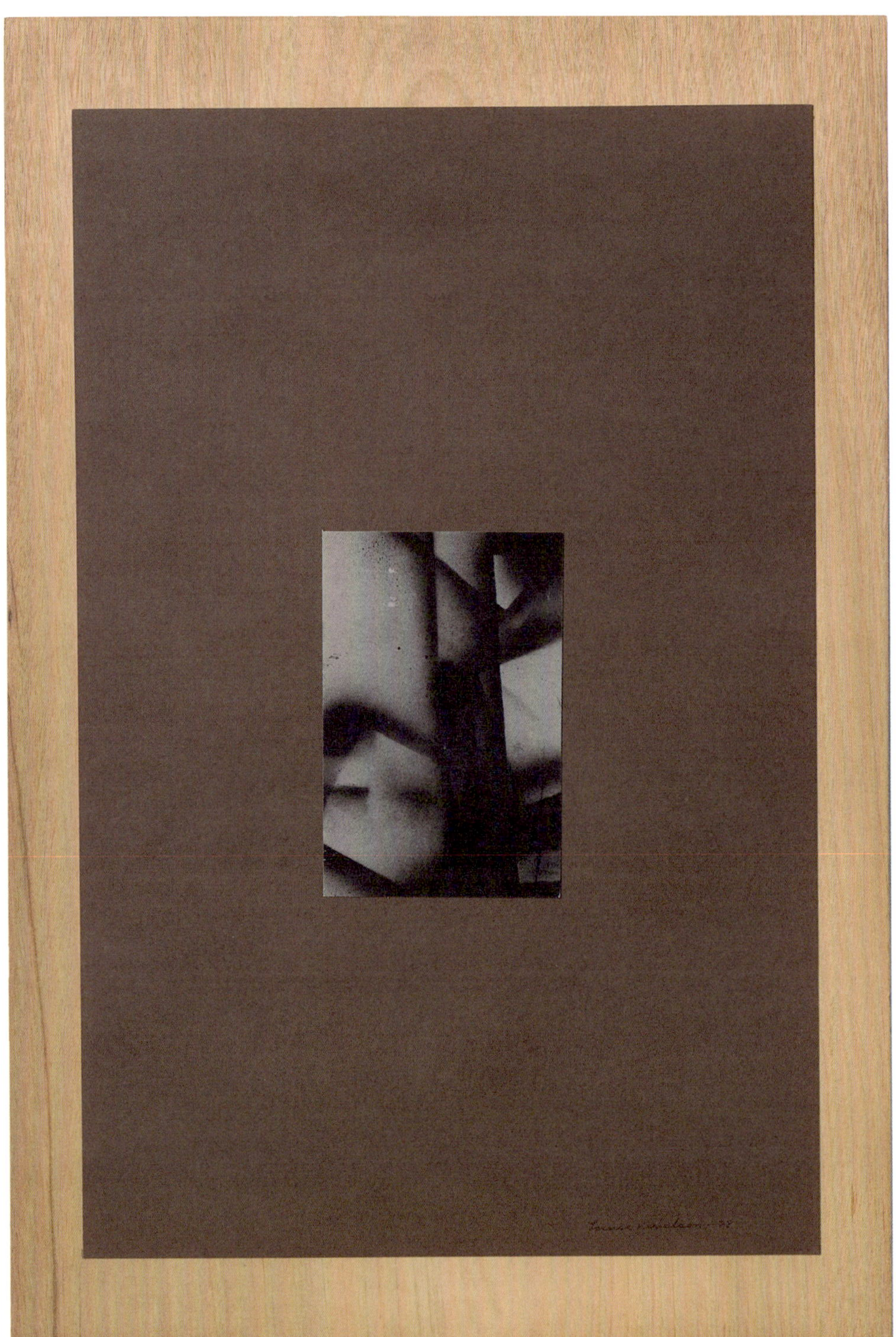

1.4 Untitled 1978, cardboard and spray paint on board, 88.8 × 60.8 × 0.9 cm

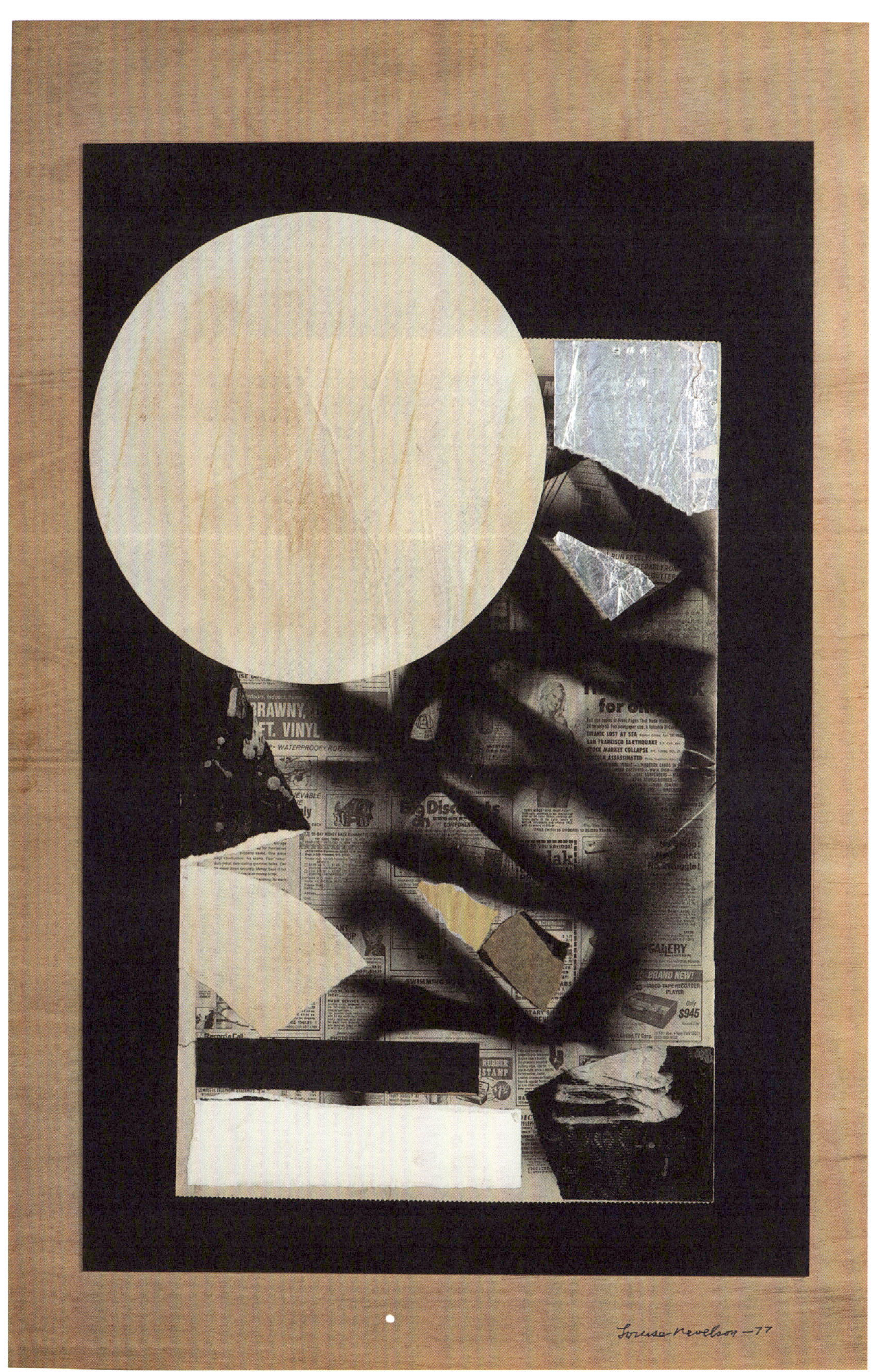

1.5 Untitled 1977, cardboard, spray paint, metal foil, newsprint, lithograph and paper on board, 91.5 × 61 cm

1.6 Night Sun I 1959, wood painted black,
293 × 164 × 27.5 cm

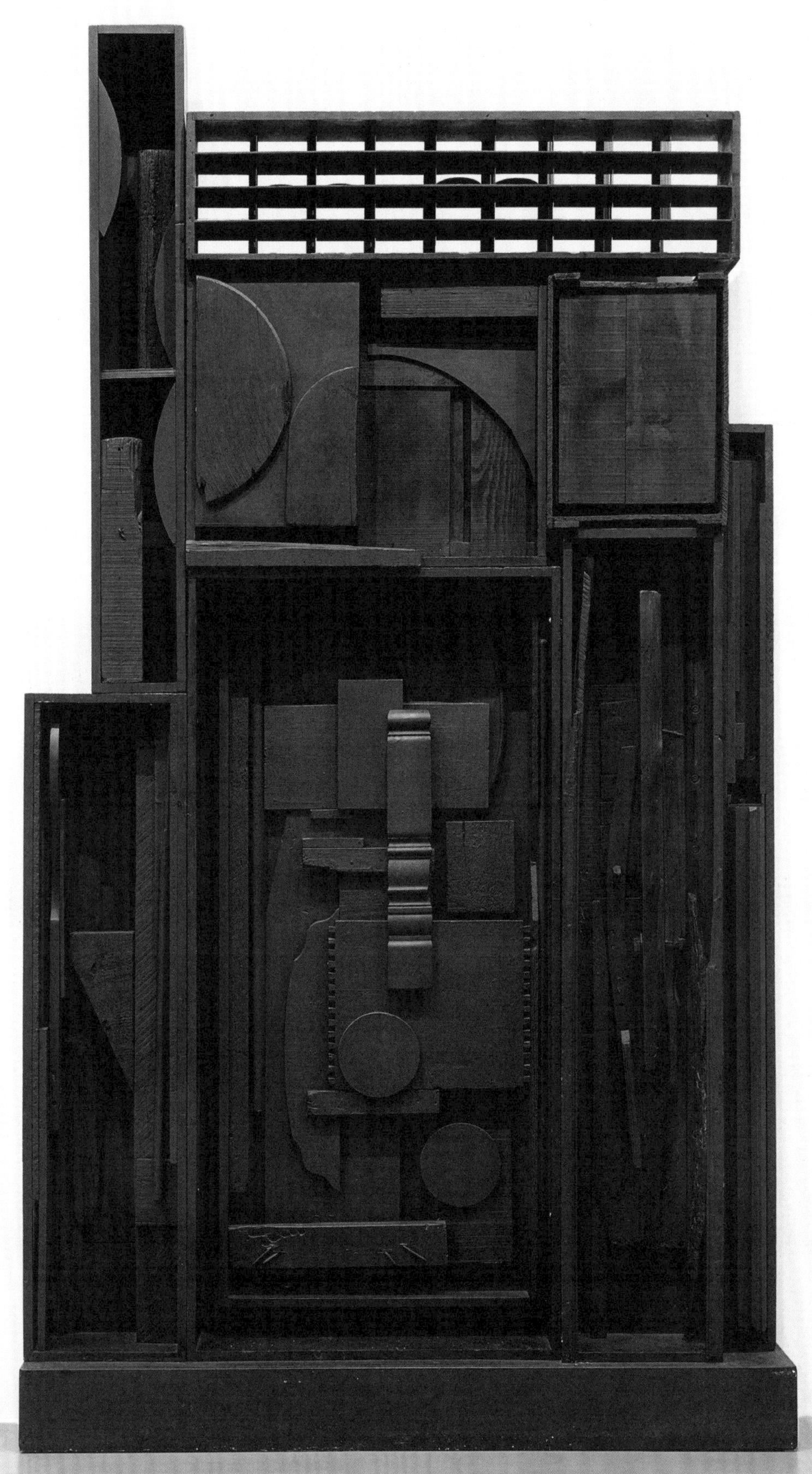

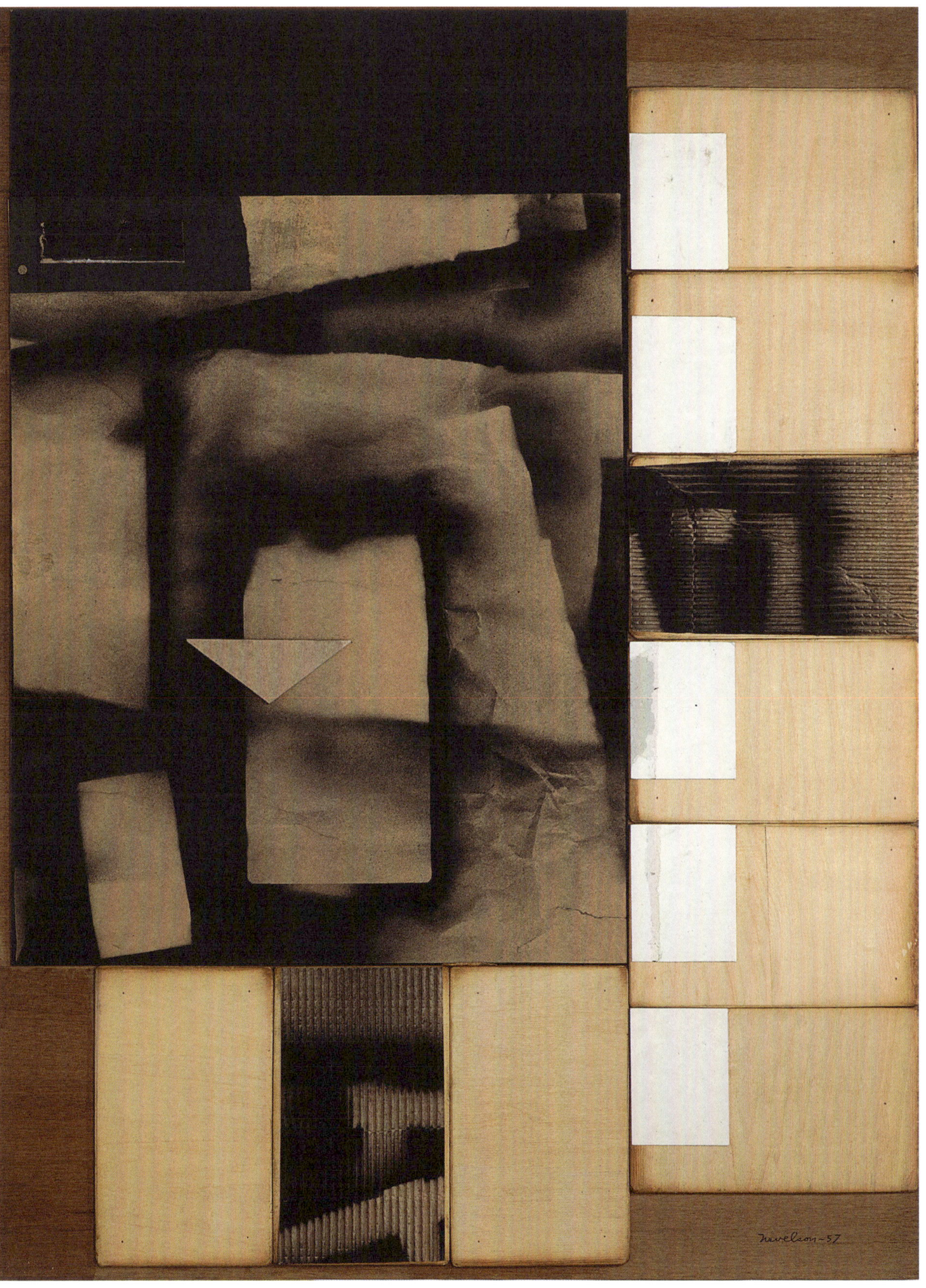

1.7 Untitled 1957, cardboard, spray paint, paper and wood on board, 102 × 76 cm

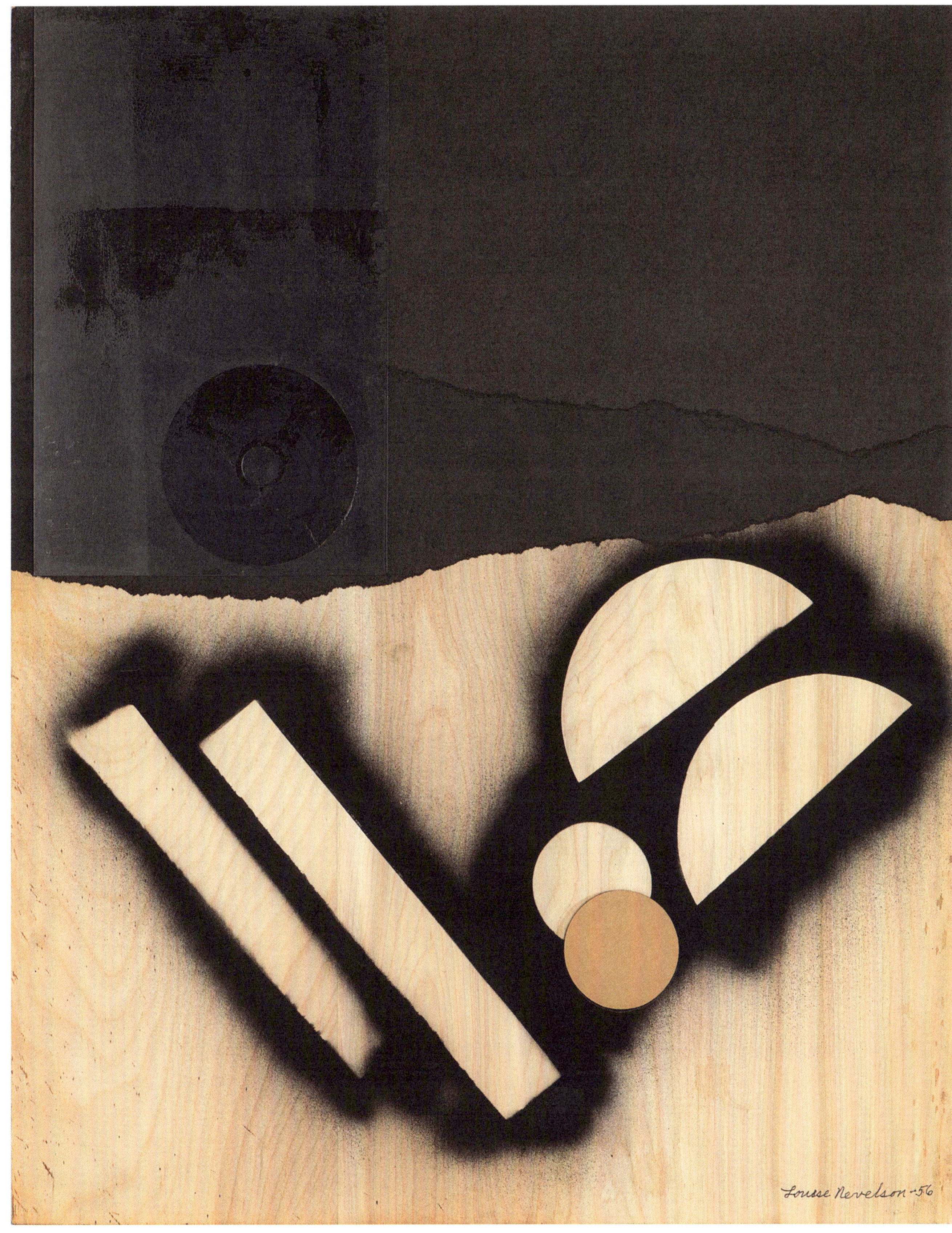

1.8 Untitled 1956, cardboard, spray paint, plastic and wood on board, 76 × 61 cm

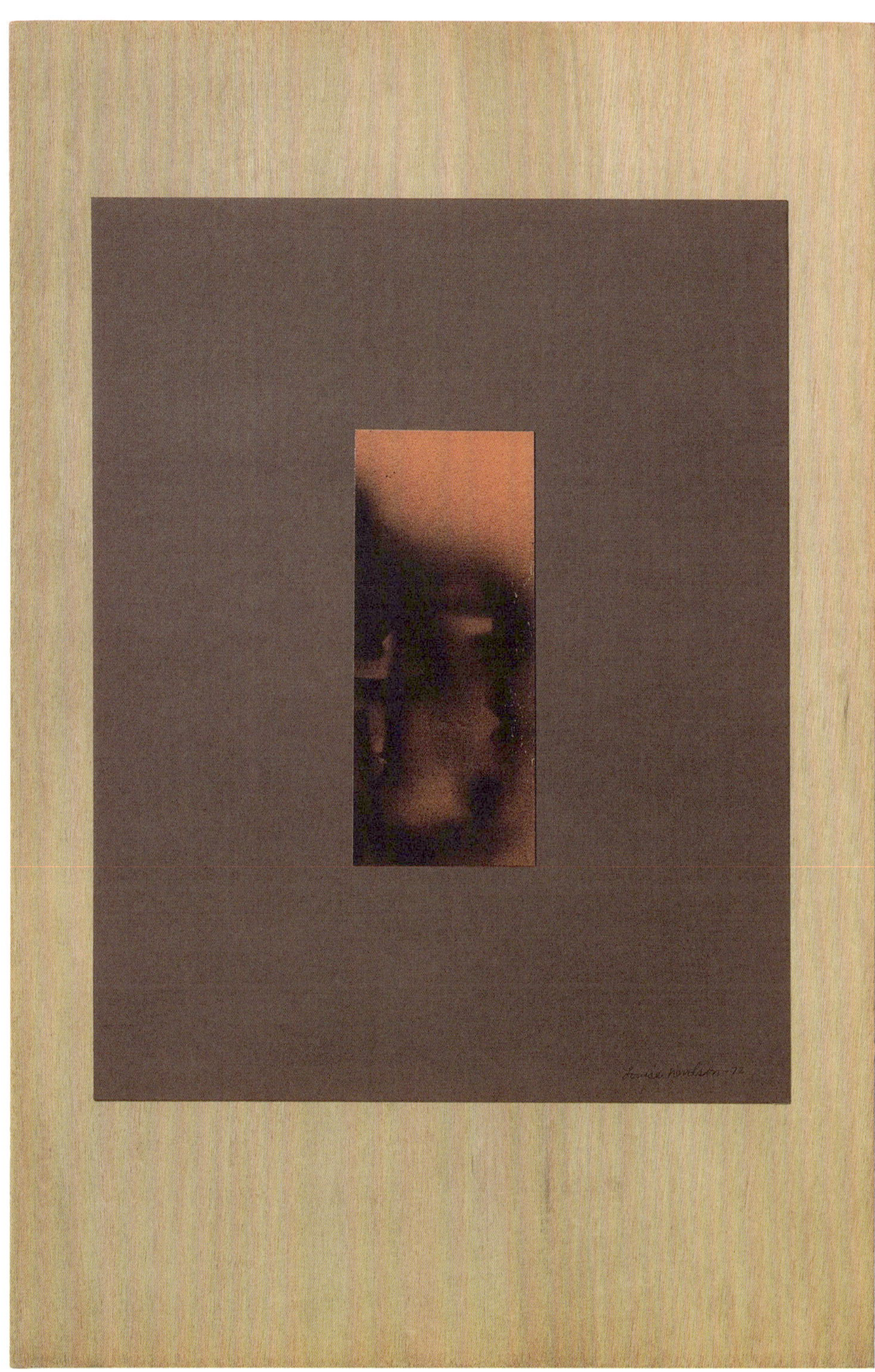

1.9 Untitled 1972, cardboard and spray paint on board, 76.1 × 50.1 × 0.9 cm

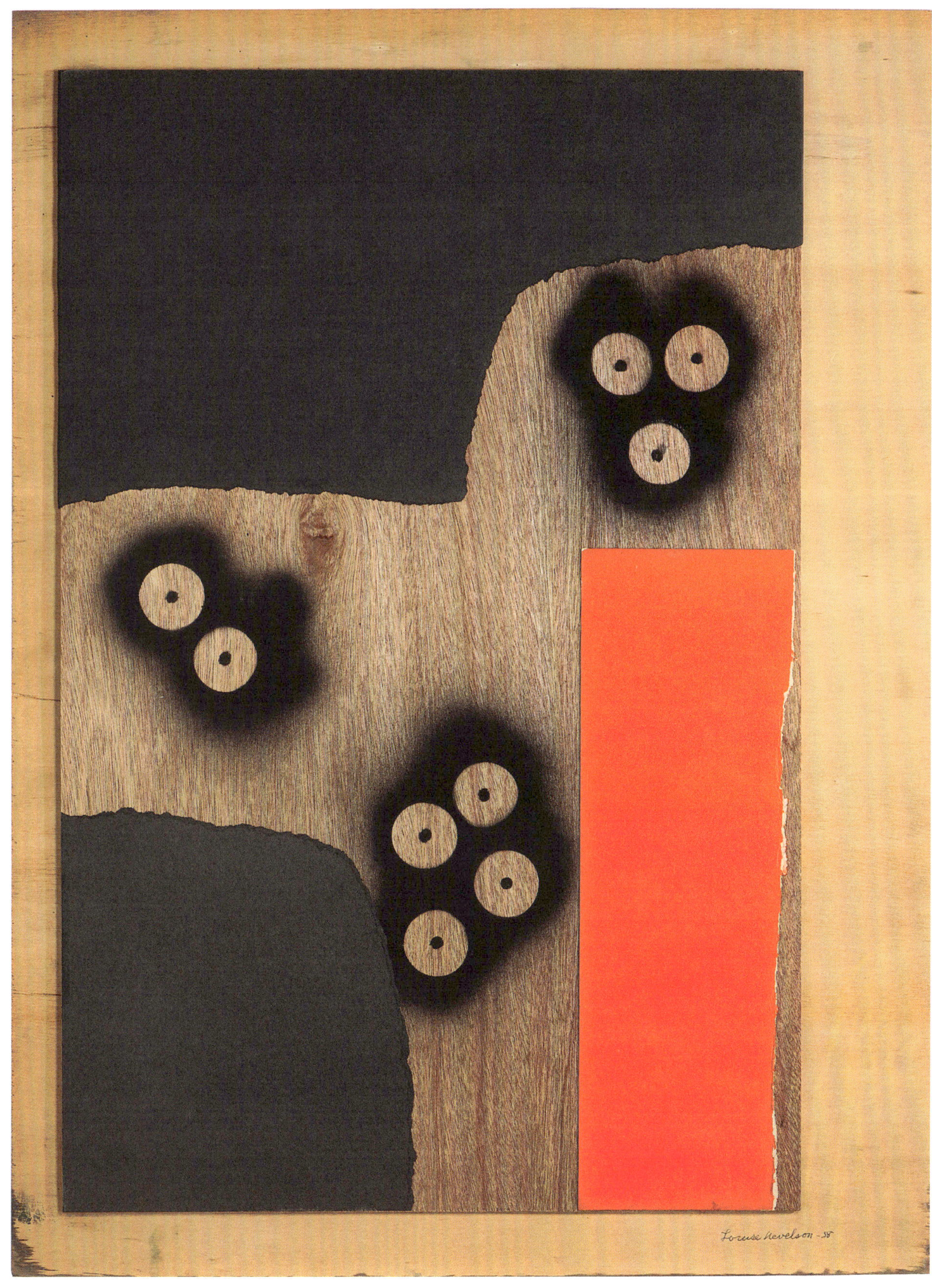

1.10 Untitled 1958, cardboard, spray paint, paint, paper and wood on board, 102 × 76 cm

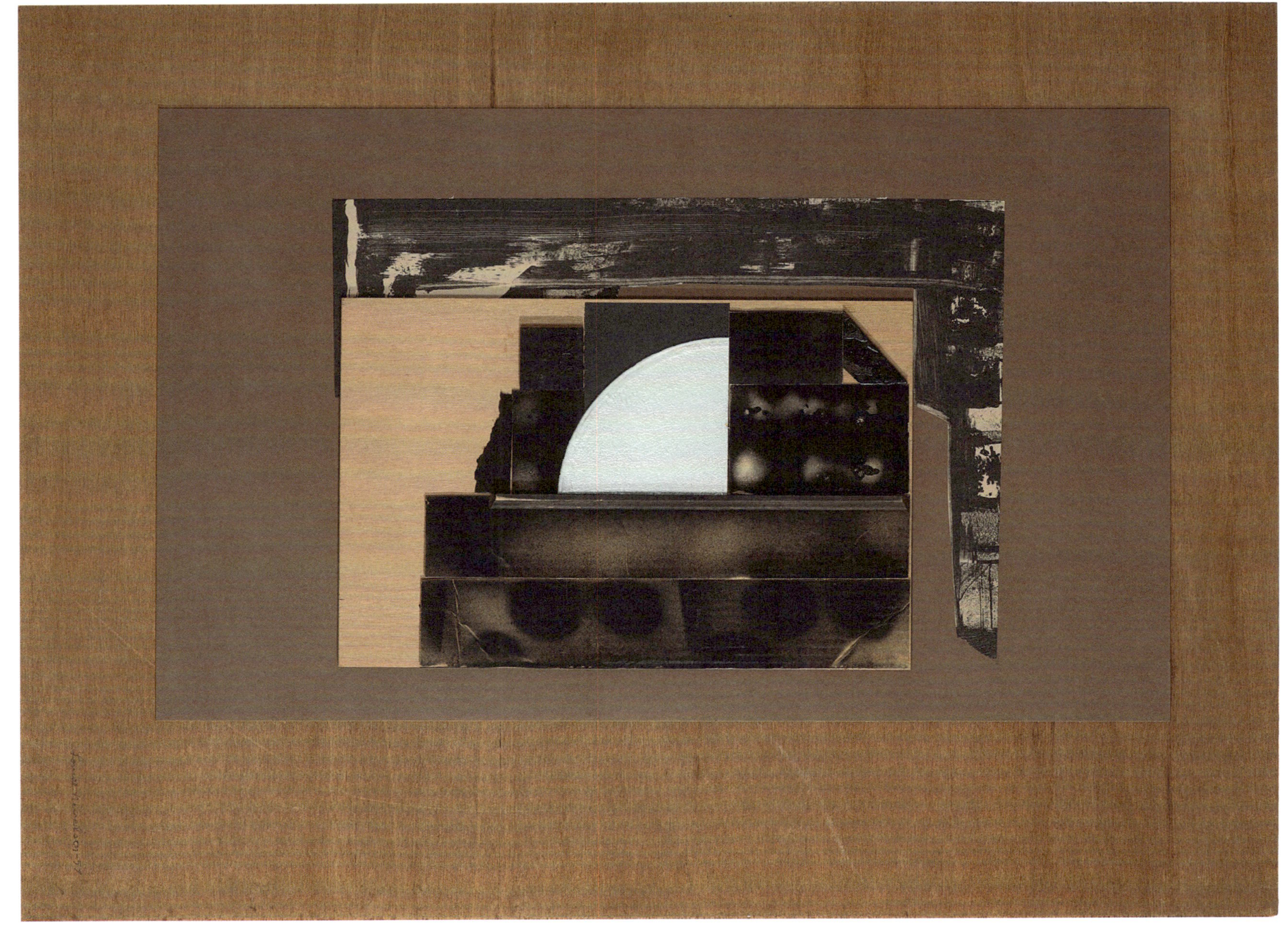

1.11 Untitled 1957, cardboard, spray paint, lithograph and wood on board, 102 × 76 cm

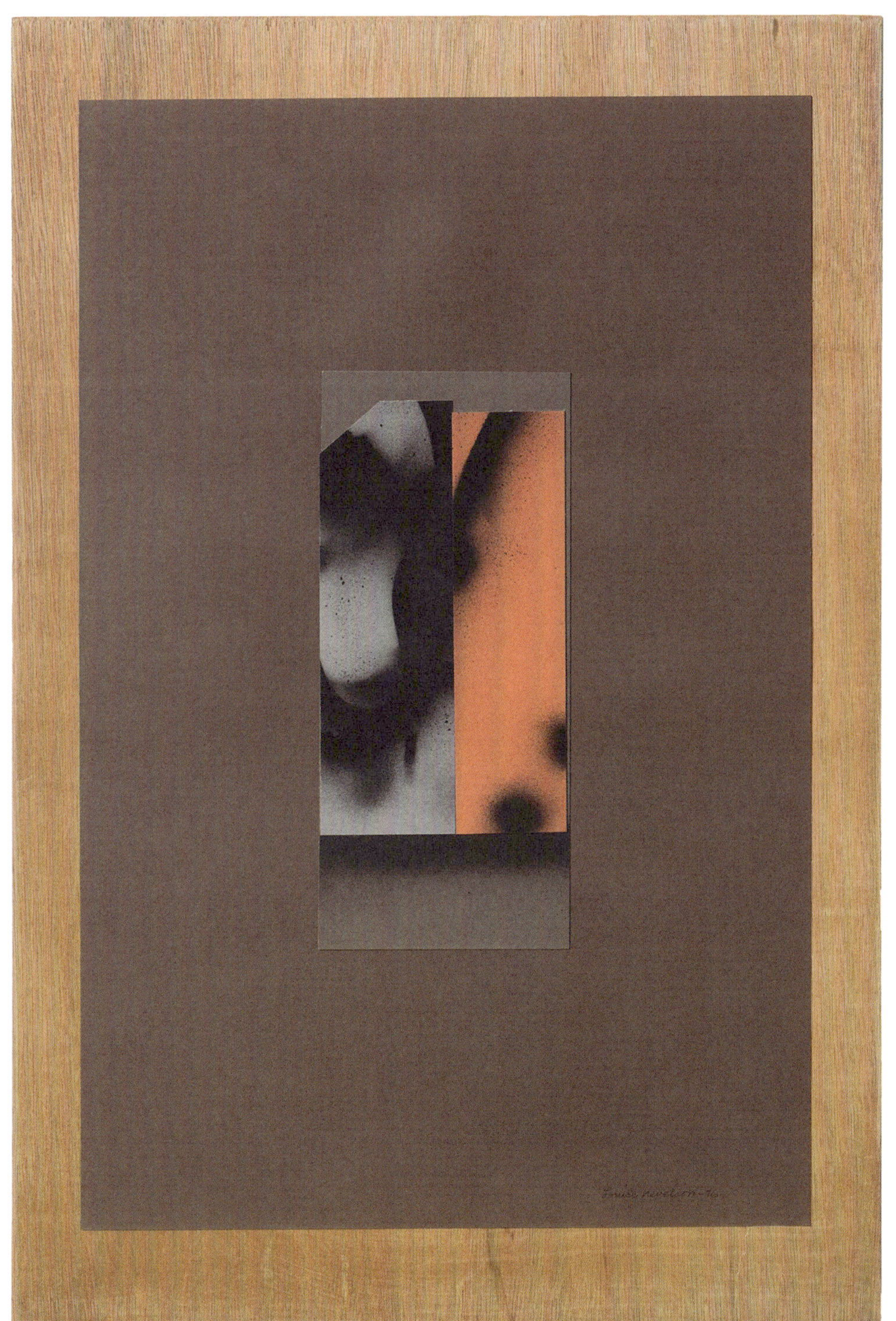

1.12 Untitled 1976, cardboard and spray paint on board, 88.8 × 60.6 × 1 cm

1.13 Untitled ca. 1976, wood painted black,
203 × 111.5 cm

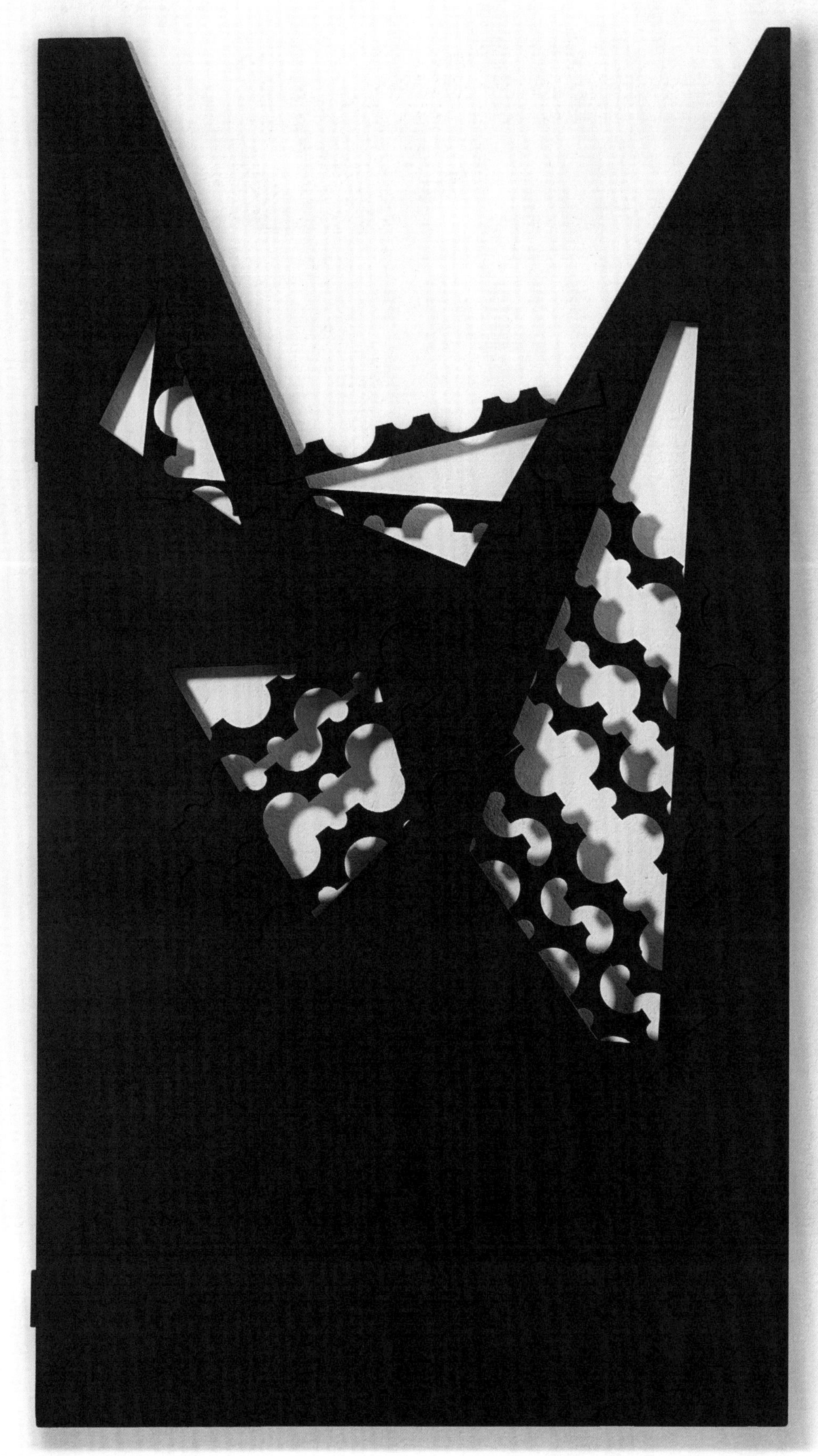

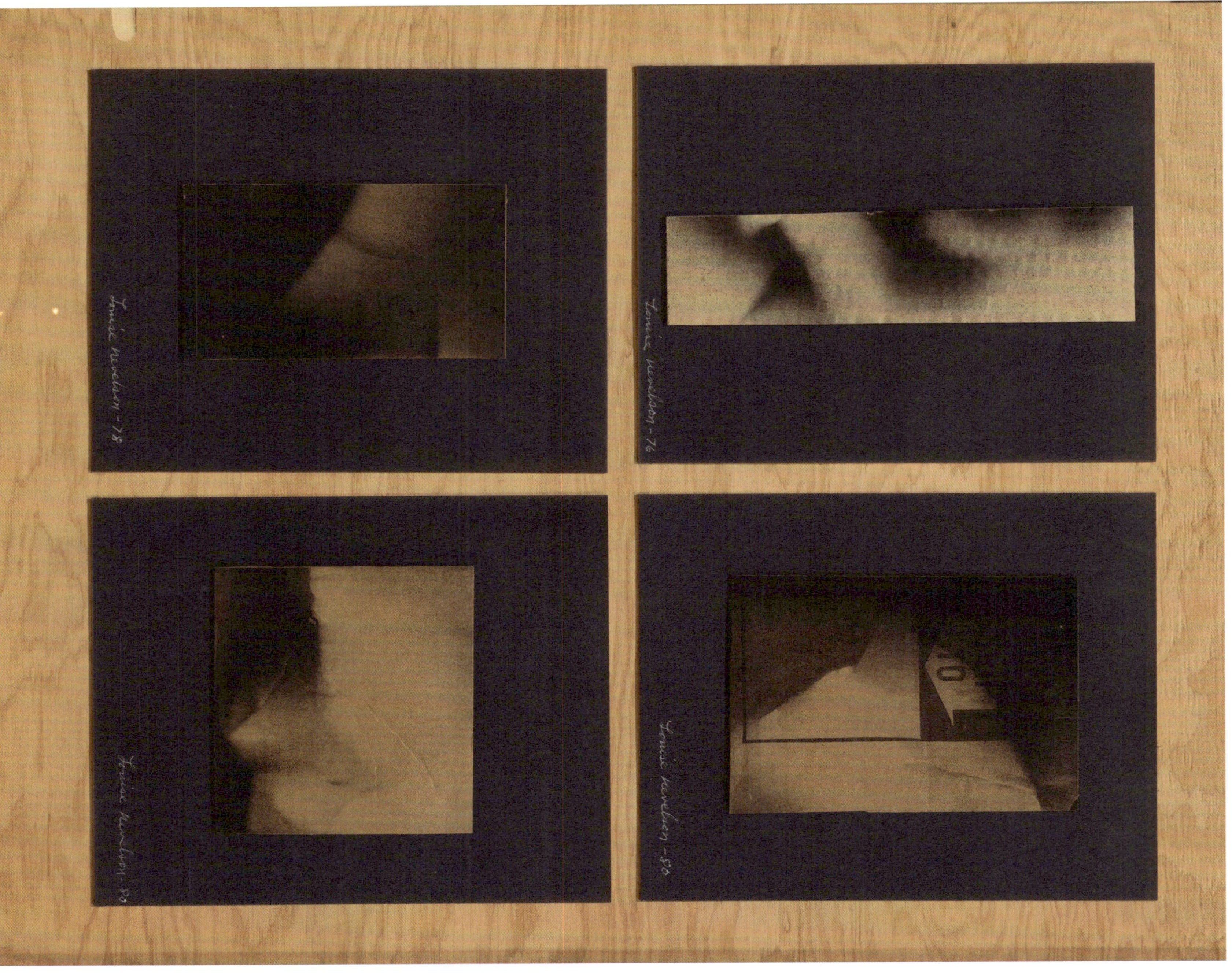

1.14 Untitled 1976–1978–1980 (dated), cardboard and spray paint on board, 60.7 × 48.5 × 1 cm

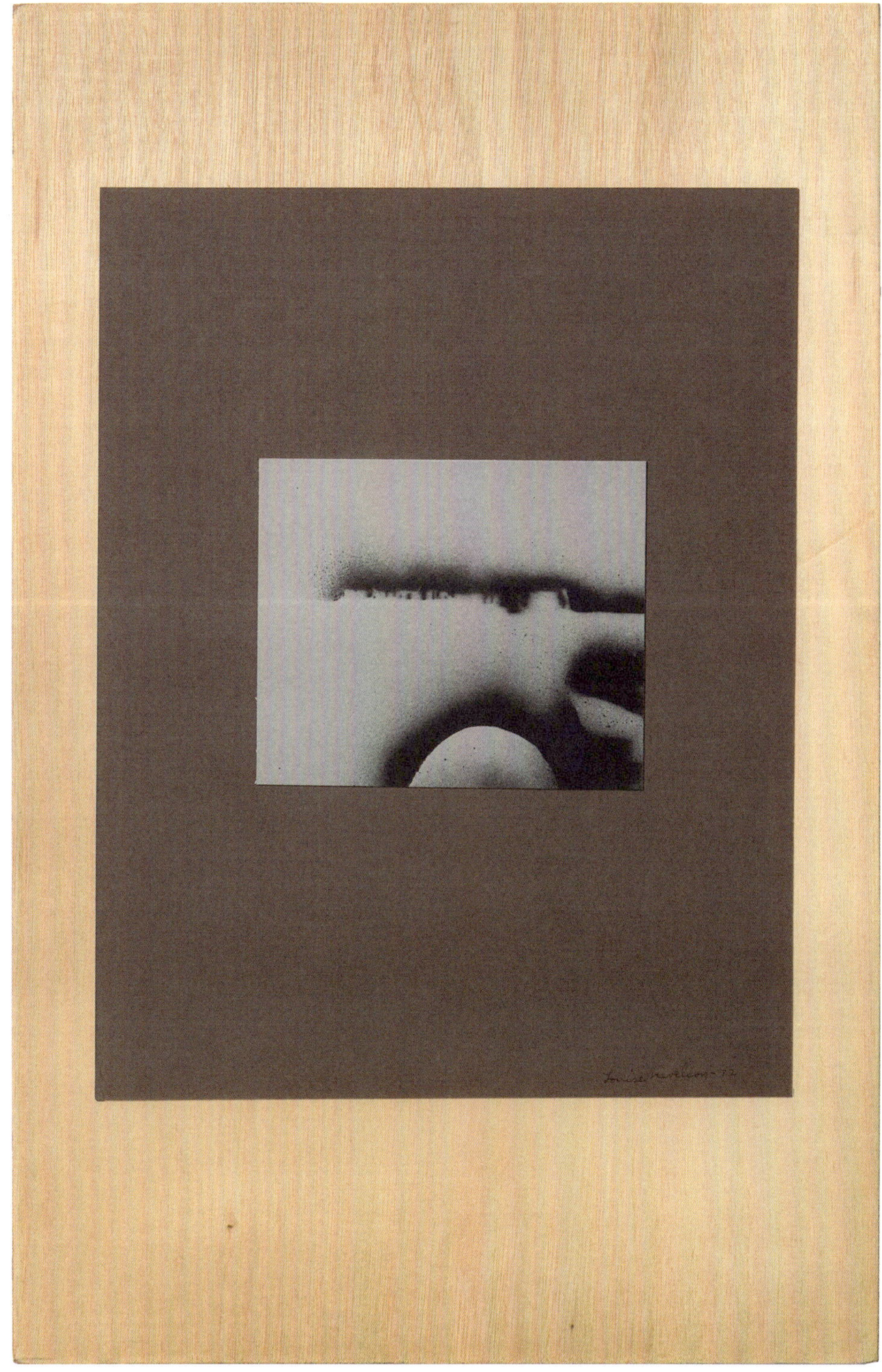

1.15 Untitled 1972, cardboard and spray paint on board, 76 × 50 × 0.9 cm

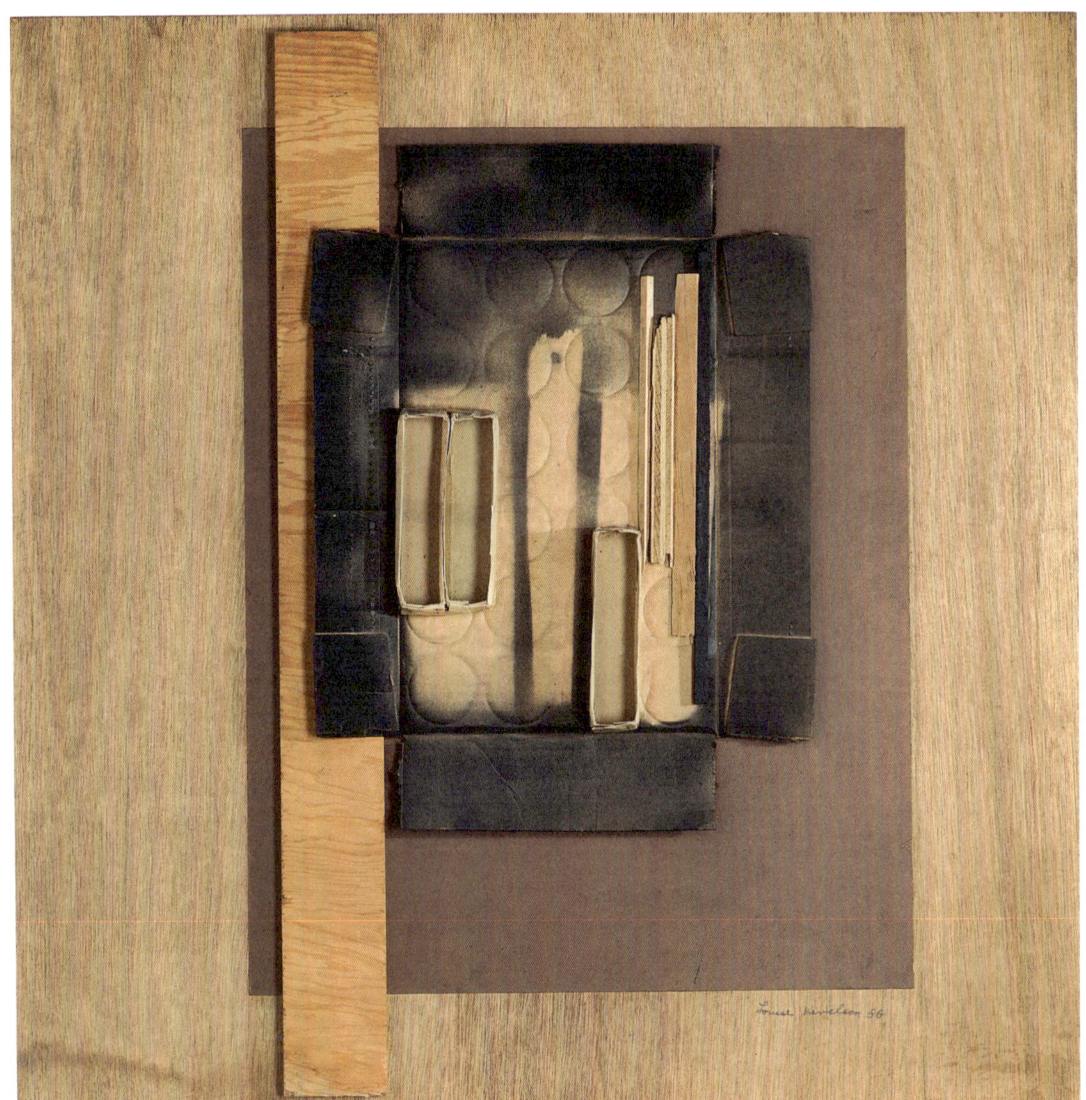

1.16 Untitled 1956, cardboard, spray paint and wood on board, 90.6 × 90.7 × 3.8 cm

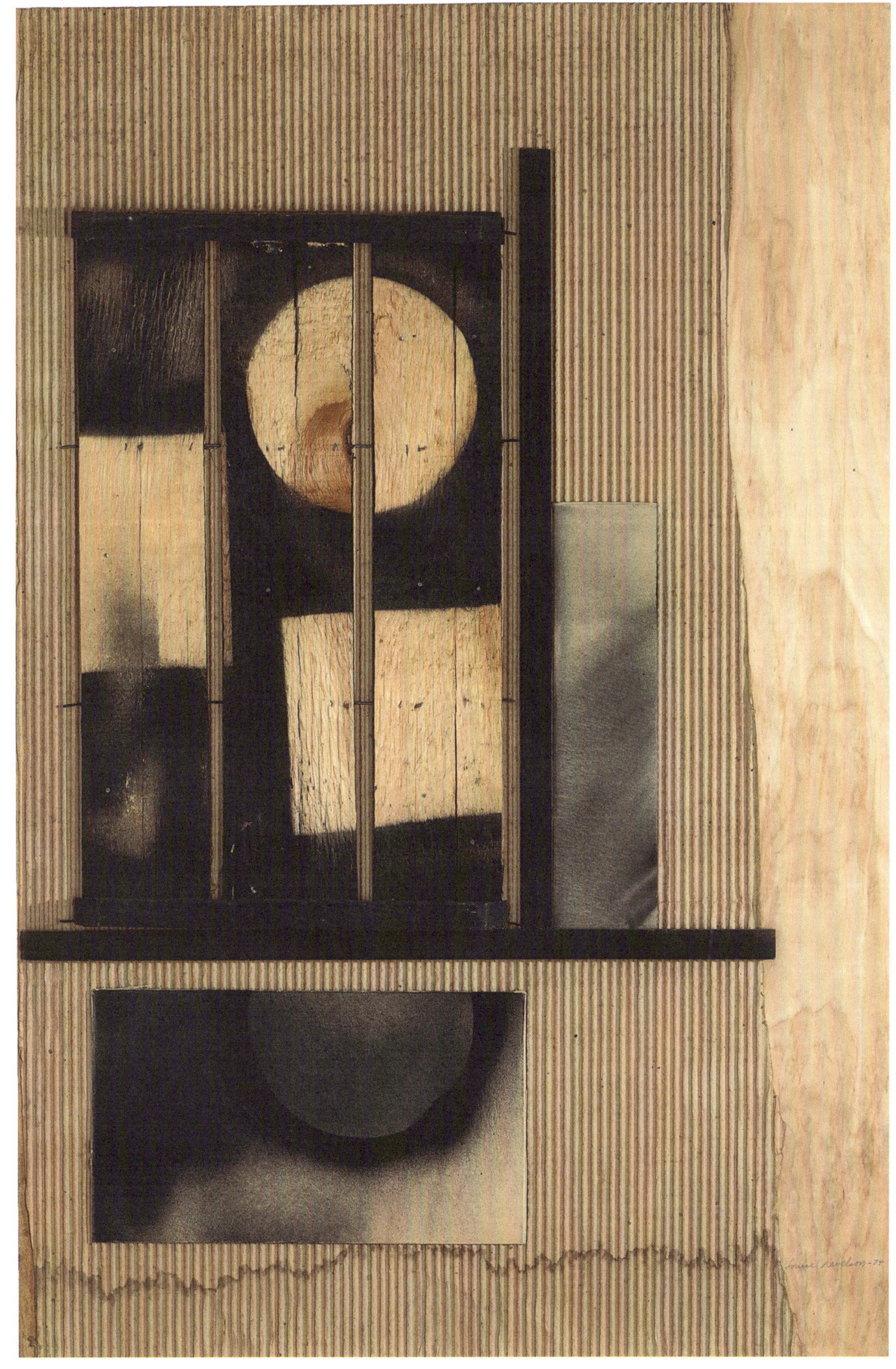

1.17 Untitled 1974, cardboard, spray paint and wood on board, 91.5 × 61 cm

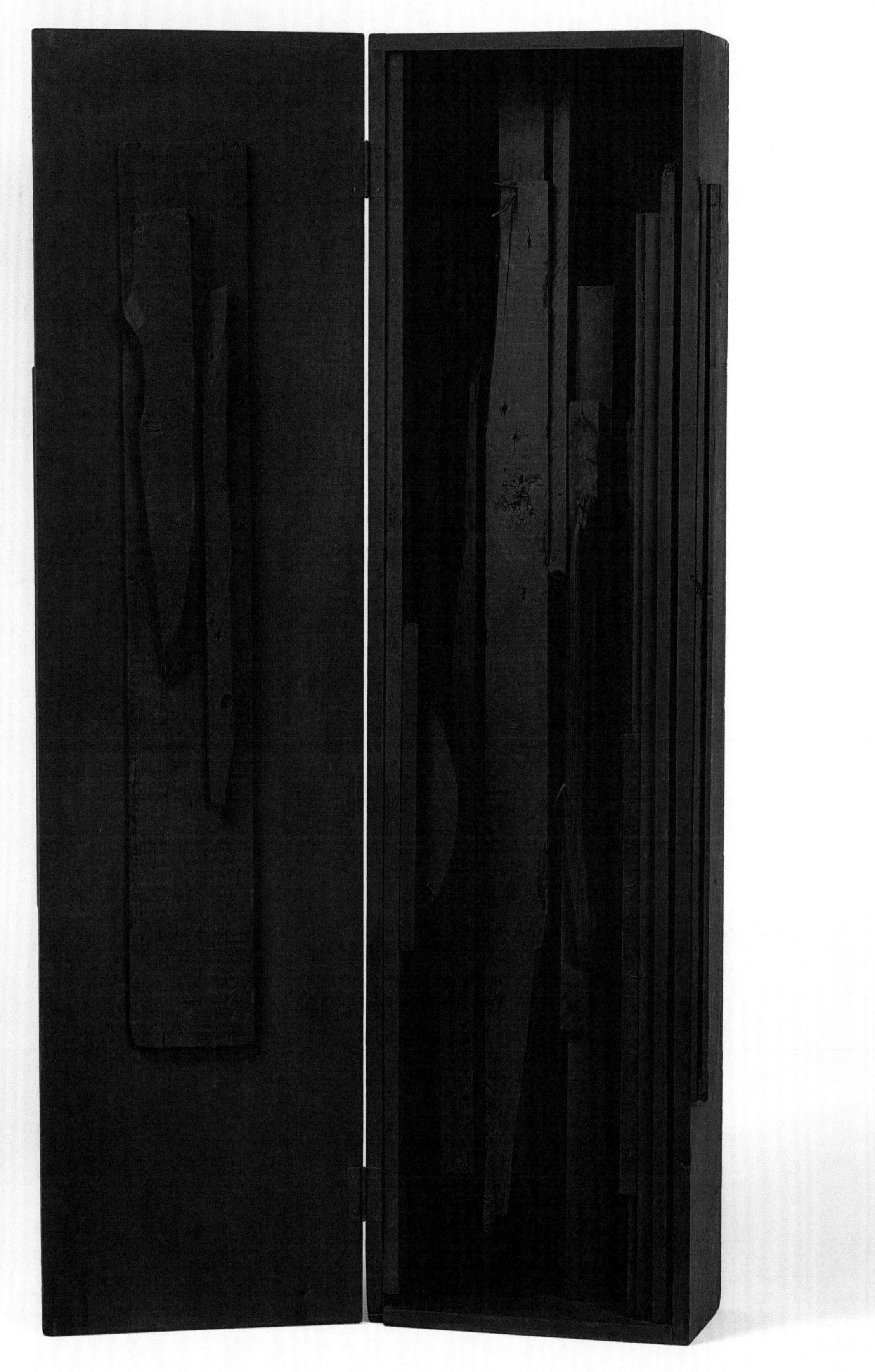

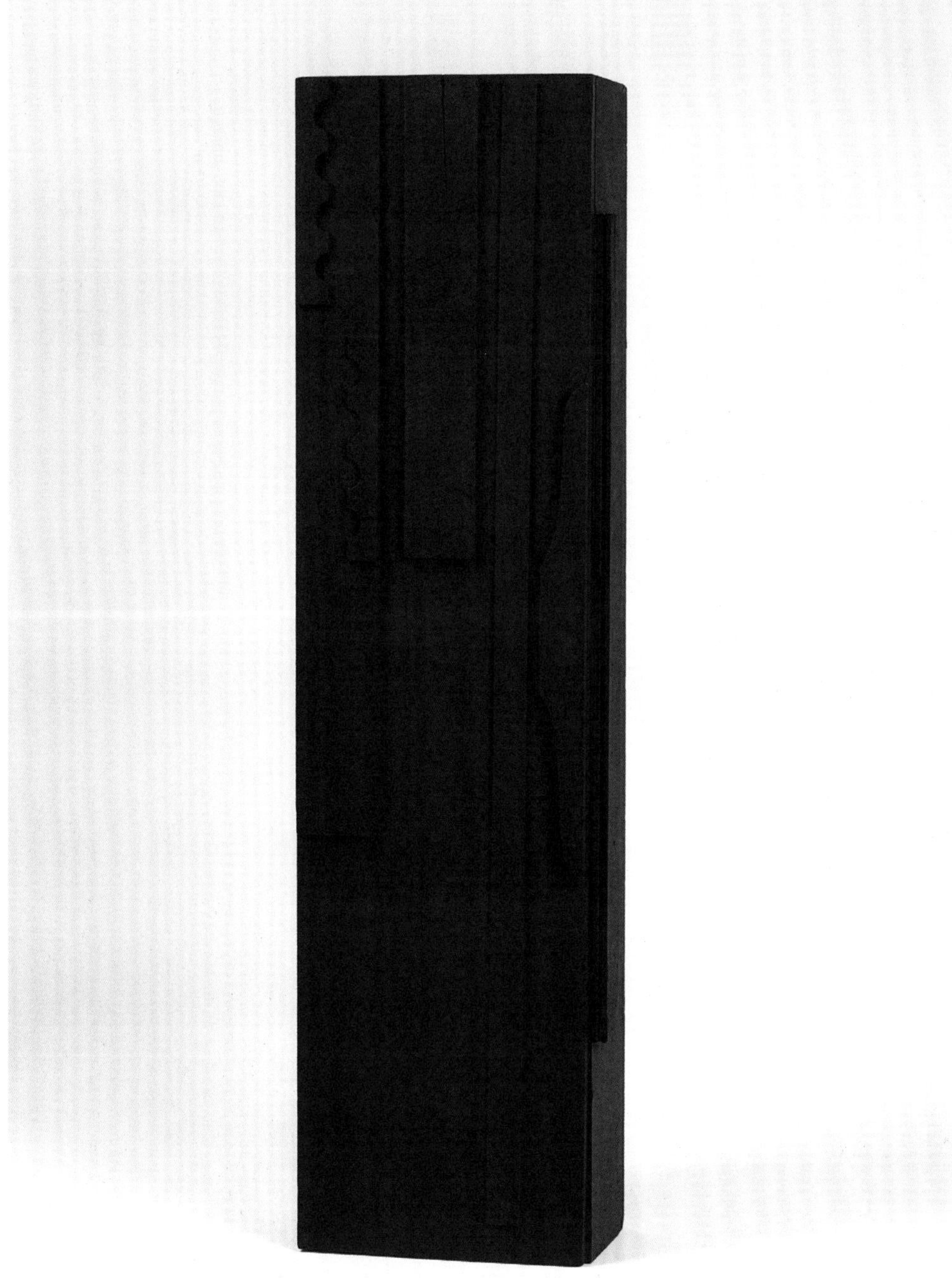

1.18 World Garden IV 1959, wood and metal painted black, 152 × 40 × 28 cm

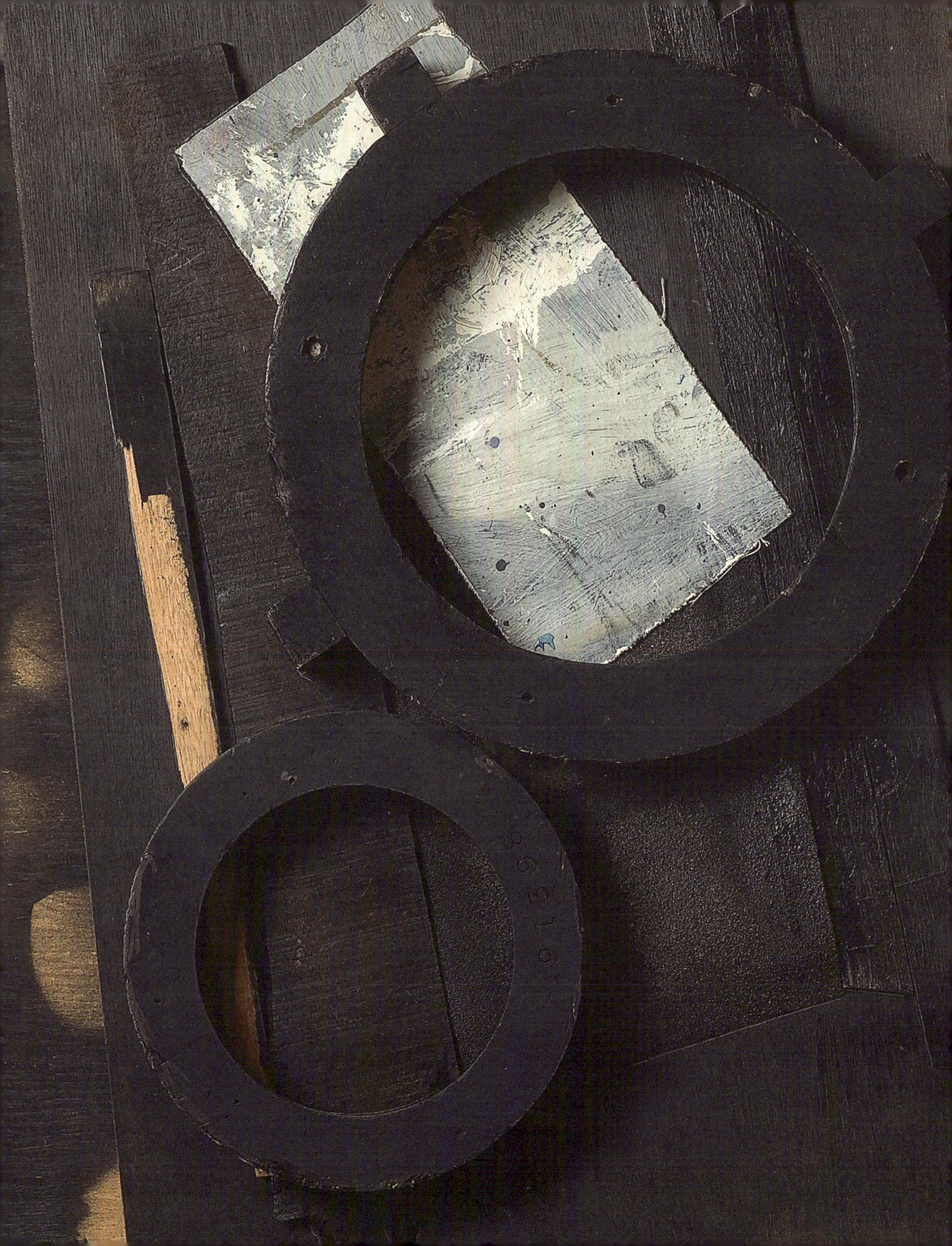

No 2

DIE SUCHE NACH DEM ALLTÄGLICHEN

THE SEARCH FOR THE EVERYDAY

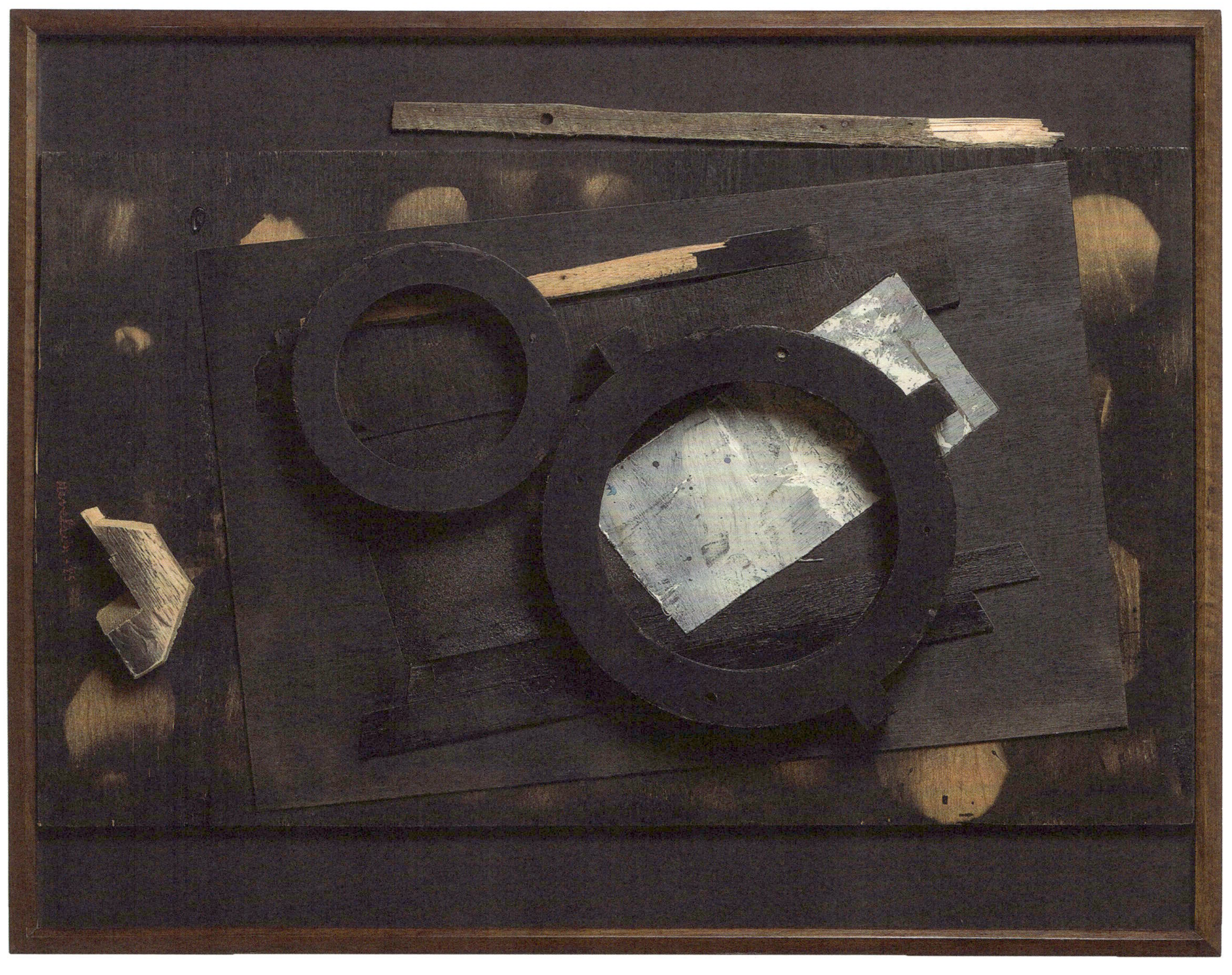

2.1 Volcanic Magic XIII 1985, cardboard, spray paint, paint and wood on board, 101 × 80.7 × 8 cm

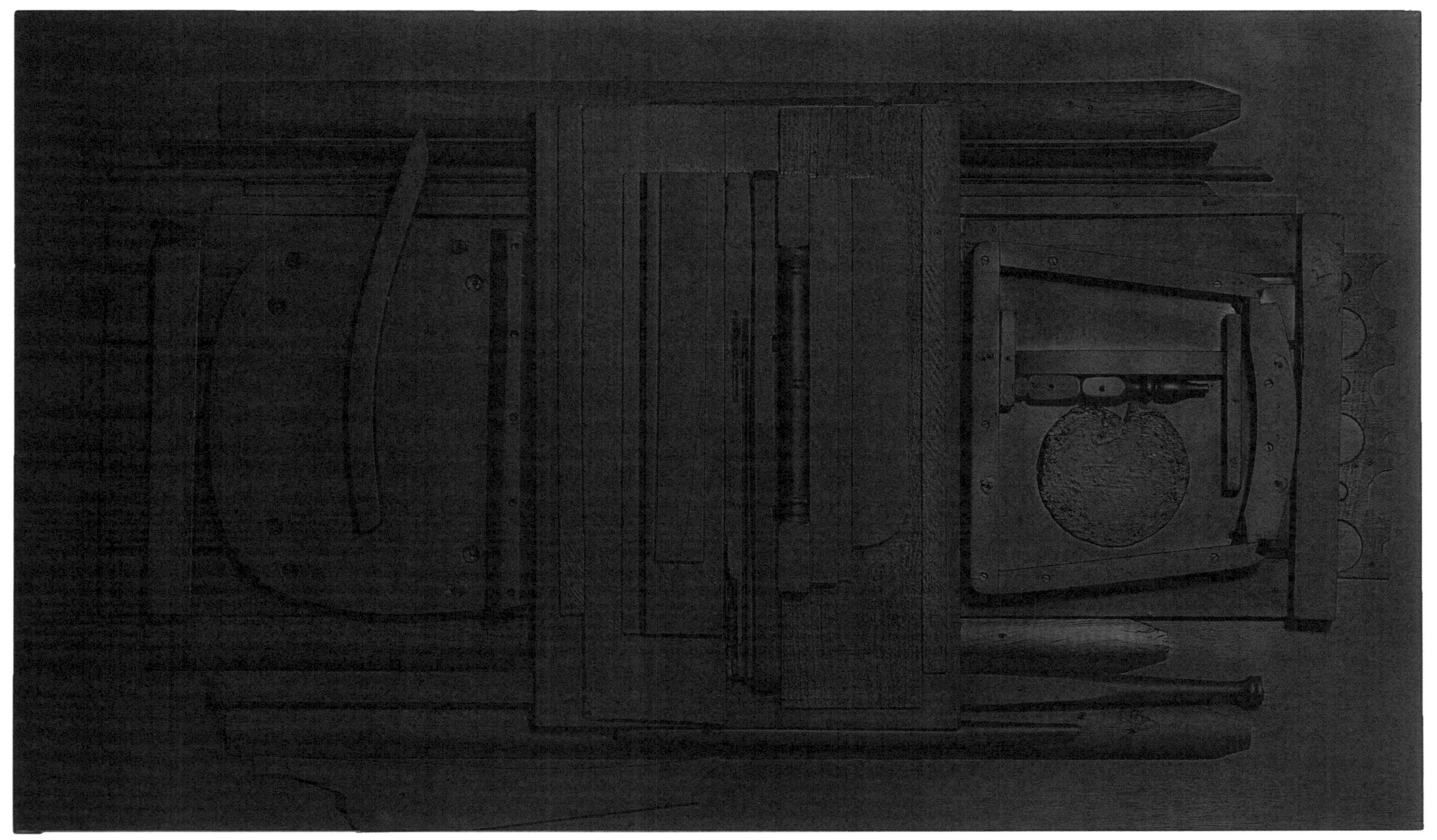

2.2 Untitled 1976, wood painted black,
203.2 × 122 × 15.5 cm

2.3 Untitled 1976–1978, wood painted black,
203.2 × 122 × 24.5 cm

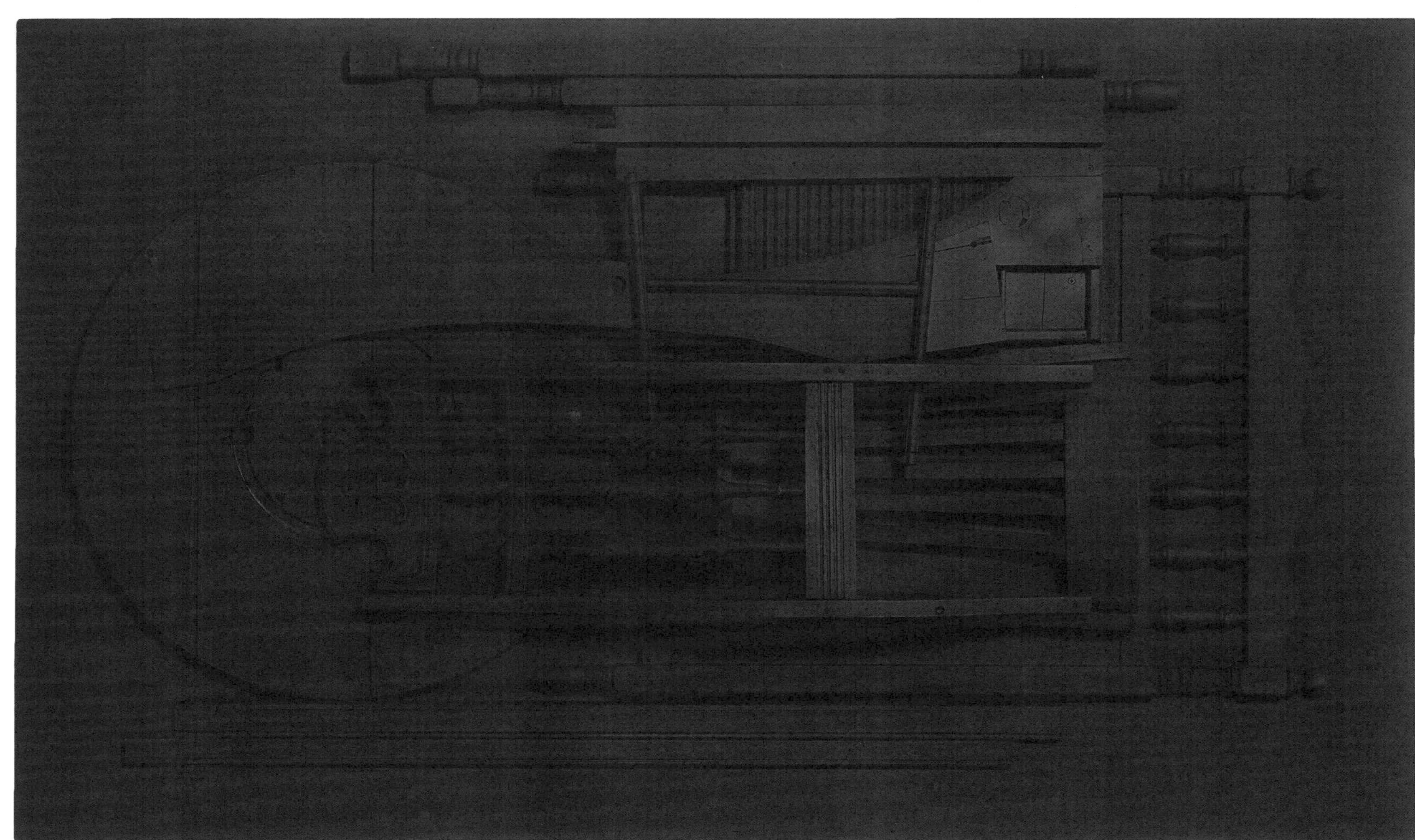

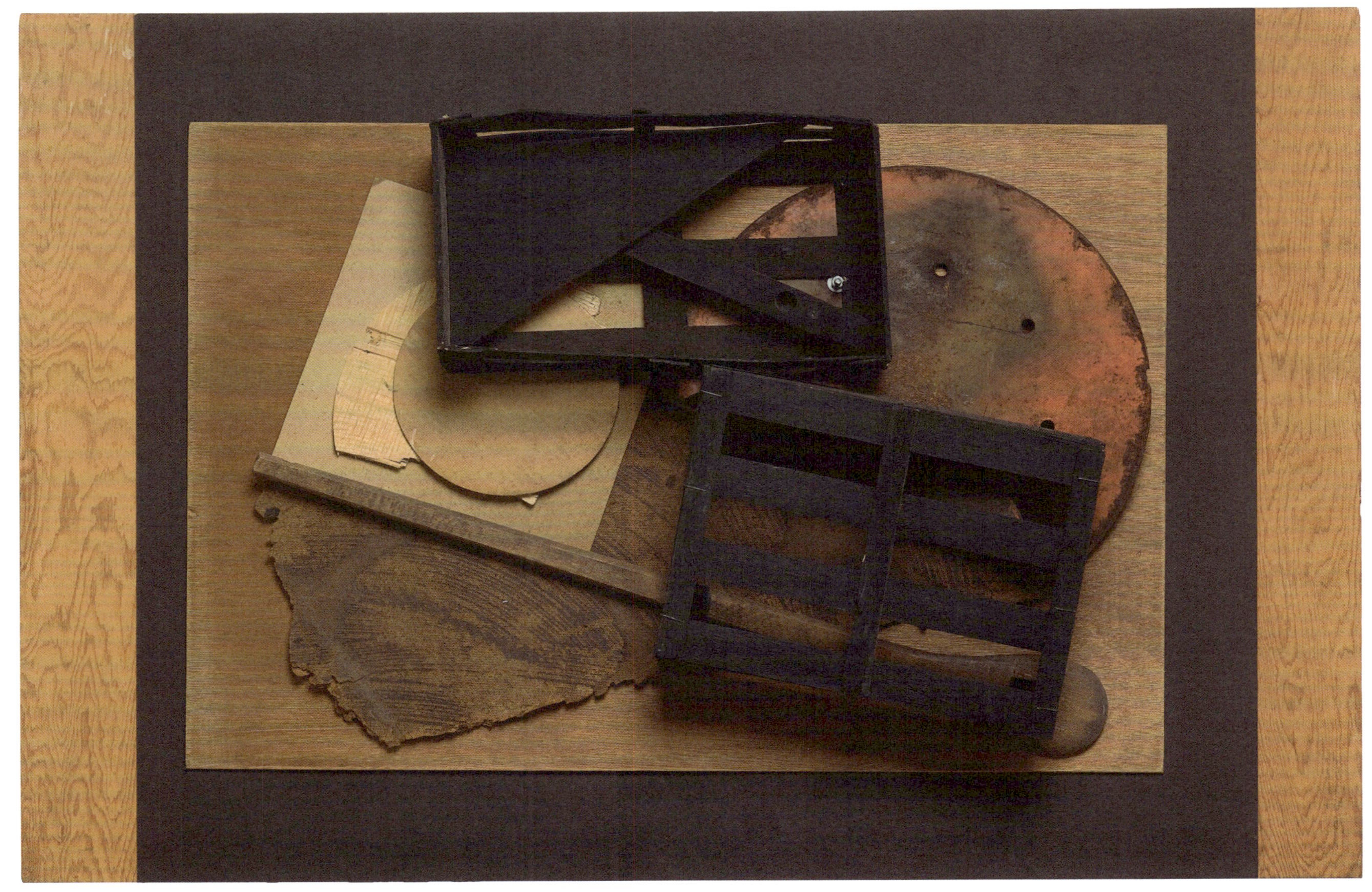

2.4 Untitled 1986, cardboard, paint, metal, wood, wooden spoon, fiber building board and wood on board, 122 × 81.7 × 15 cm

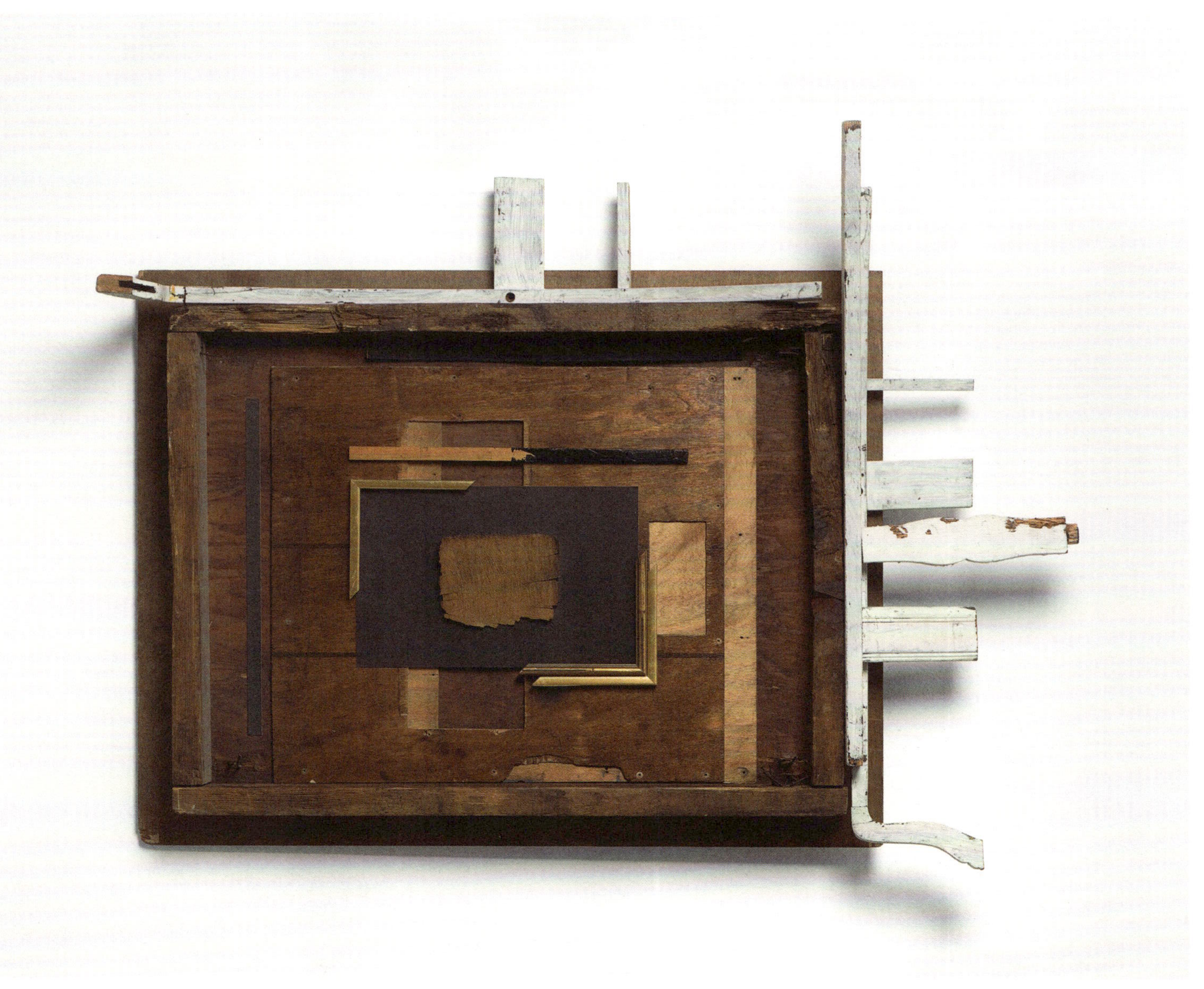

2.5 Volcanic Magic XXXII 1985, cardboard, paint and wood on board, 129 × 100.5 × 9.5 cm

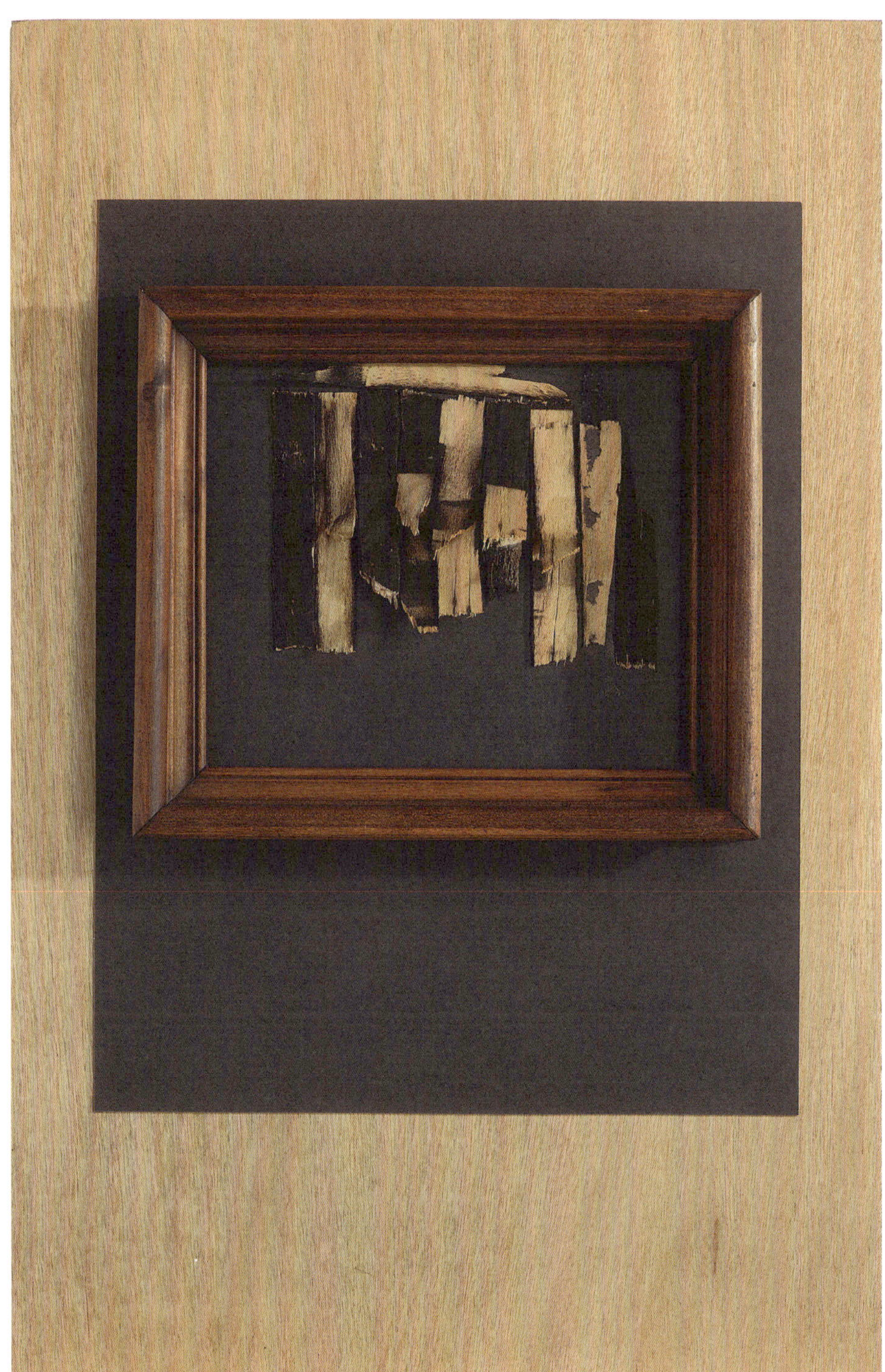

2.6 Untitled 1982, cardboard, paint and wood on board, 76 × 51 cm

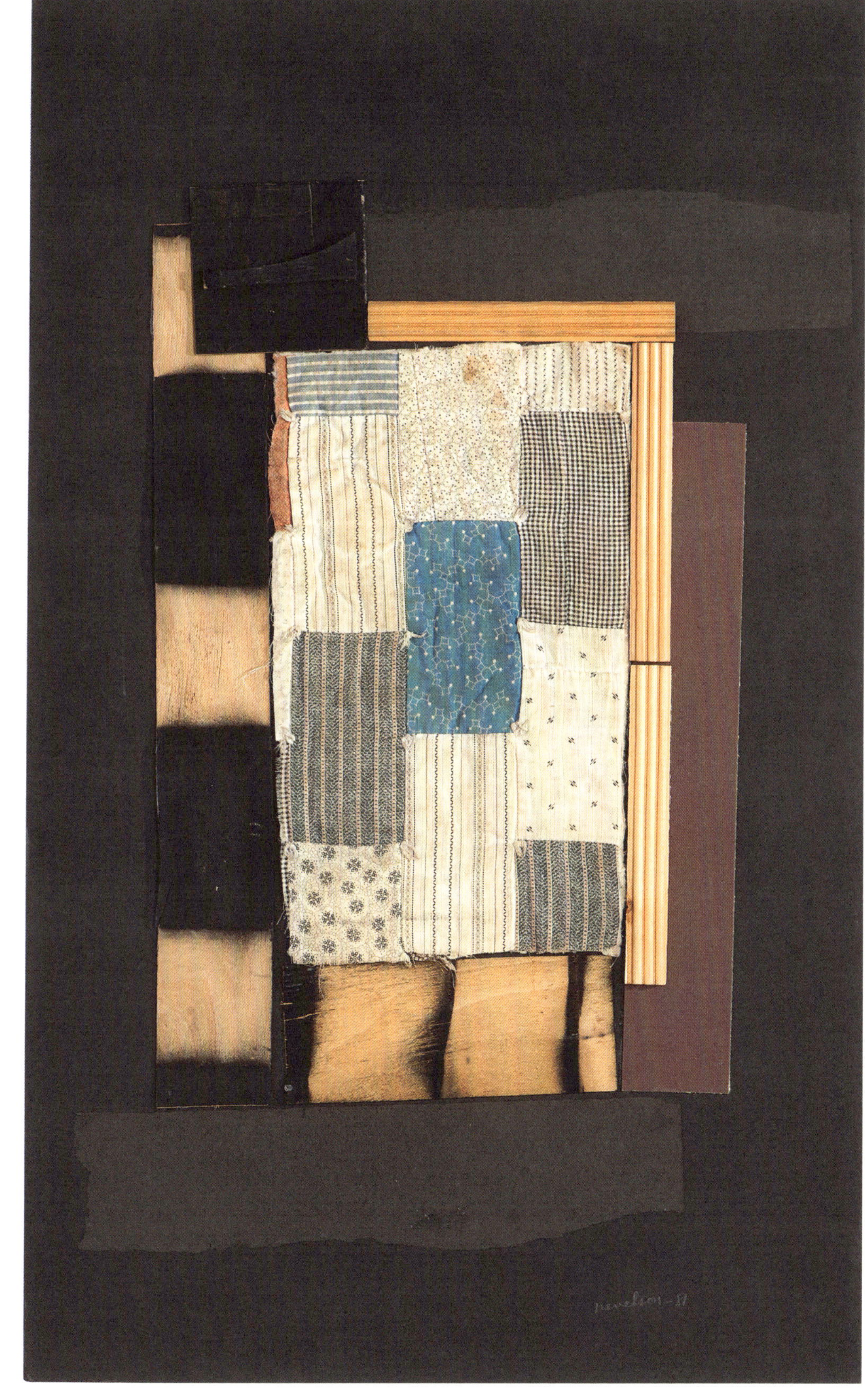

2.7 Untitled 1981, fabric, paint, paper and wood on board, 81 × 51 cm

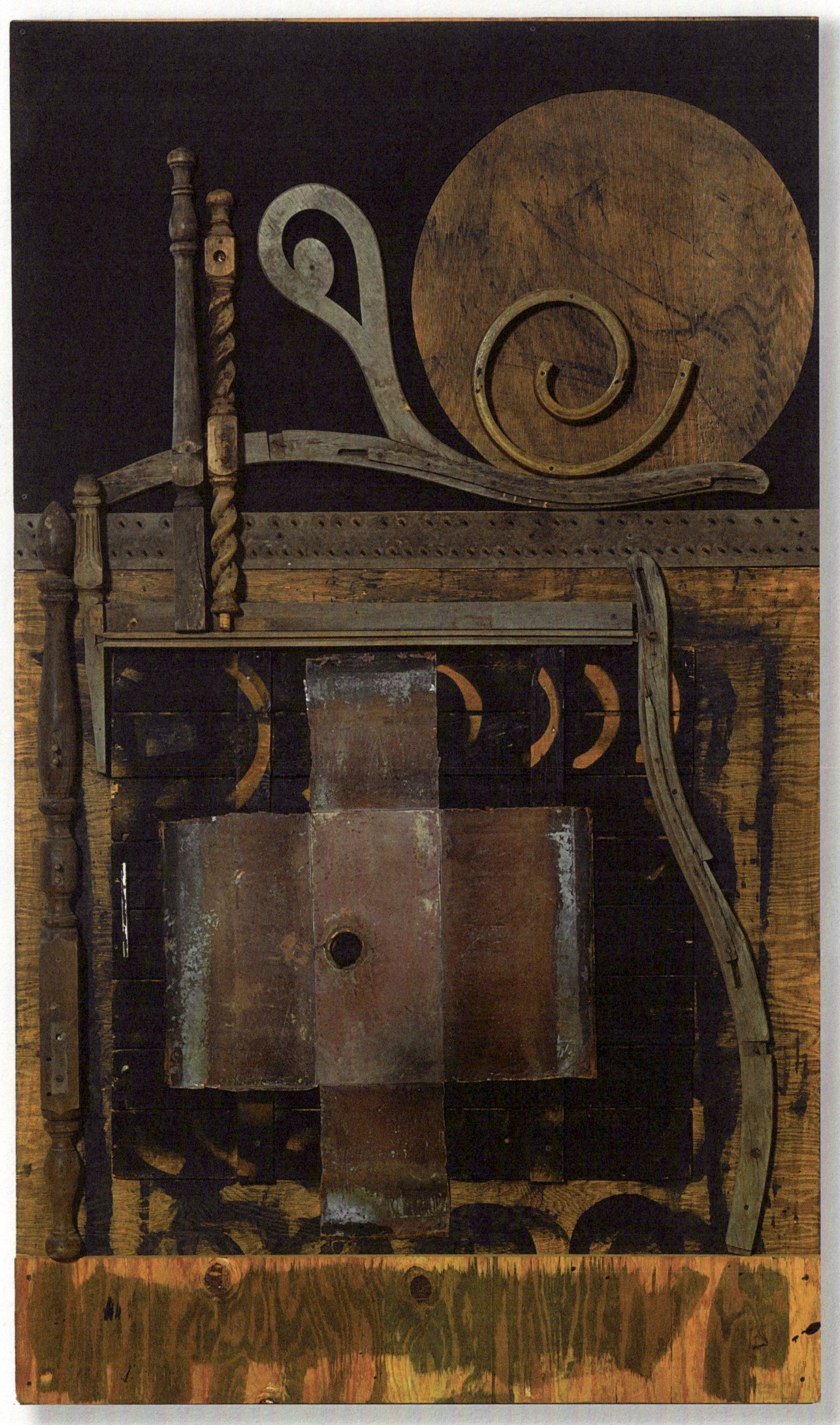

2.8 Untitled 1980, collage on painted wood,
202.7 × 122 × 14 cm

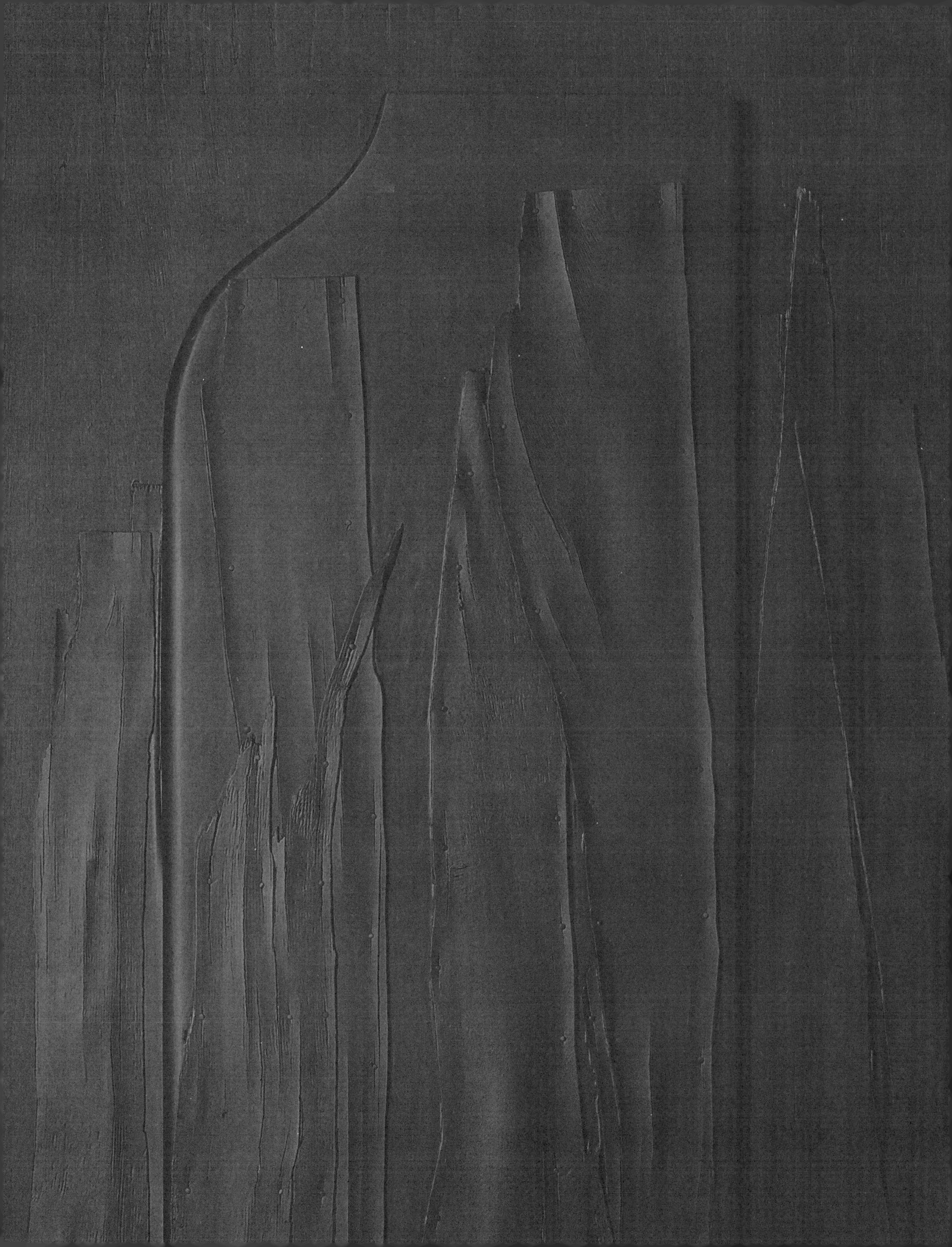

VOM SUCHEN UND FINDEN

No3

SEARCHING AND FINDING

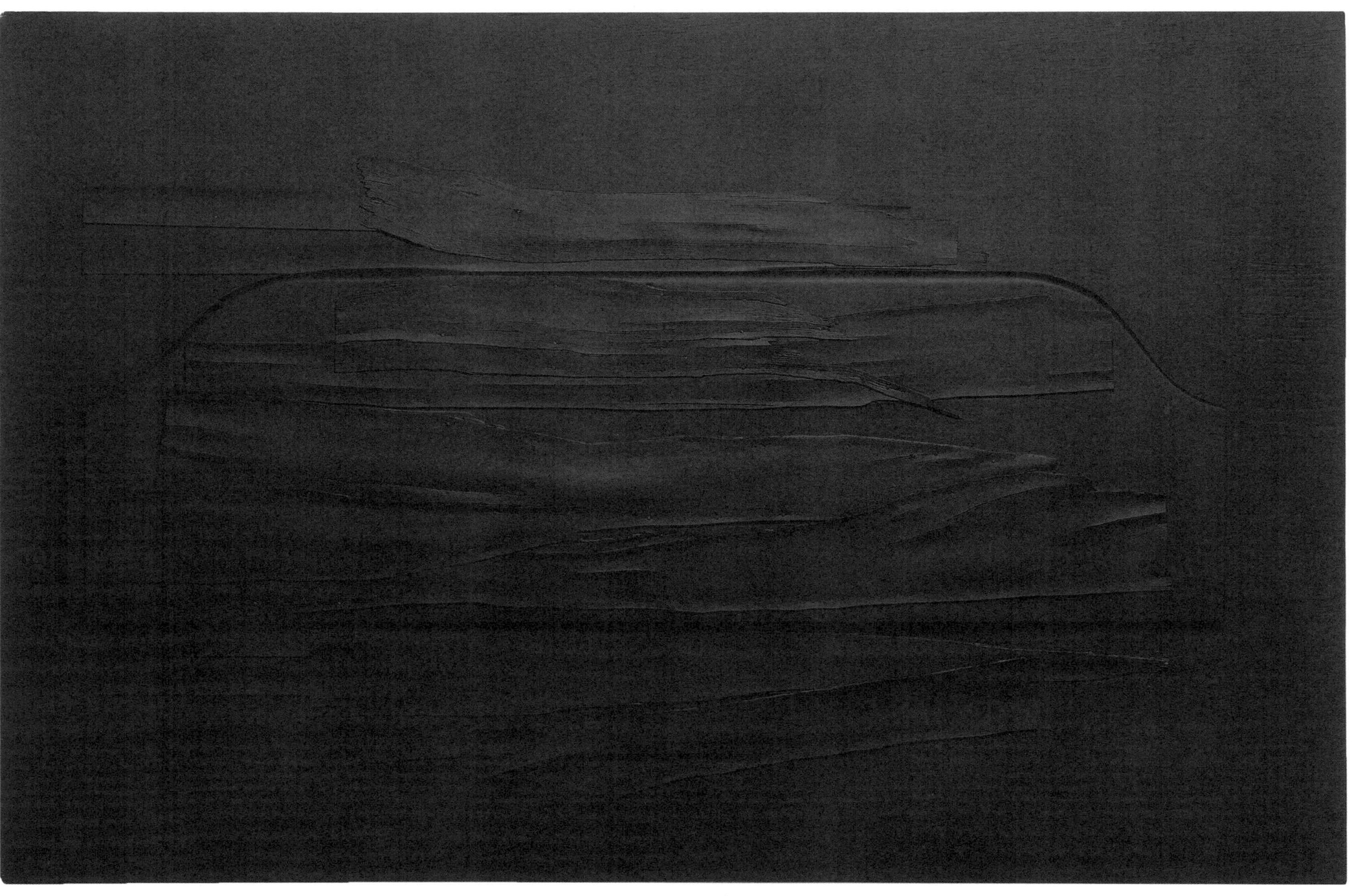

3.1 Untitled 1985, paint and wood on board,
136.9 × 91.3 × 2.5 cm

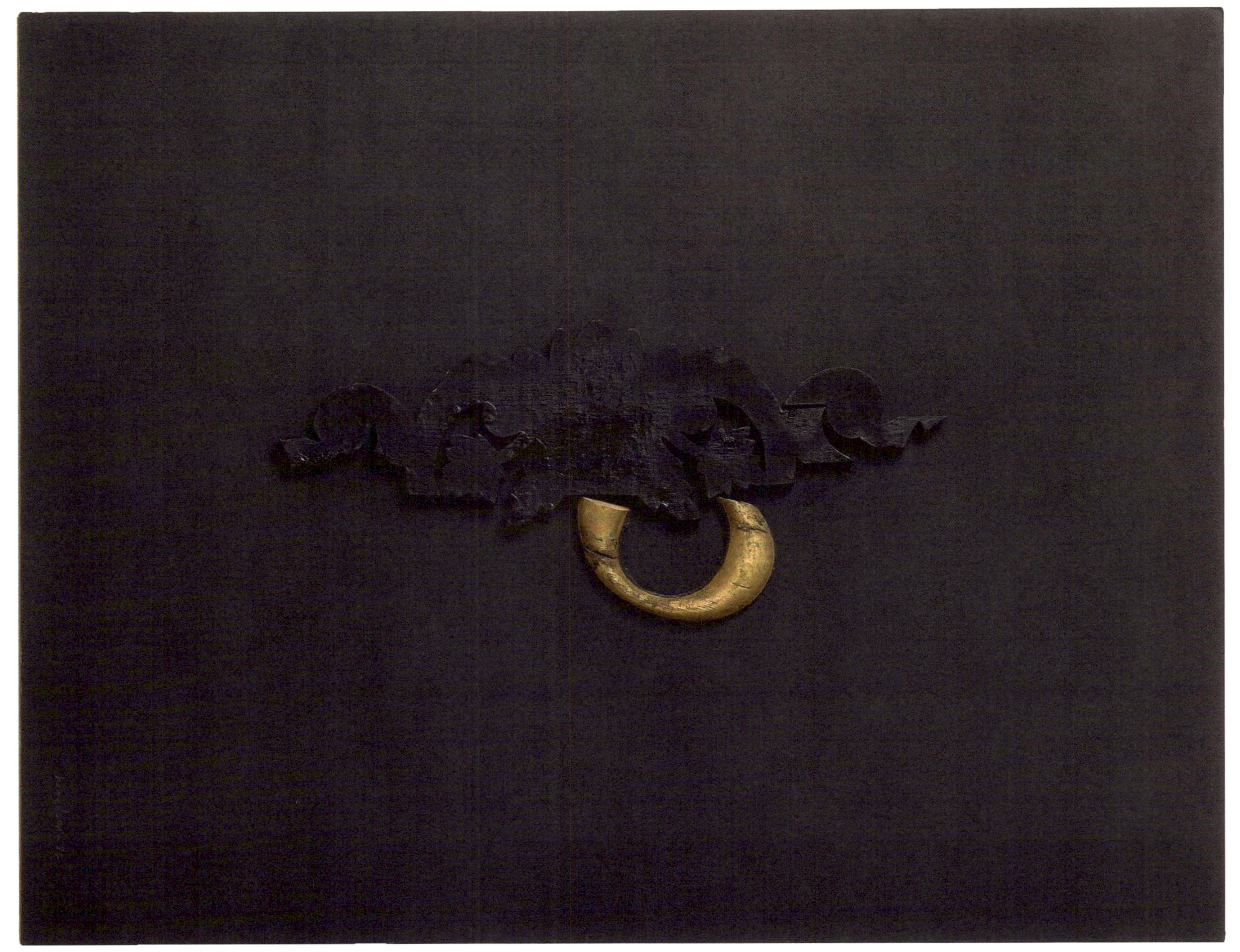

3.2 Untitled 1982, wood and paint on board, 101.5 × 81.2 × 3 cm

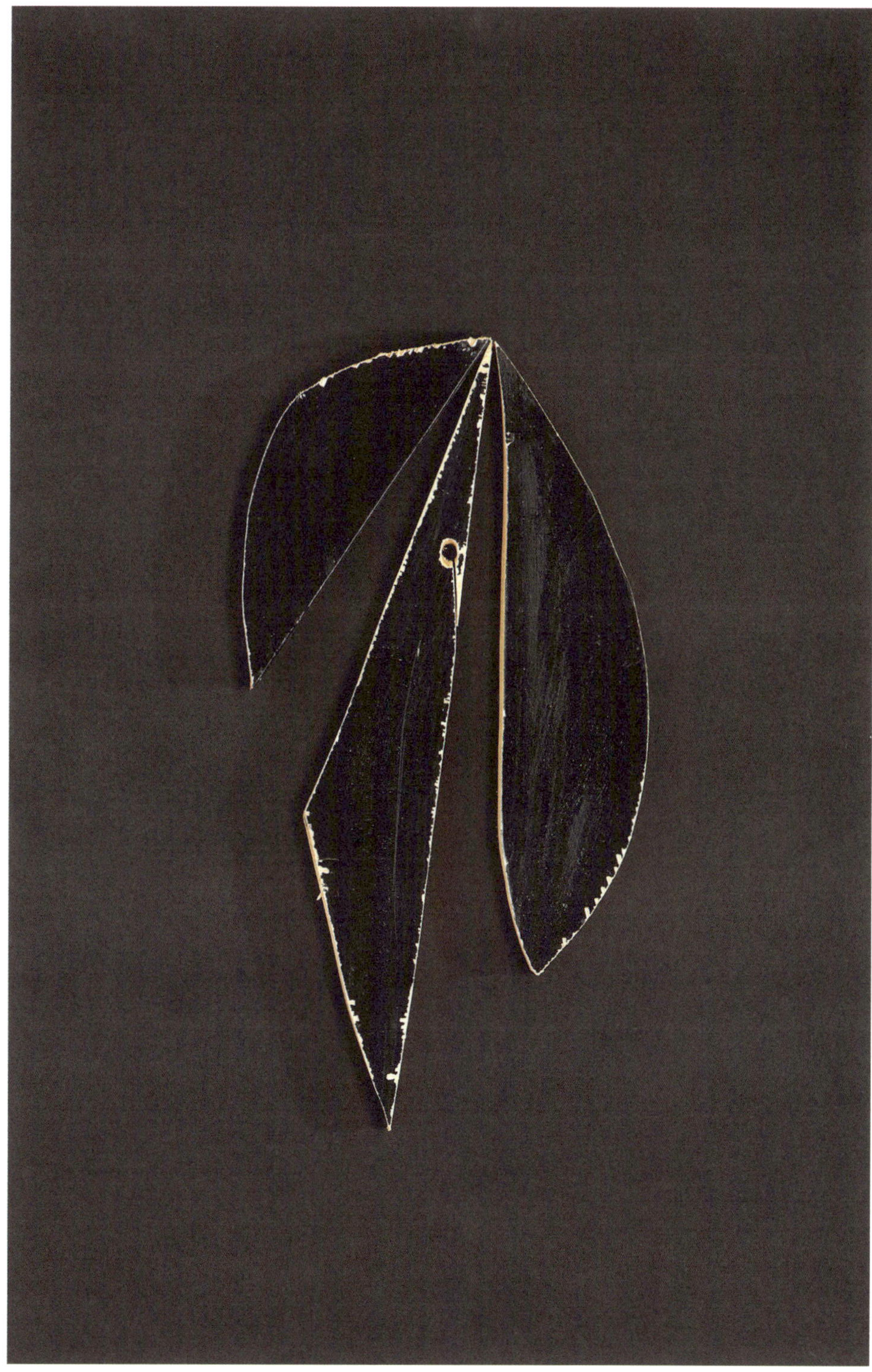

3.3 Untitled 1970, cardboard, paint and wood on board, 76 × 51 cm

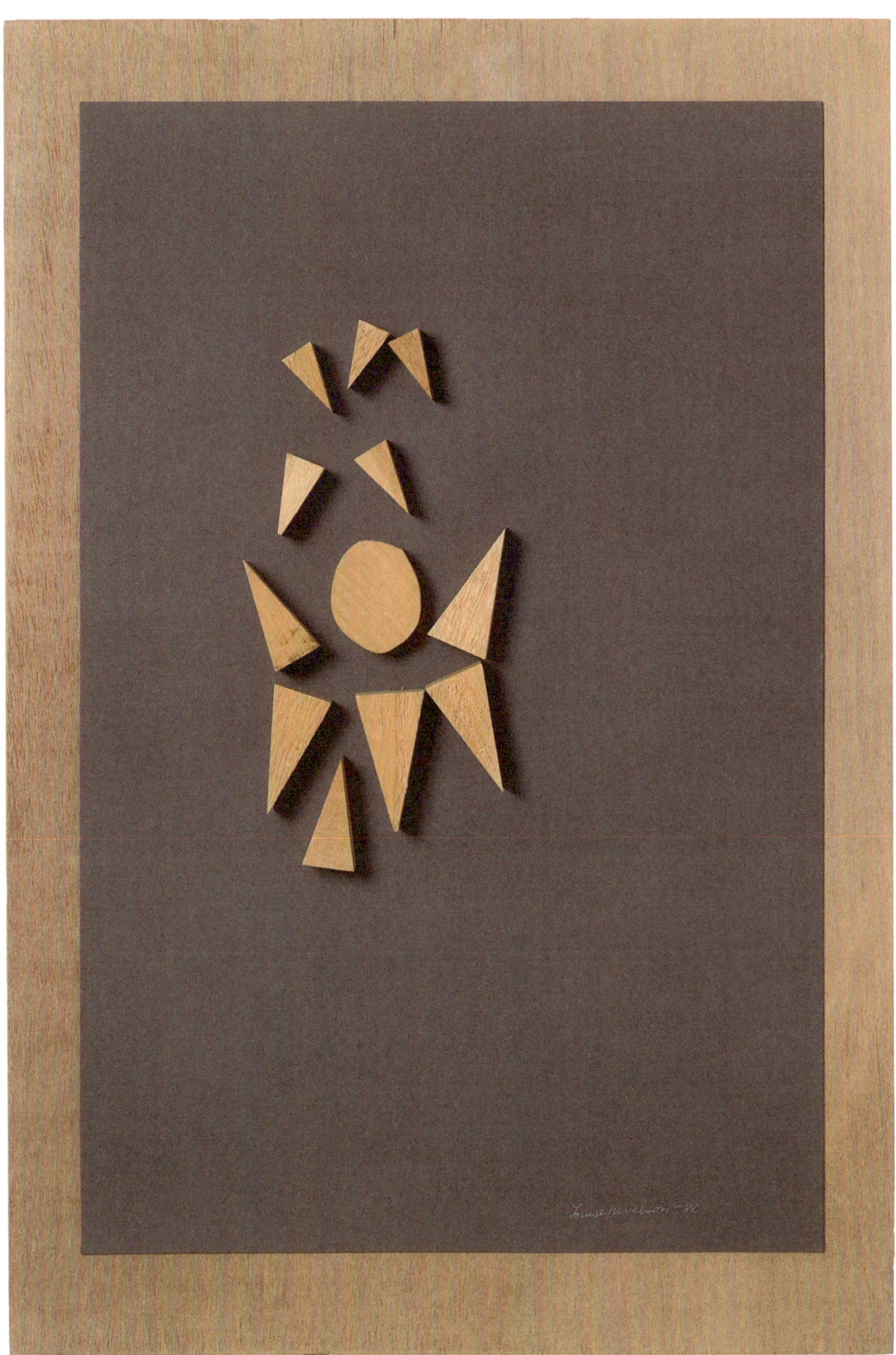

3.4 Untitled 1980, cardboard and wood on board, 88.8 × 60.6 × 3.8 cm

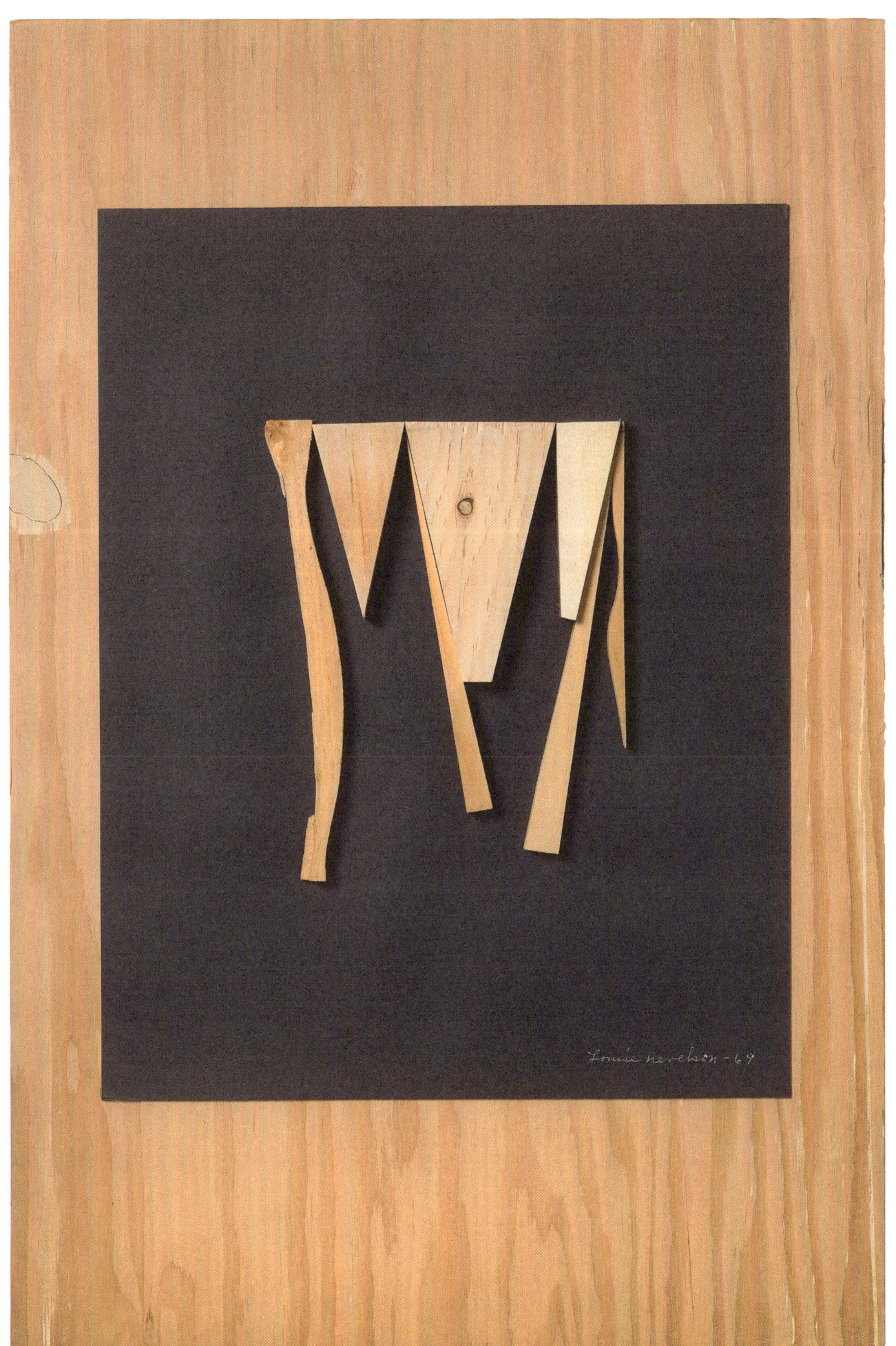

3.5 Untitled 1969, cardboard and wood on board, 76.2 × 51.3 × 2.8 cm

3.6 Untitled 1980, wood painted black,
ca. 212 × 85 × 68 cm

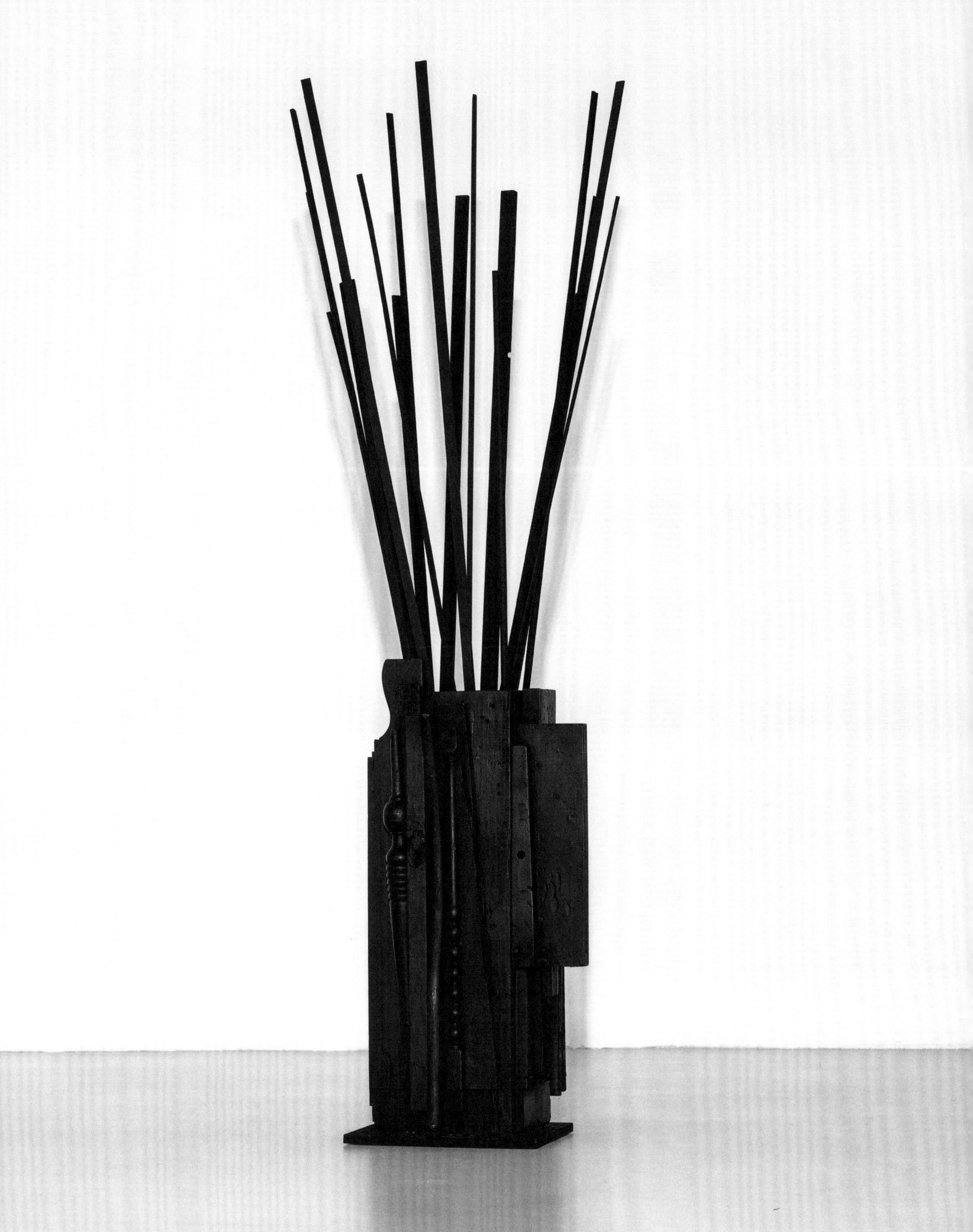

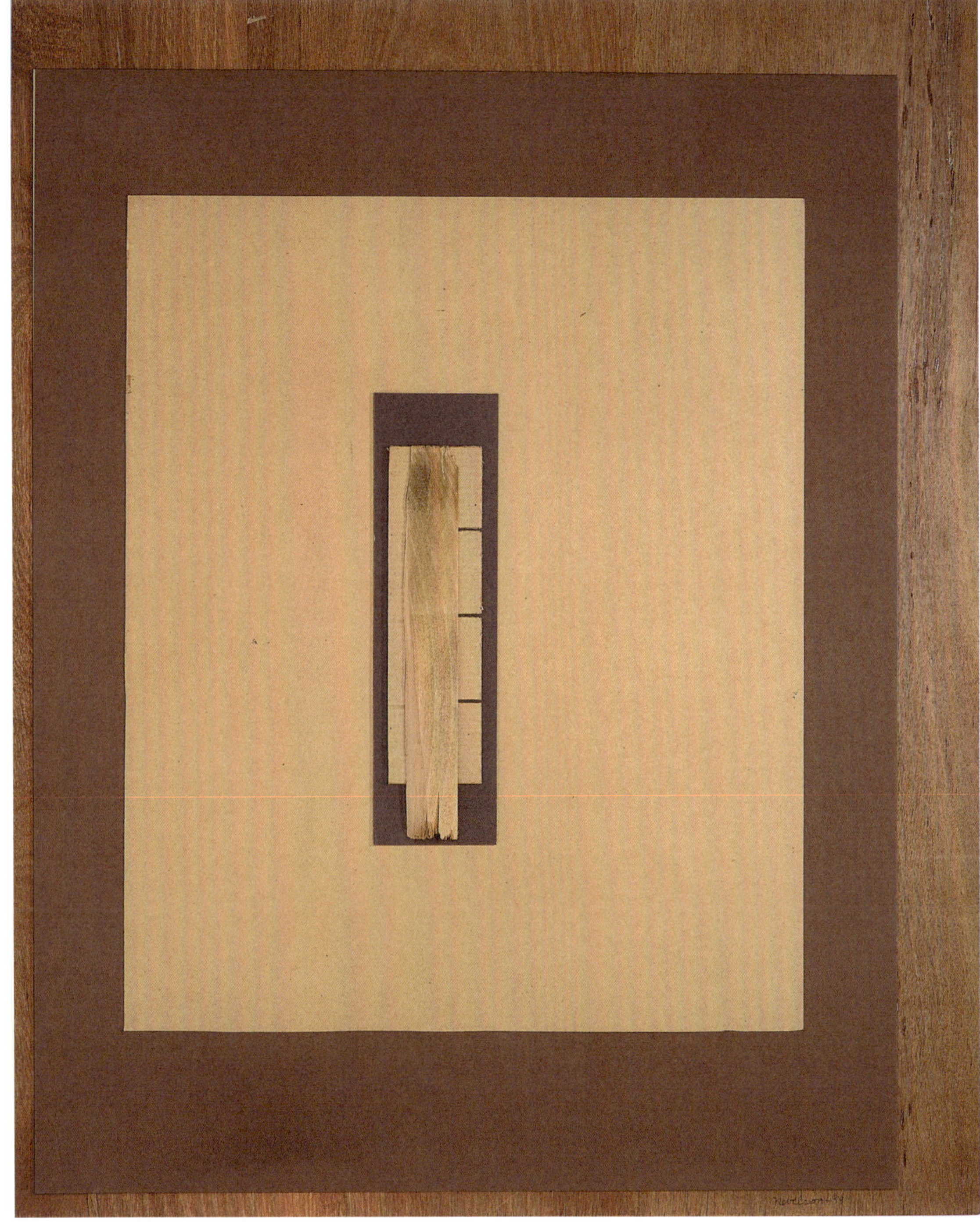

3.7 Untitled 1959, cardboard and wood on board, 112 × 91.5 cm

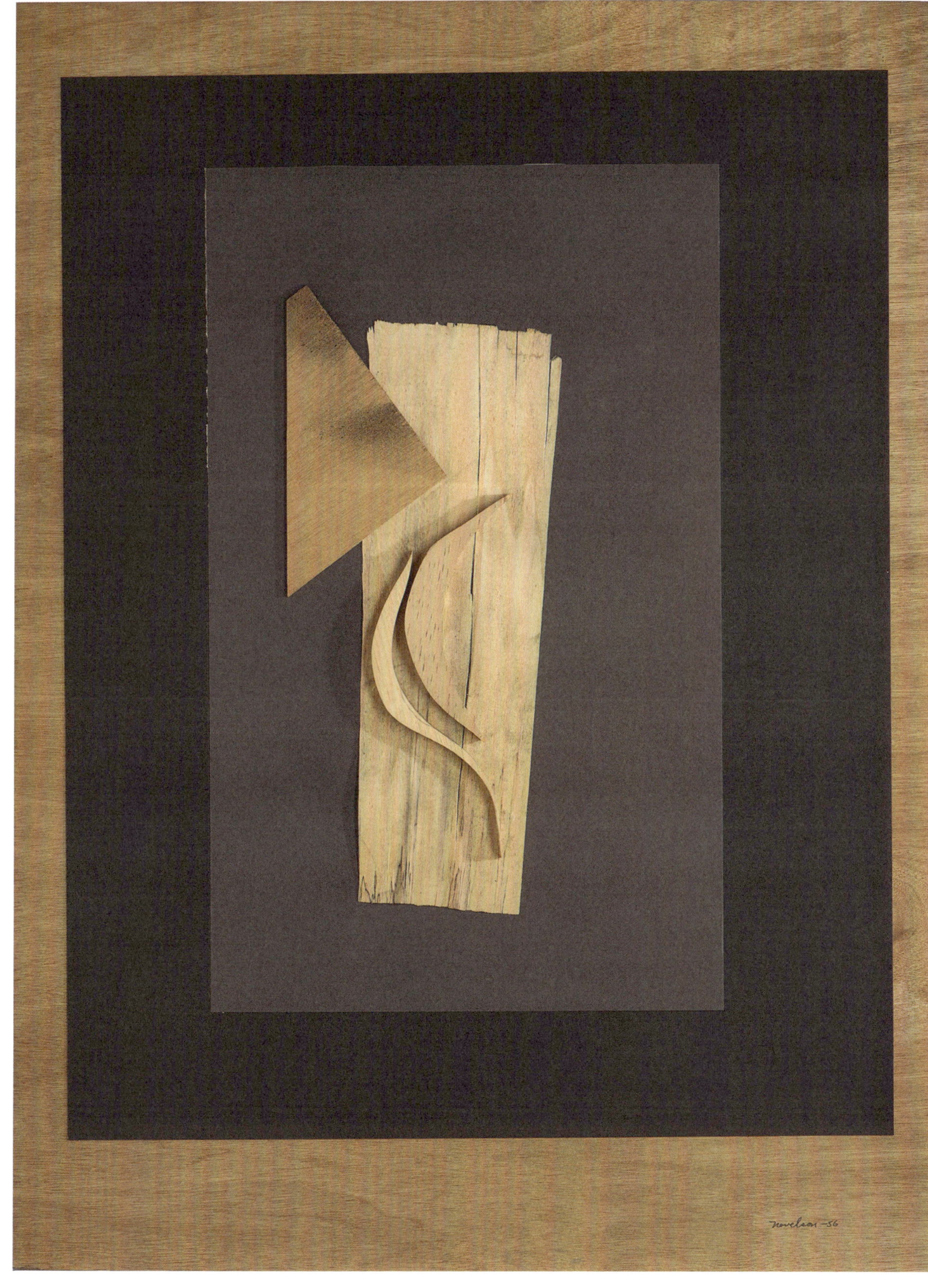

3.8 Untitled 1956, cardboard, spray paint and wood on board, 122 × 91 cm

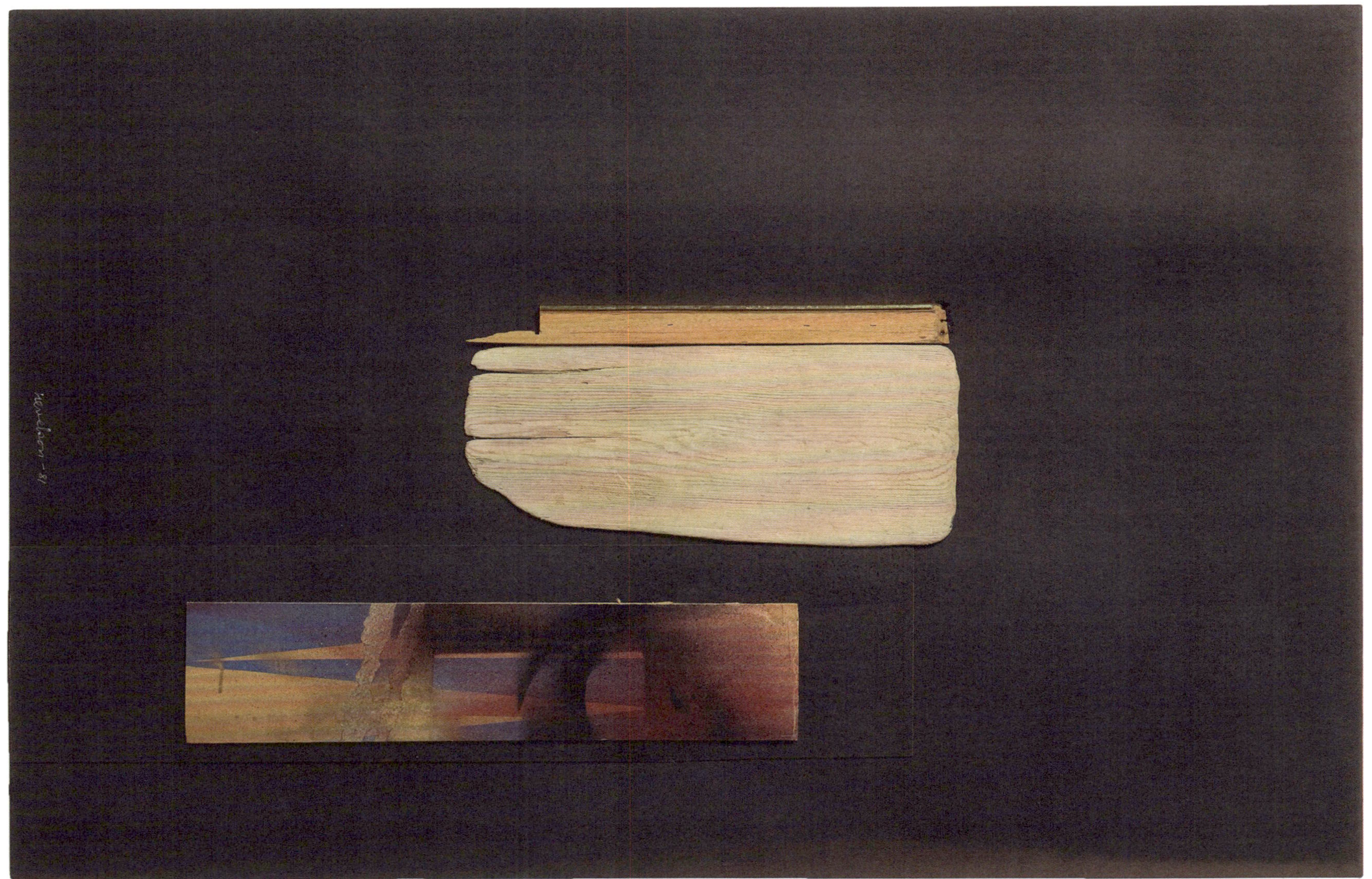

3.9 Untitled 1981, cardboard, spray paint, paint and wood on board, 76 × 50.5 × 1.4 cm

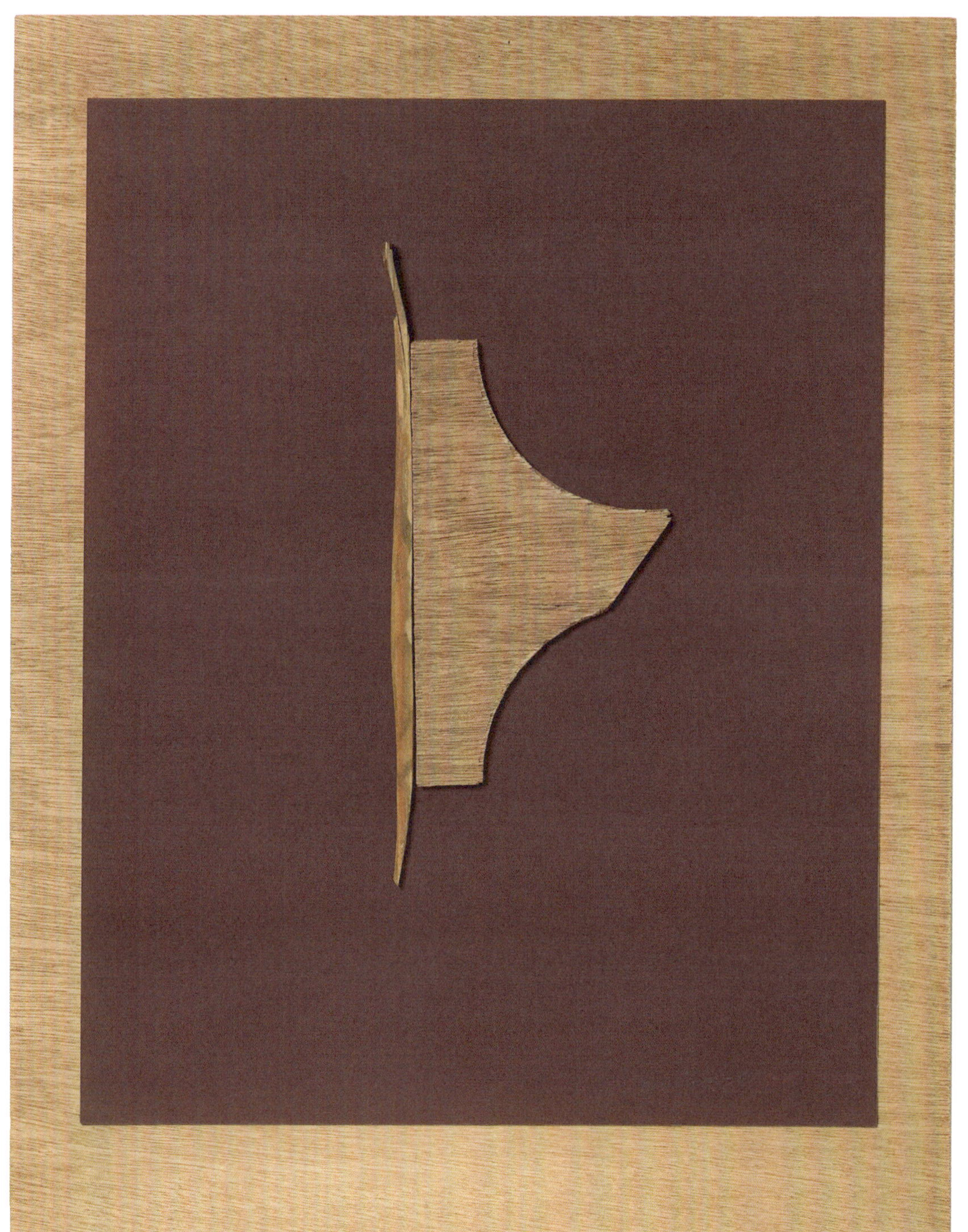

3.10 Untitled 1980, cardboard and wood on board, 60.6 × 48.5 × 1.4 cm

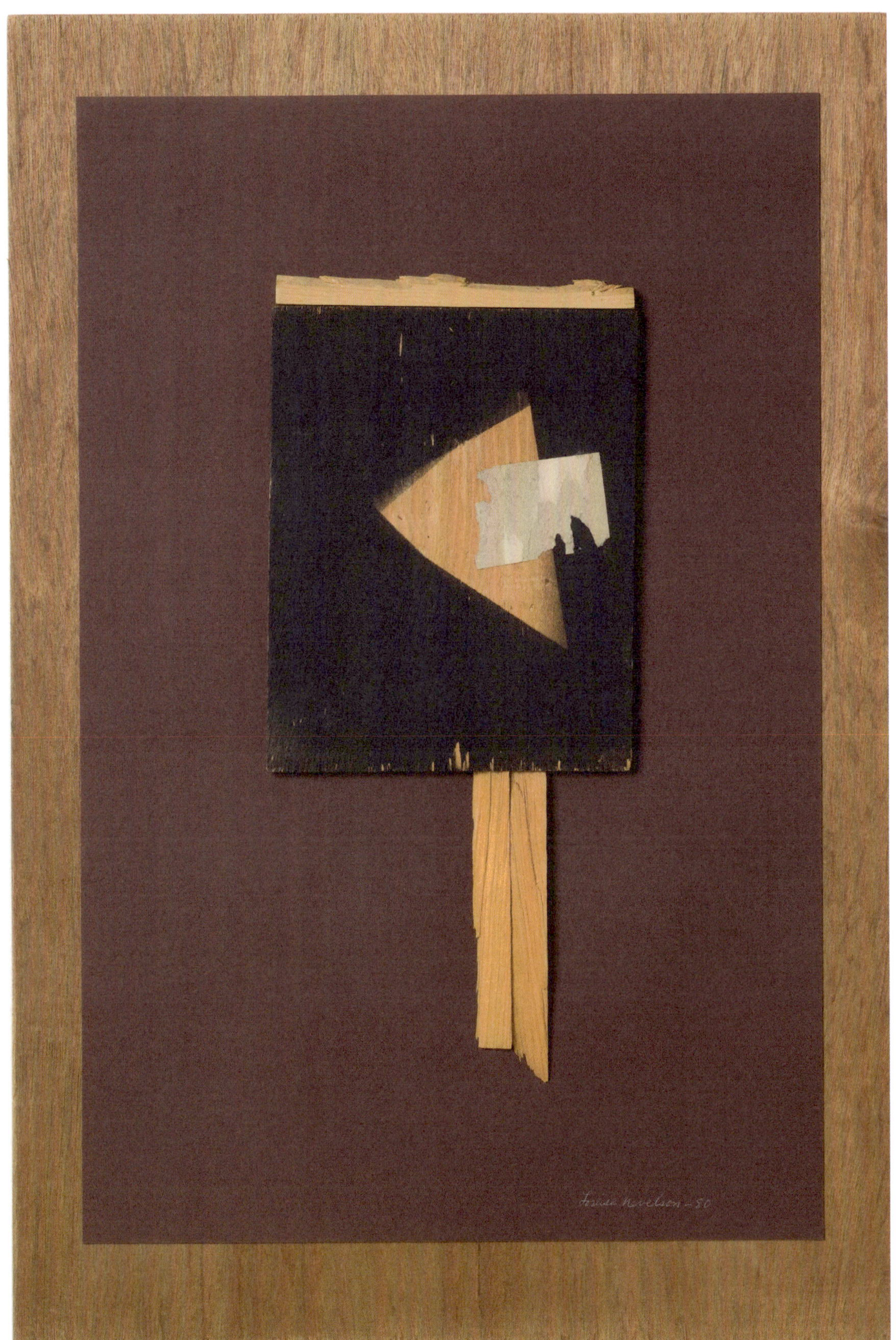

3.11 Untitled 1980, cardboard, paint, paper and wood on board, 88.8 × 60.6 × 2.2 cm

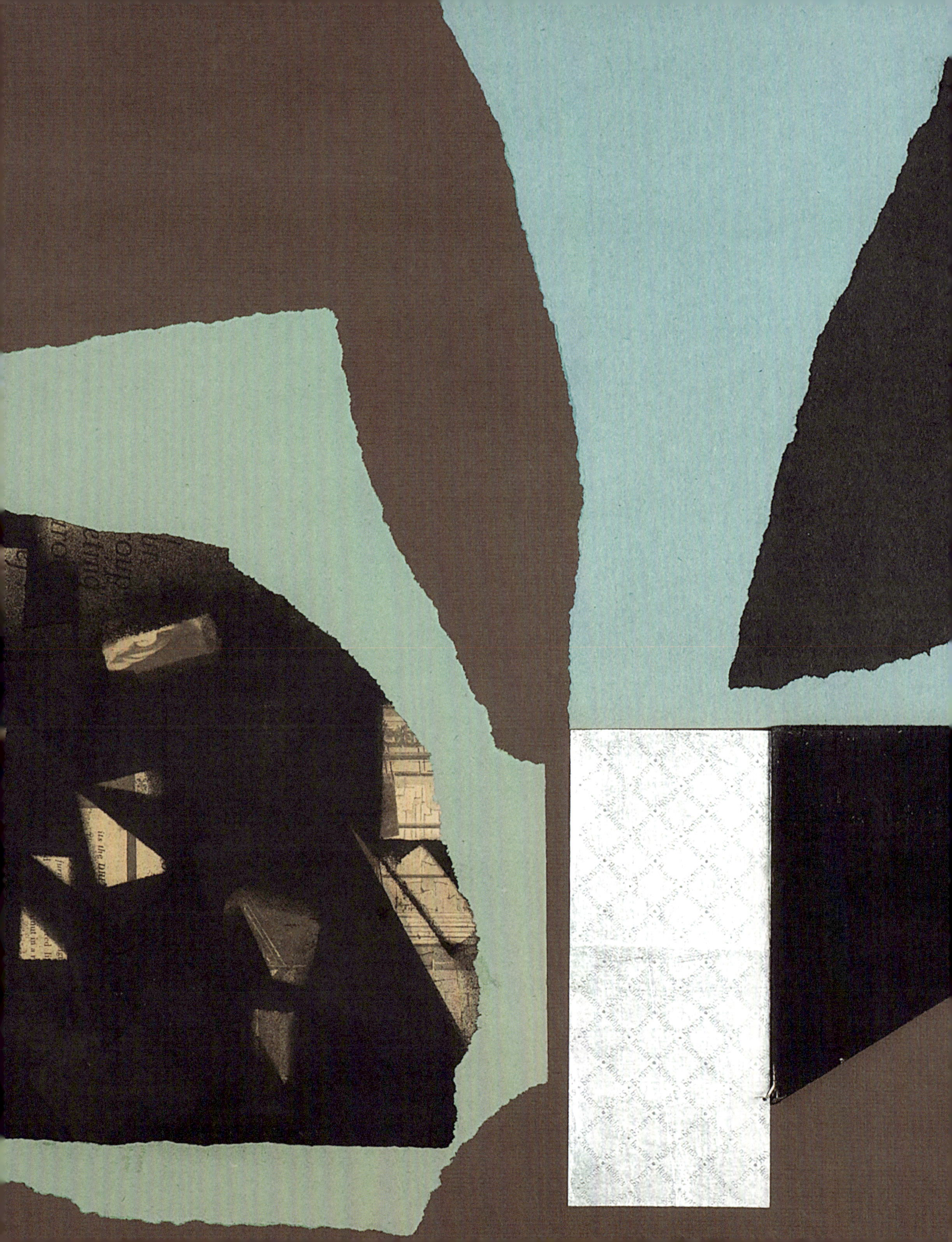

No 4

DAS FORTWÄHRENDE ENTDECKEN
THE ONGOING DISCOVERY

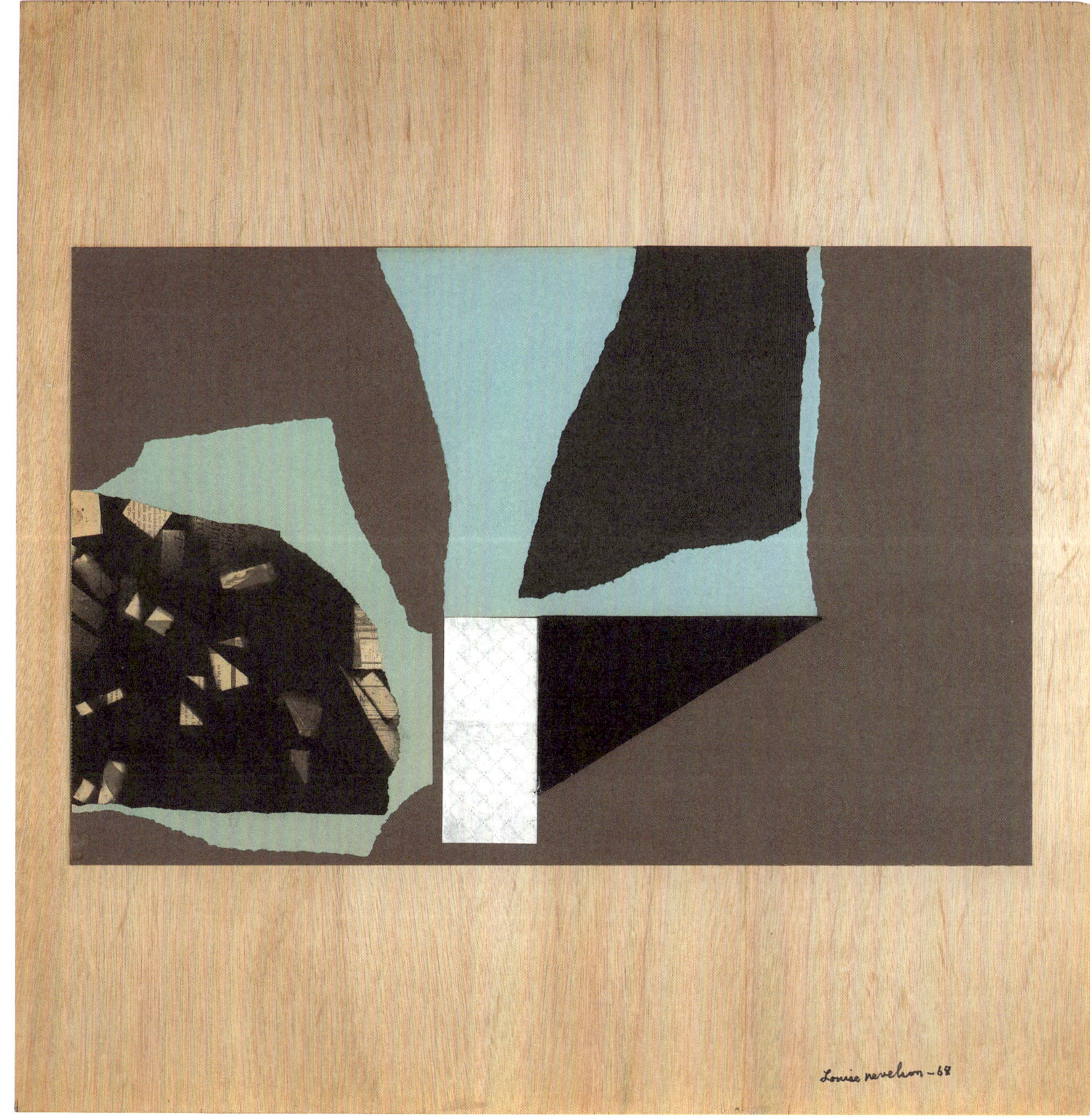

4.1 Untitled 1968, cardboard, spray paint, newsprint on board, 91.5 × 91.5 cm

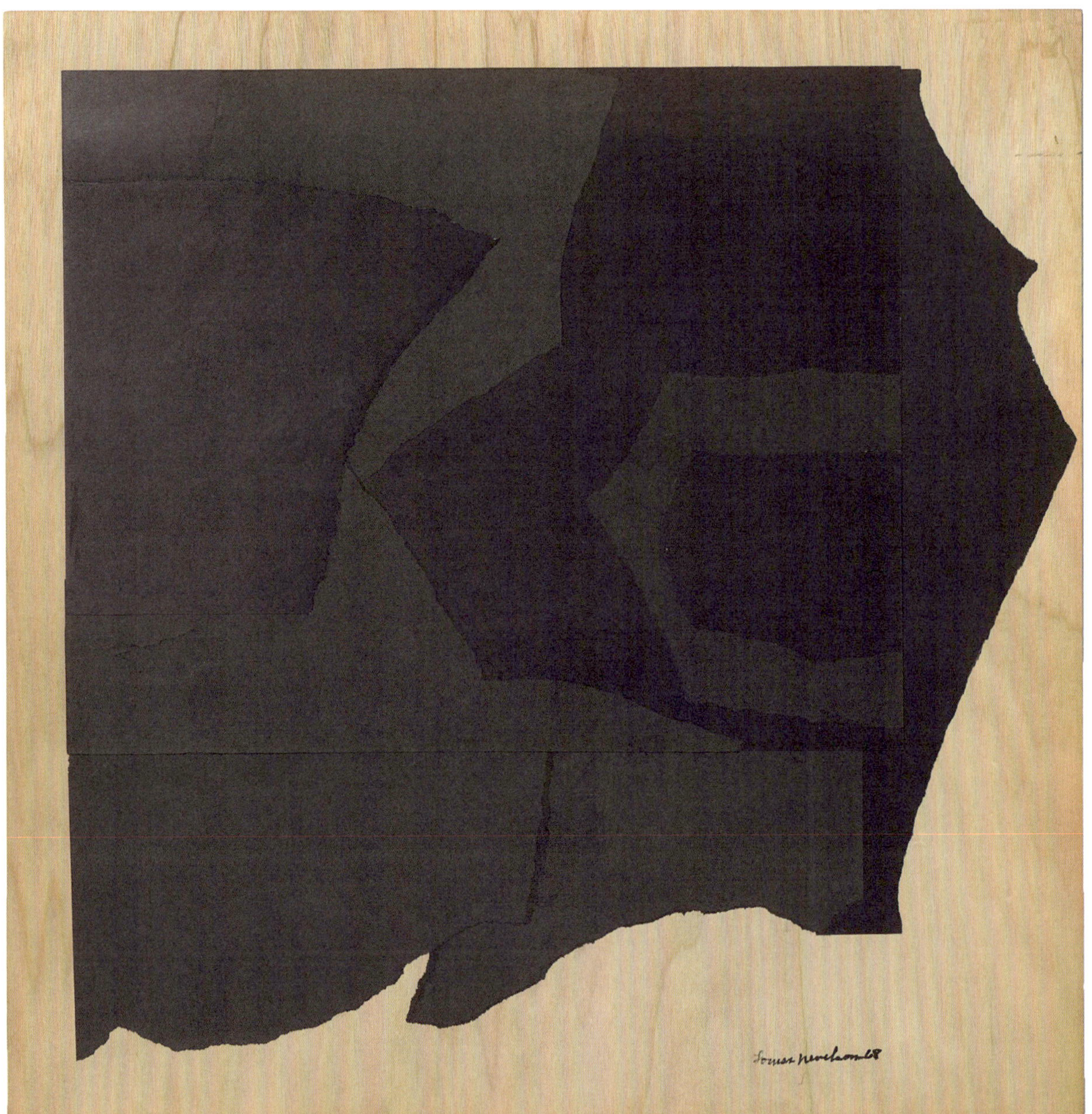

4.2 Untitled 1967, cardboard and paint on board, 91.4 × 91.2 × 0.8 cm

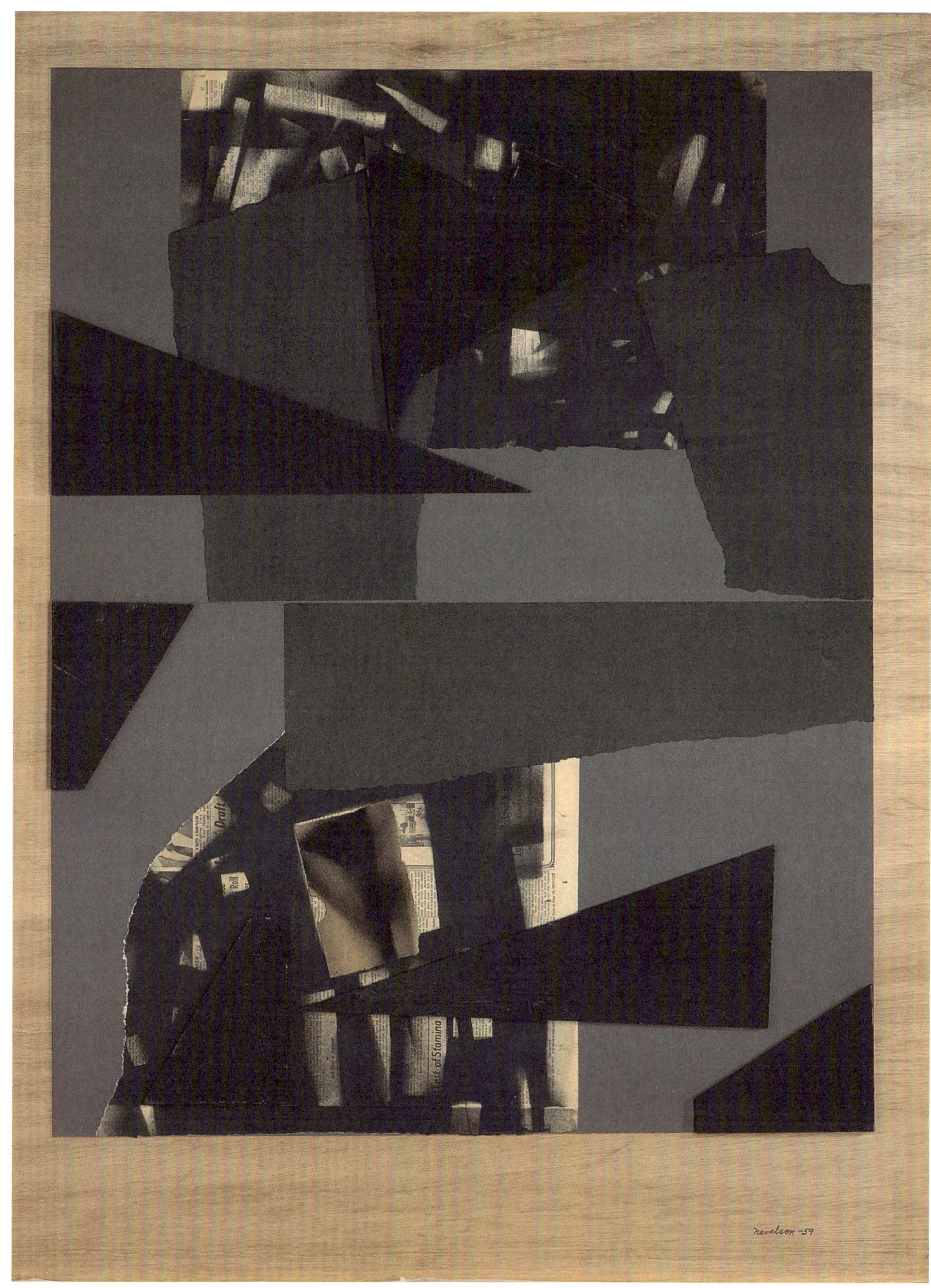

4.3 Untitled 1959, cardboard, spray paint, newsprint and wood on board, 122 × 91.5 cm

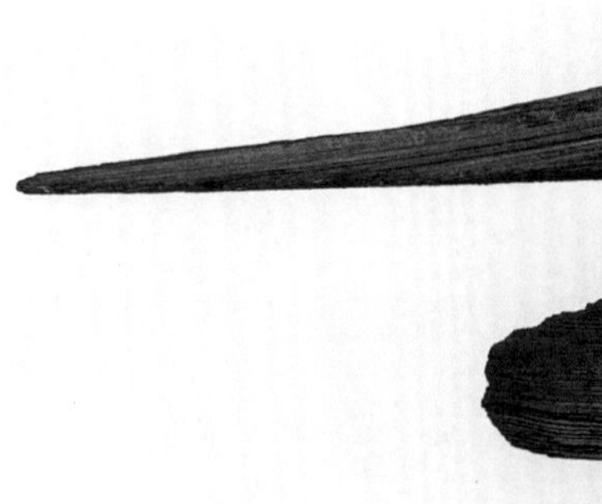

4.4 Moon Spikes IV 1955, wood painted black, 93.5 × 108.3 × 25.5 cm

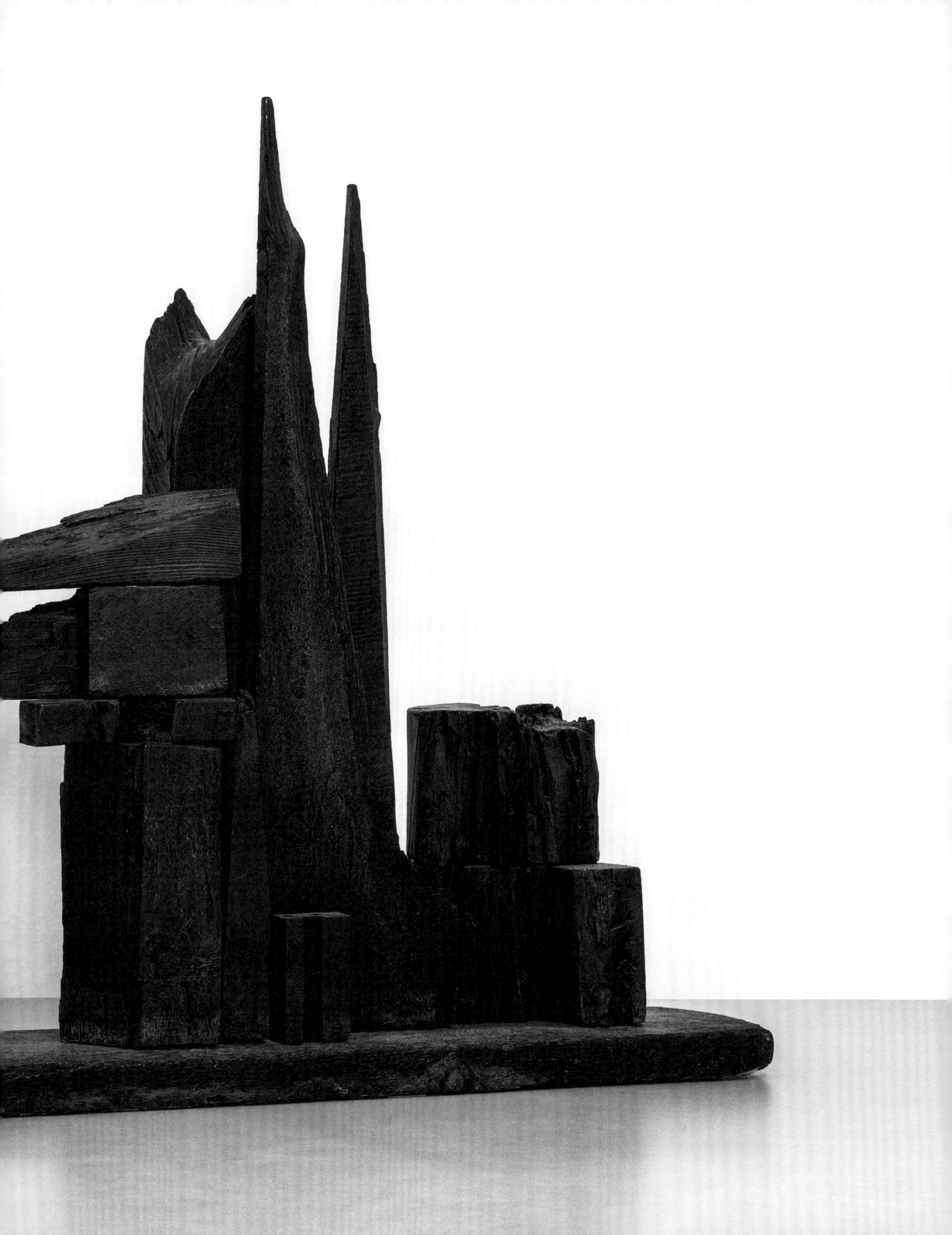

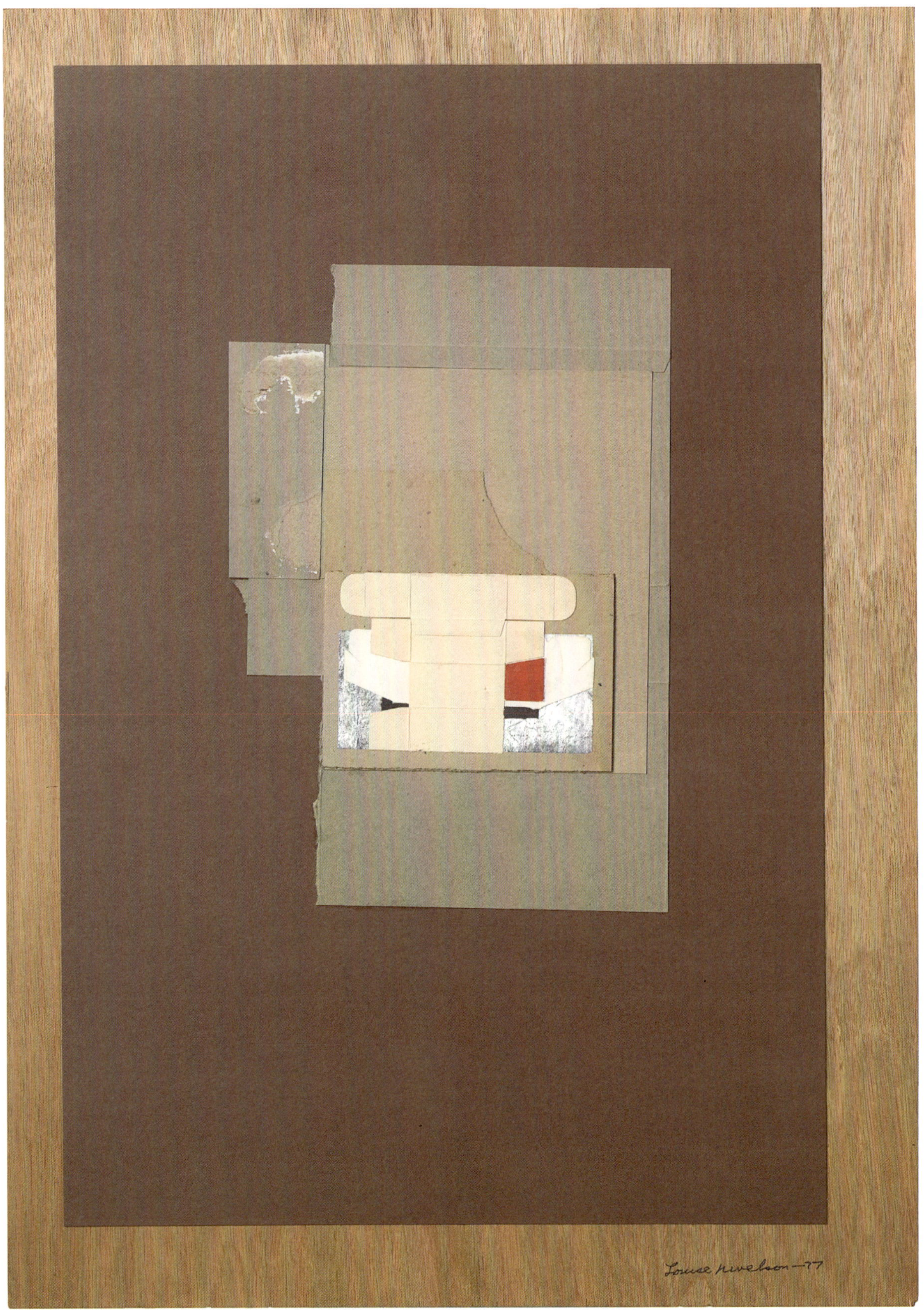

4.5 Untitled 1977, cardboard, metal foil and paper on board,91 × 60.5 × 1.4 cm

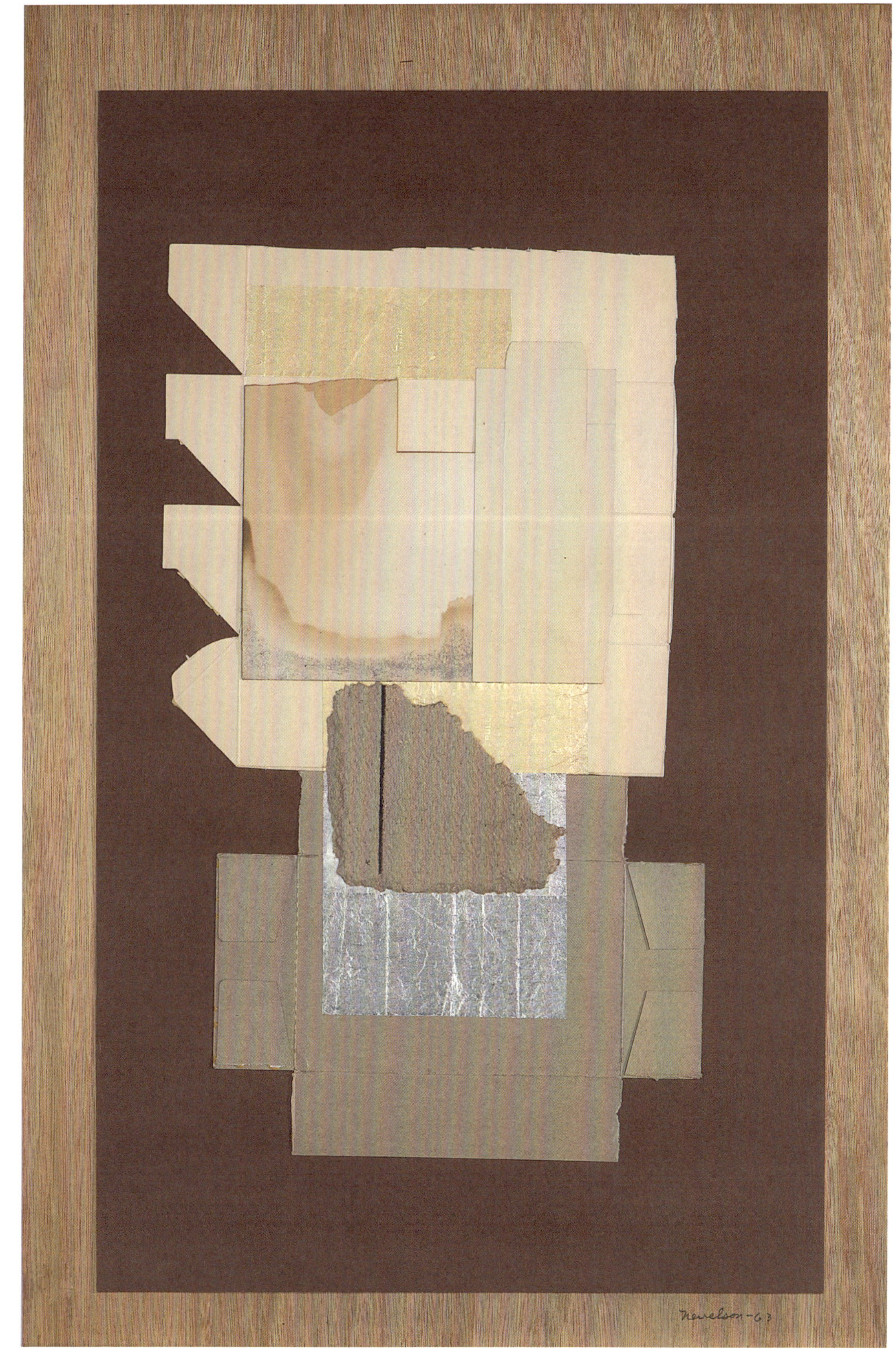

4.6 Untitled 1963, cardboard and metal foil on board, 91.5 × 61 cm

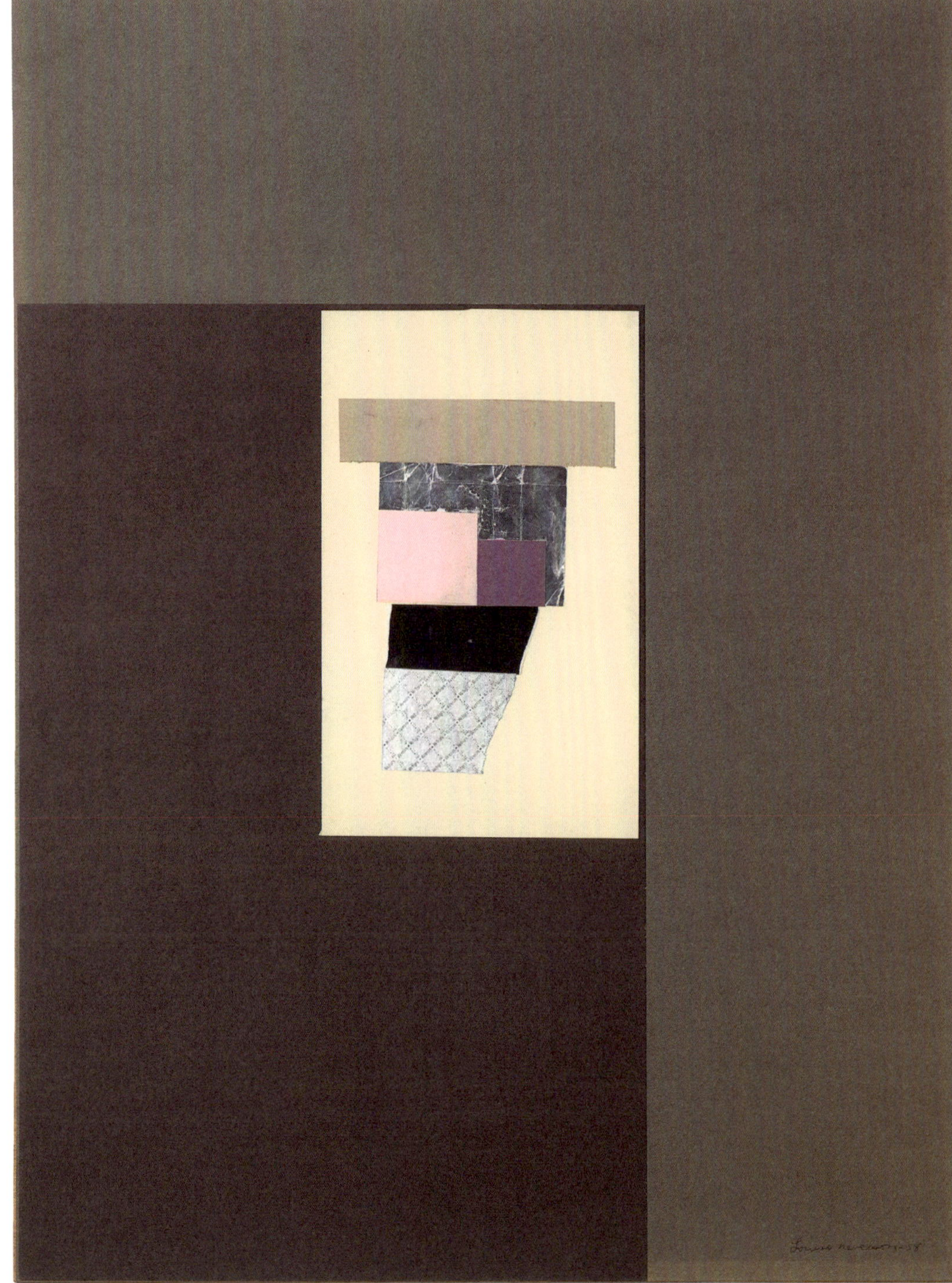

4.7 Untitled 1958, cardboard, metal foil and paper on board, 102 × 75.8 × 1.3 cm

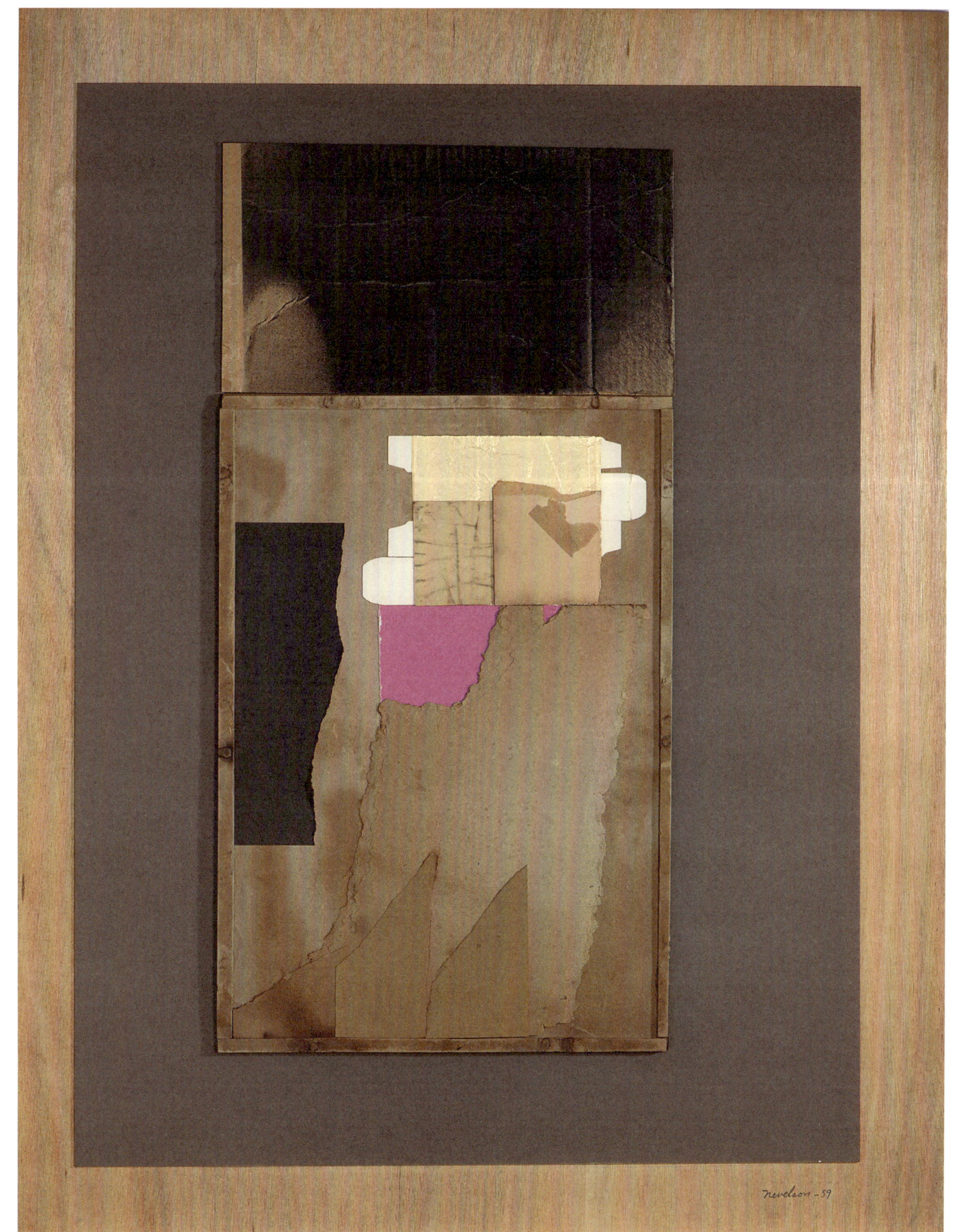

4.8 Untitled 1959, cardboard, spray paint, metal foil, paper and wood on board, 117 × 91.5 cm

4.9 Untitled 1961, cardboard and paper on board, 91.5 × 61 cm

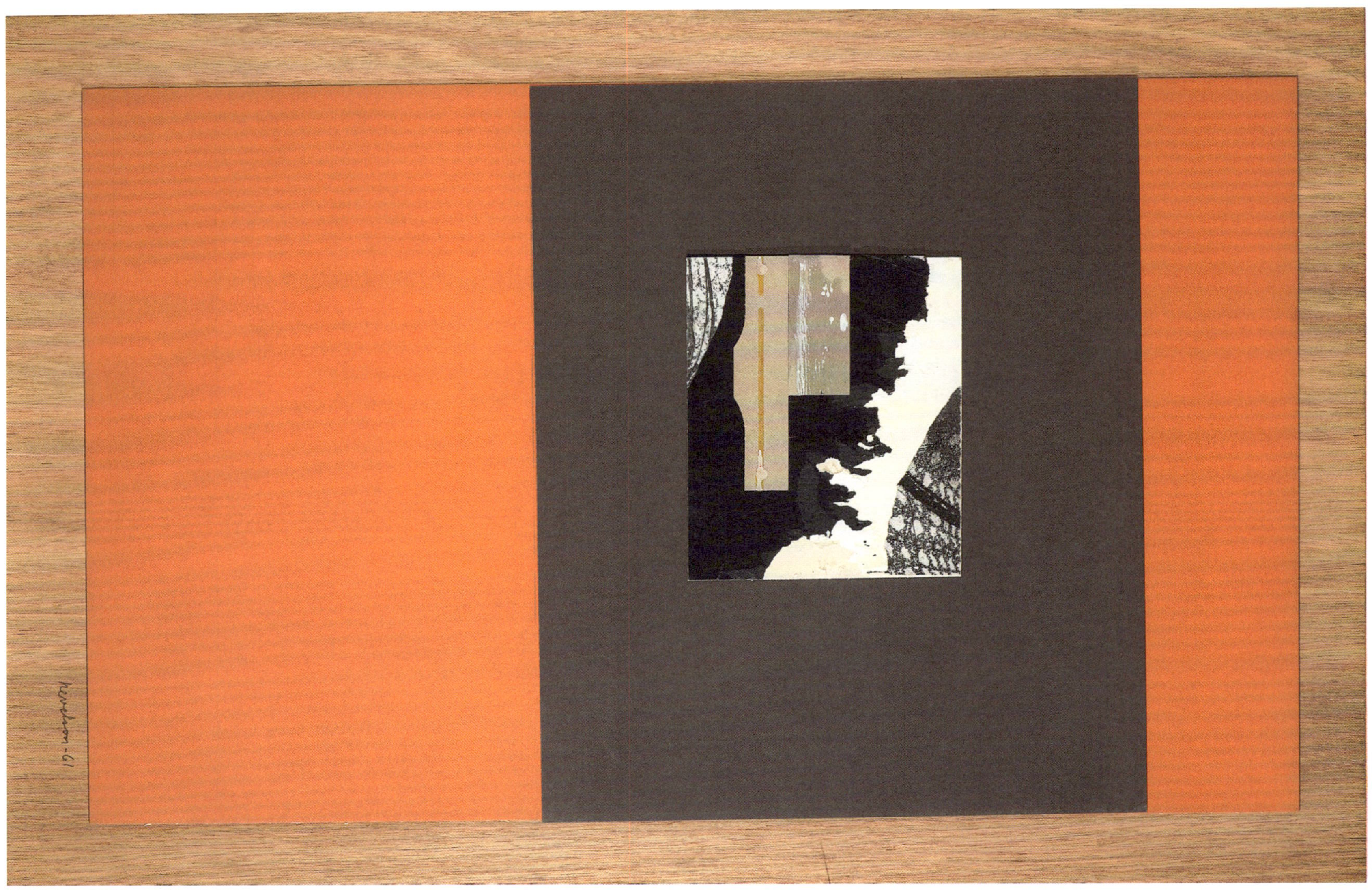

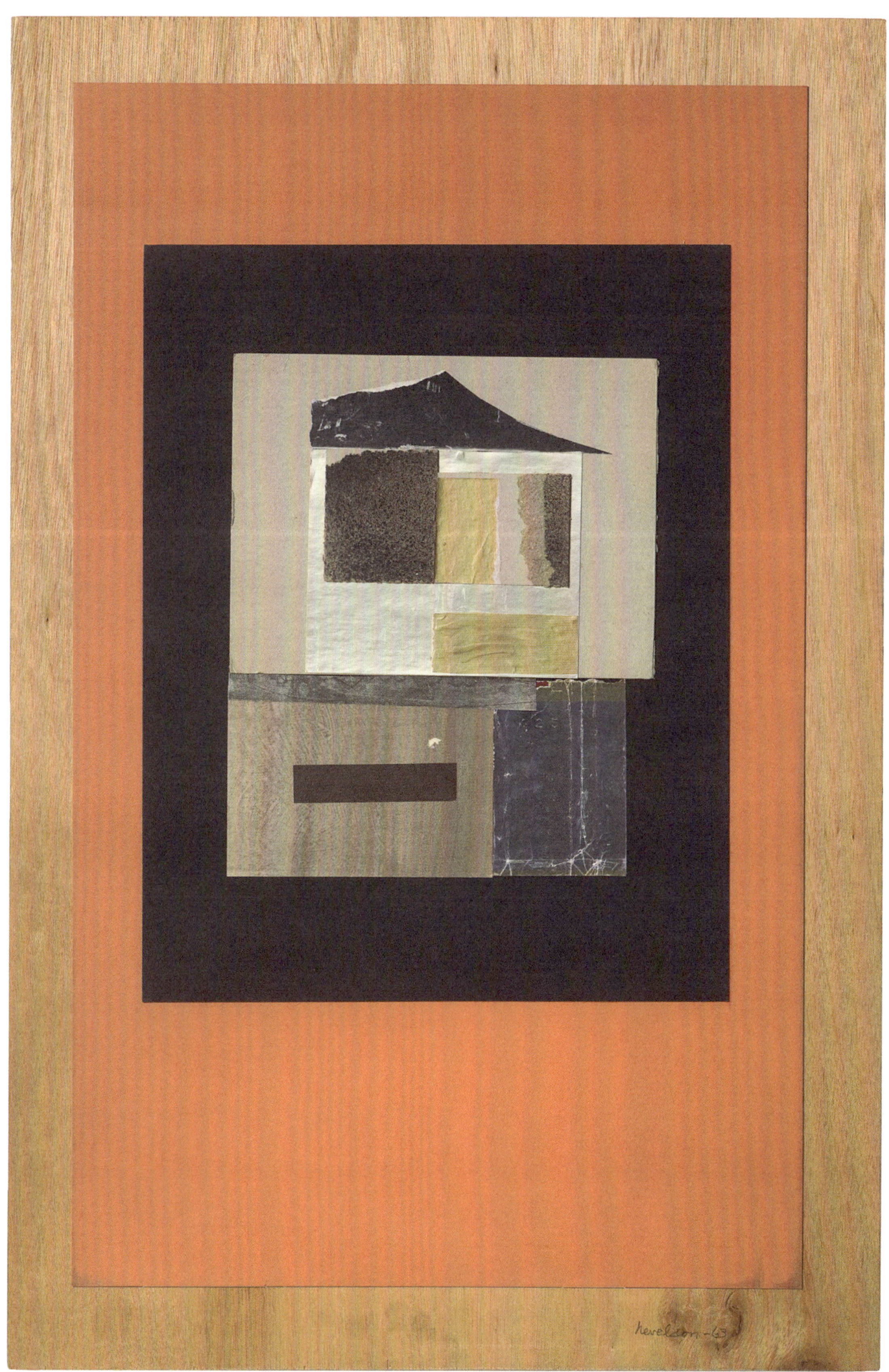

4.10 Untitled 1963, cardboard, spray paint, metal foil, paper and wood on board, 91.4 × 60.3 × 0.8 cm

4.11 Untitled 1963, cardboard, paper and wood on board, 91.2 × 60.6 × 2.2 cm

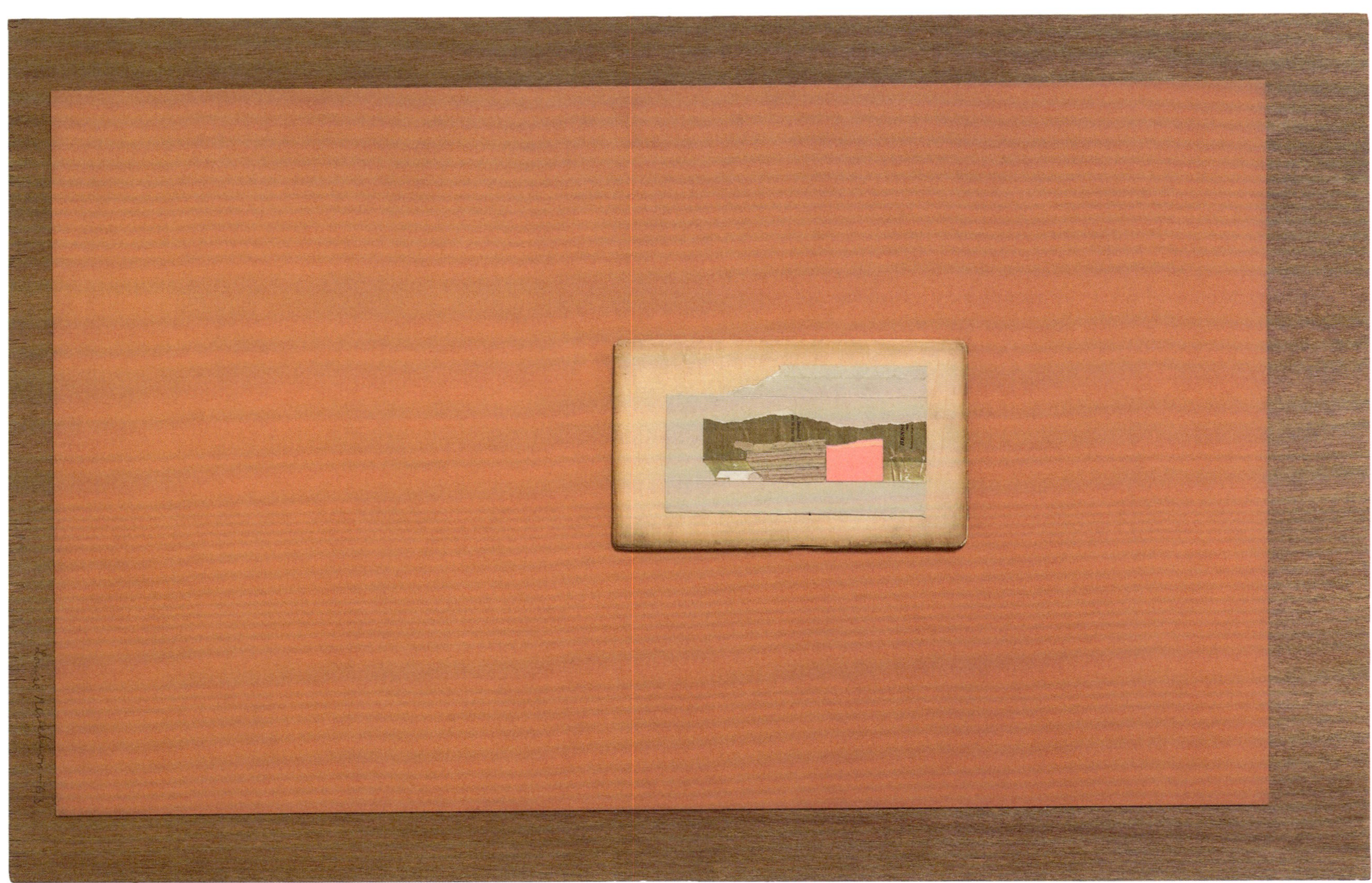

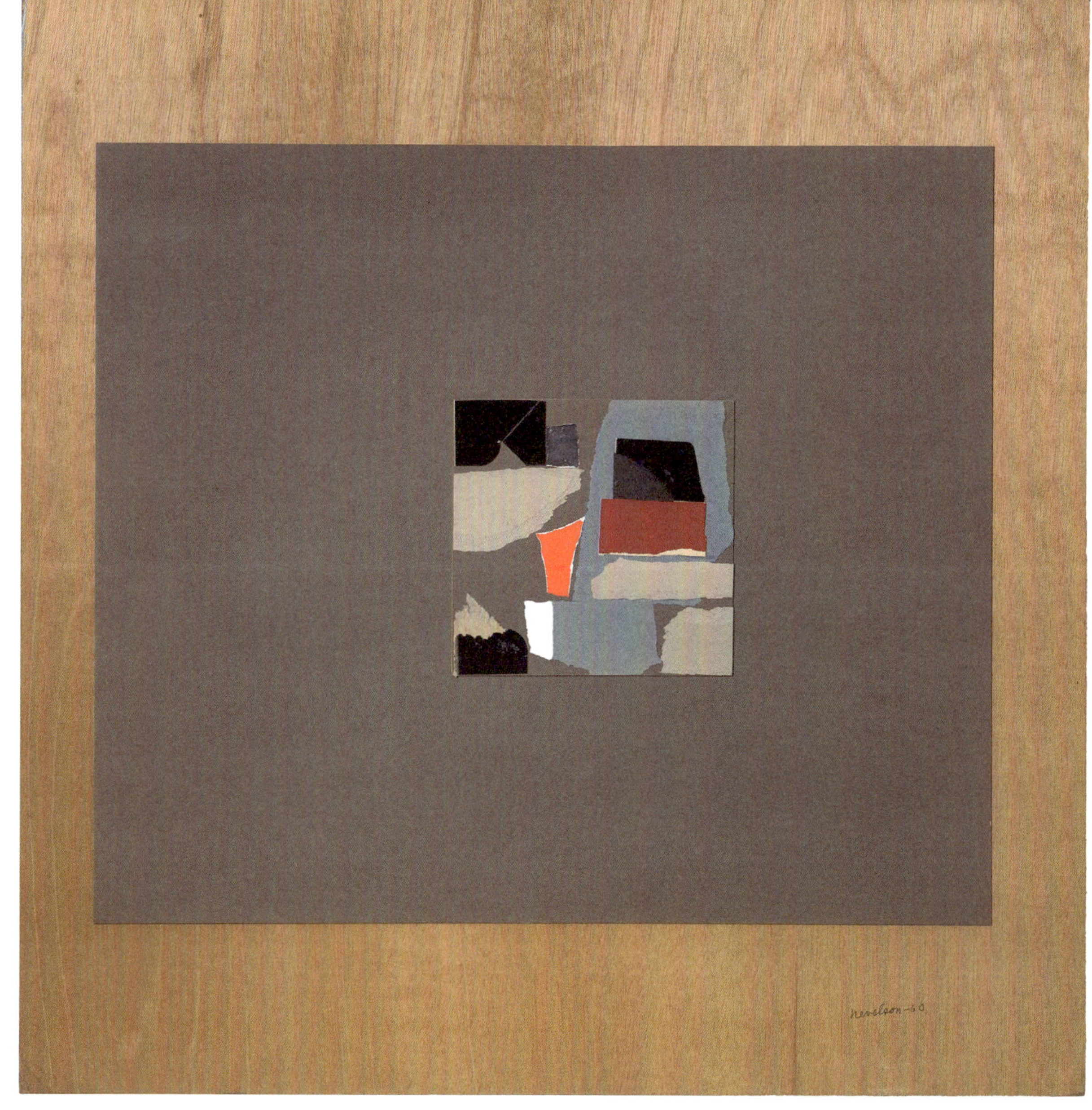

4.12 Untitled 1960, cardboard, metal foil and paper on board, 91.2 × 91.6 × 1 cm

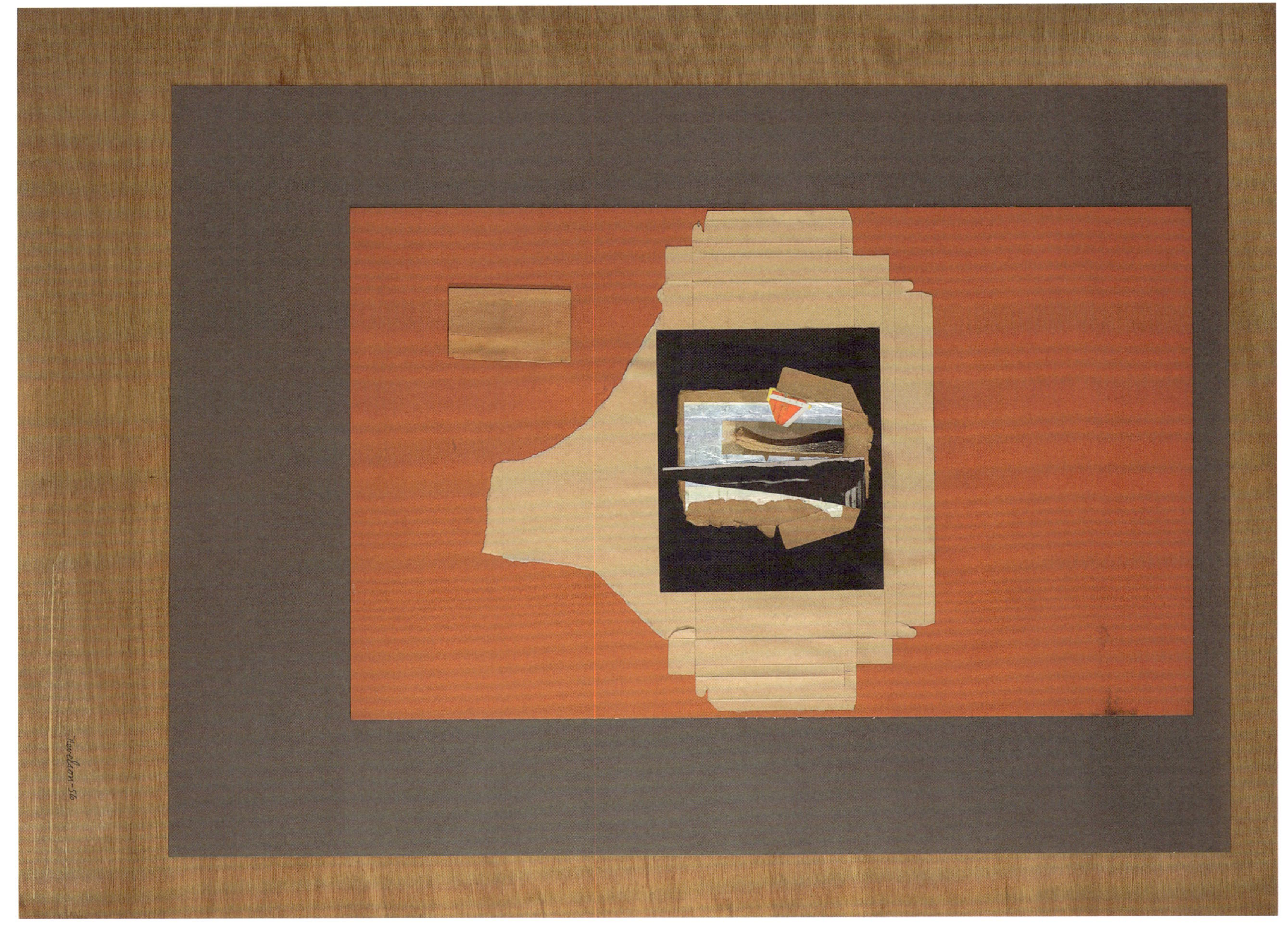

4.13 Untitled 1956, cardboard, paint, metal foil, printed paper and wood on board, 122 × 91 cm

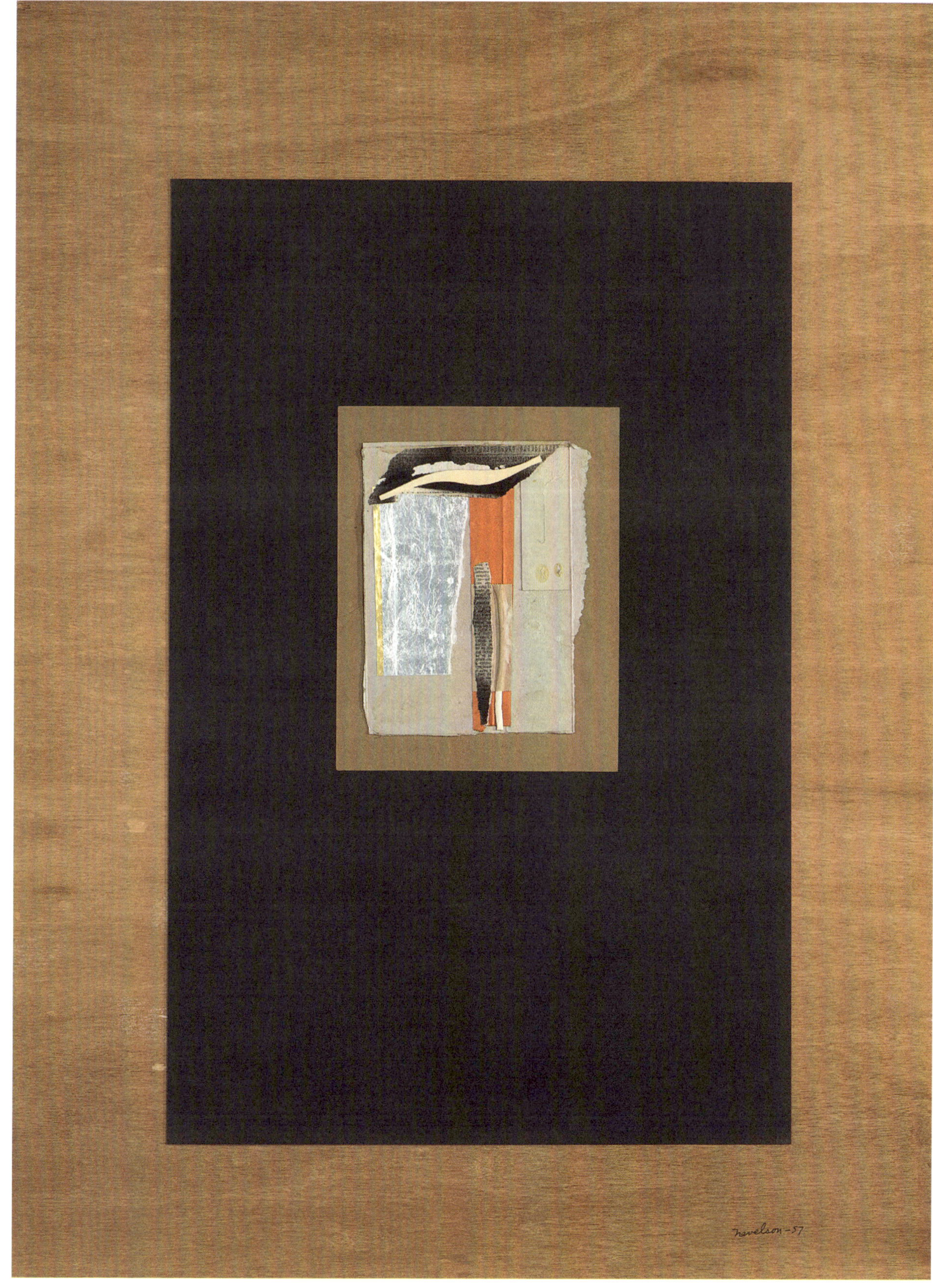

4.14 Untitled 1957, cardboard, metal foil, paper and wood on board, 102 × 76 cm

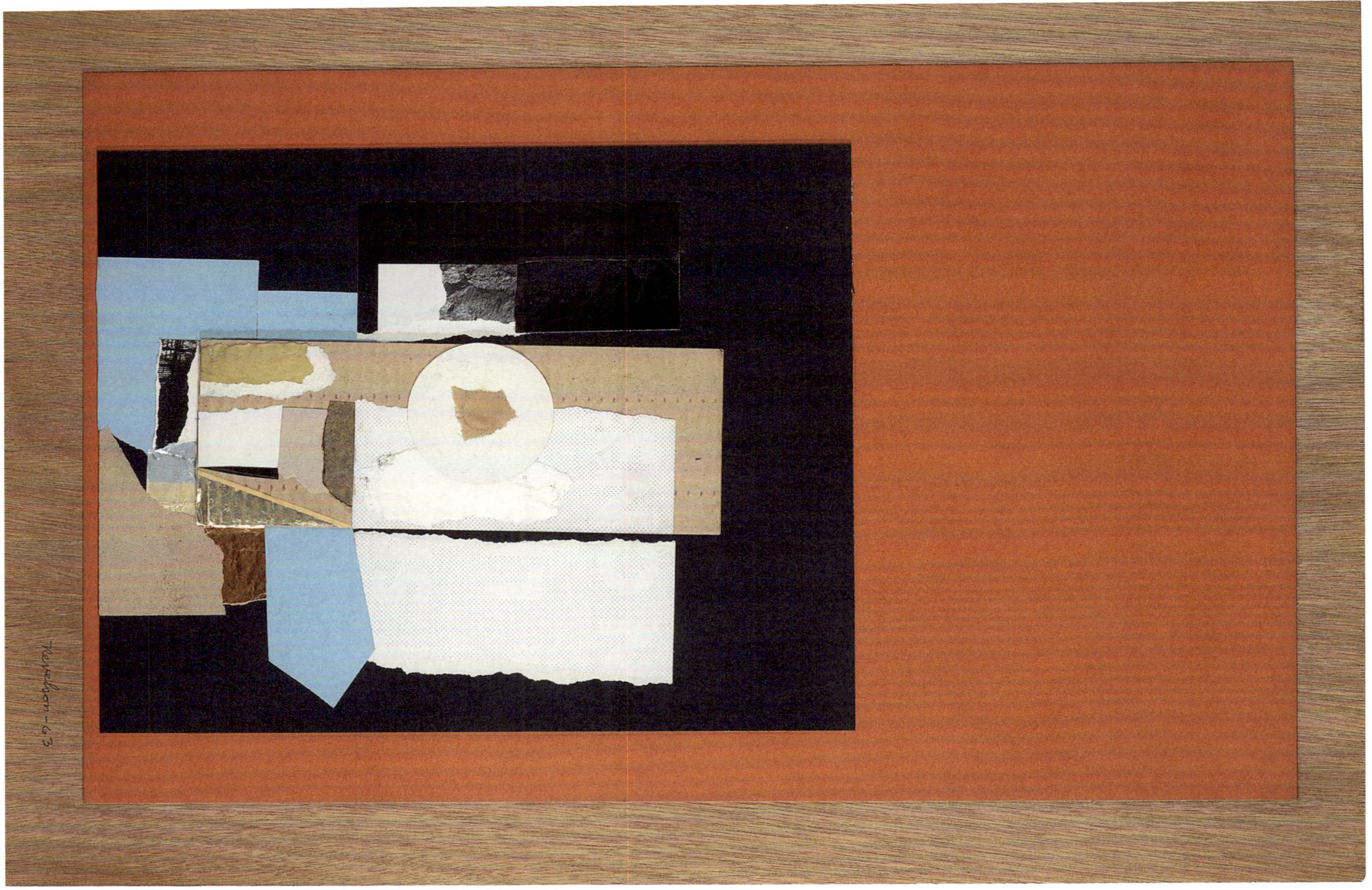

4.15 Untitled 1963, cardboard, metal foil, paper and pencil on board, 91.5 × 61 cm

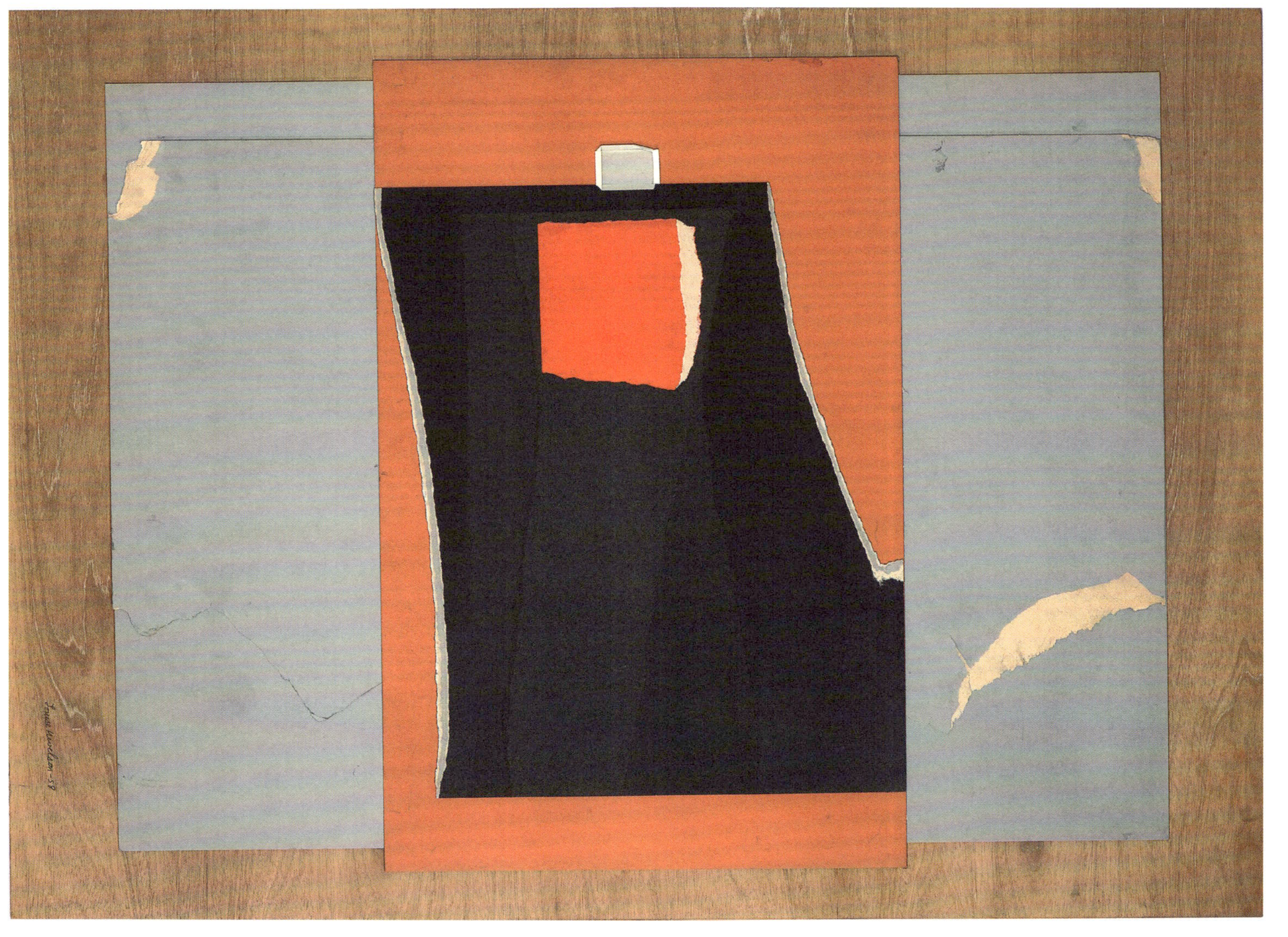

4.16 Untitled 1958, cardboard and paper on board, 122 × 91.5 cm

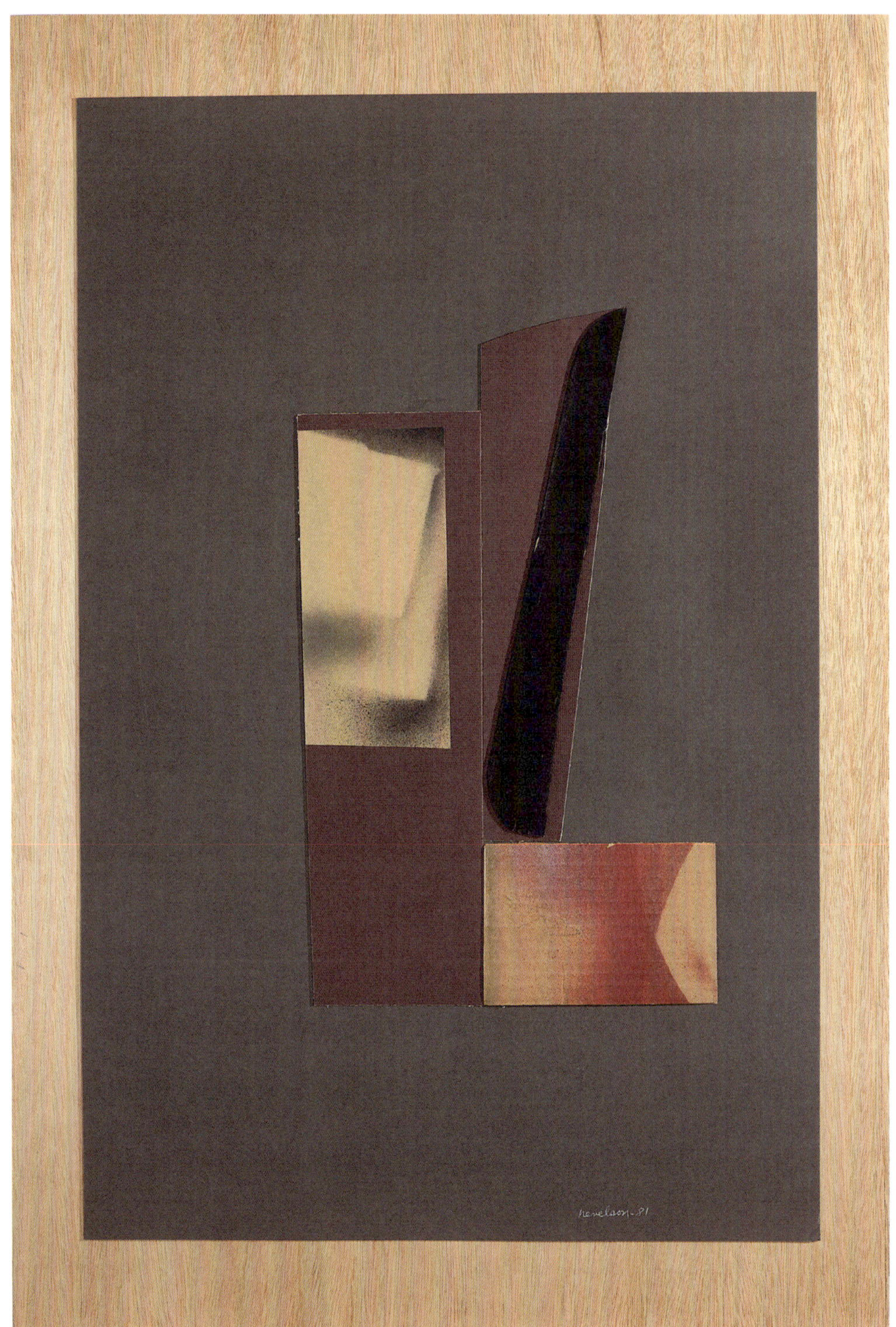

4.17 Untitled 1981, cardboard and spray paint on board, 89 × 61 cm

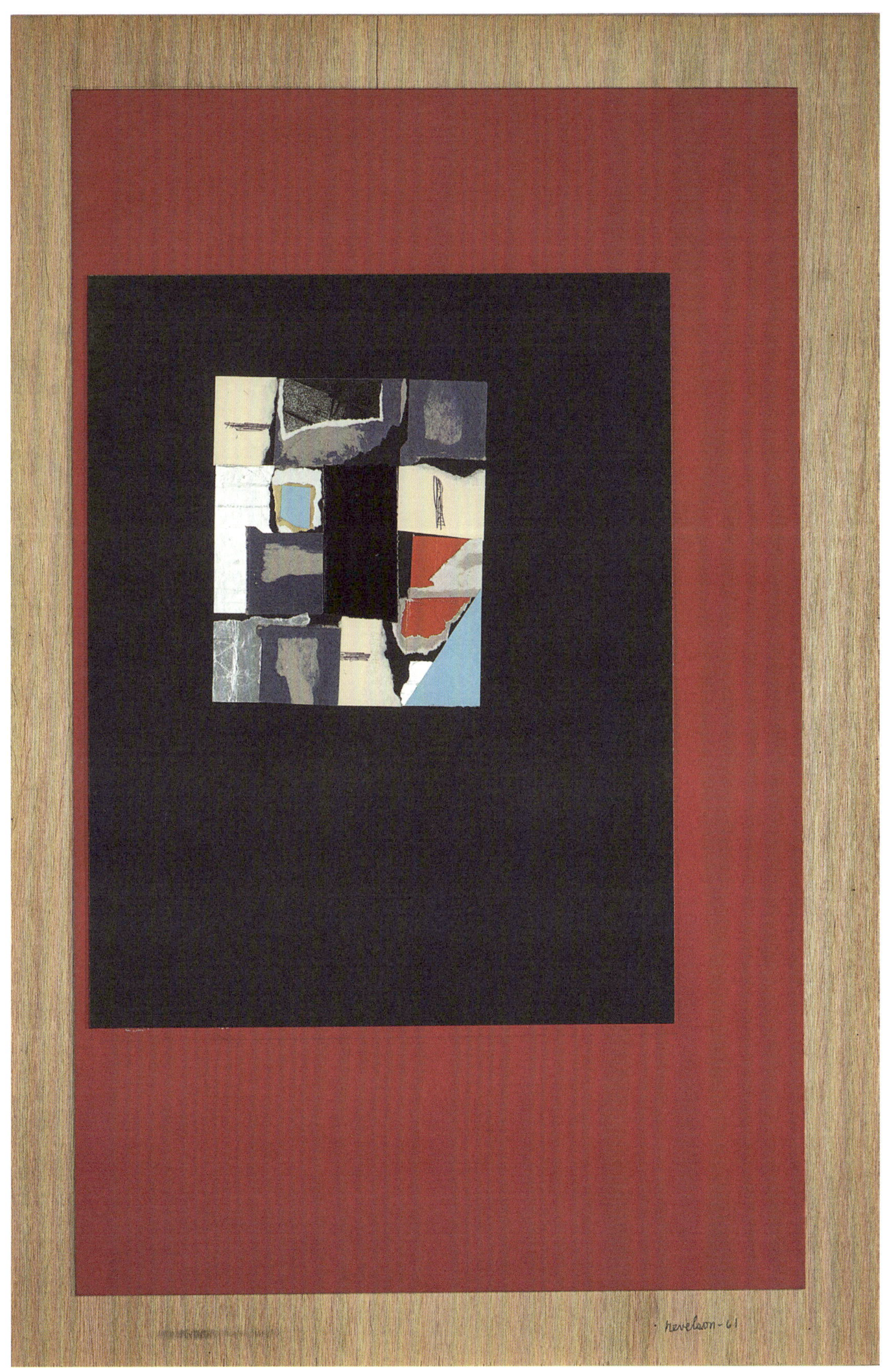

4.18 Untitled 1961, cardboard, metal foil and paper on board, 91.5 × 61 cm

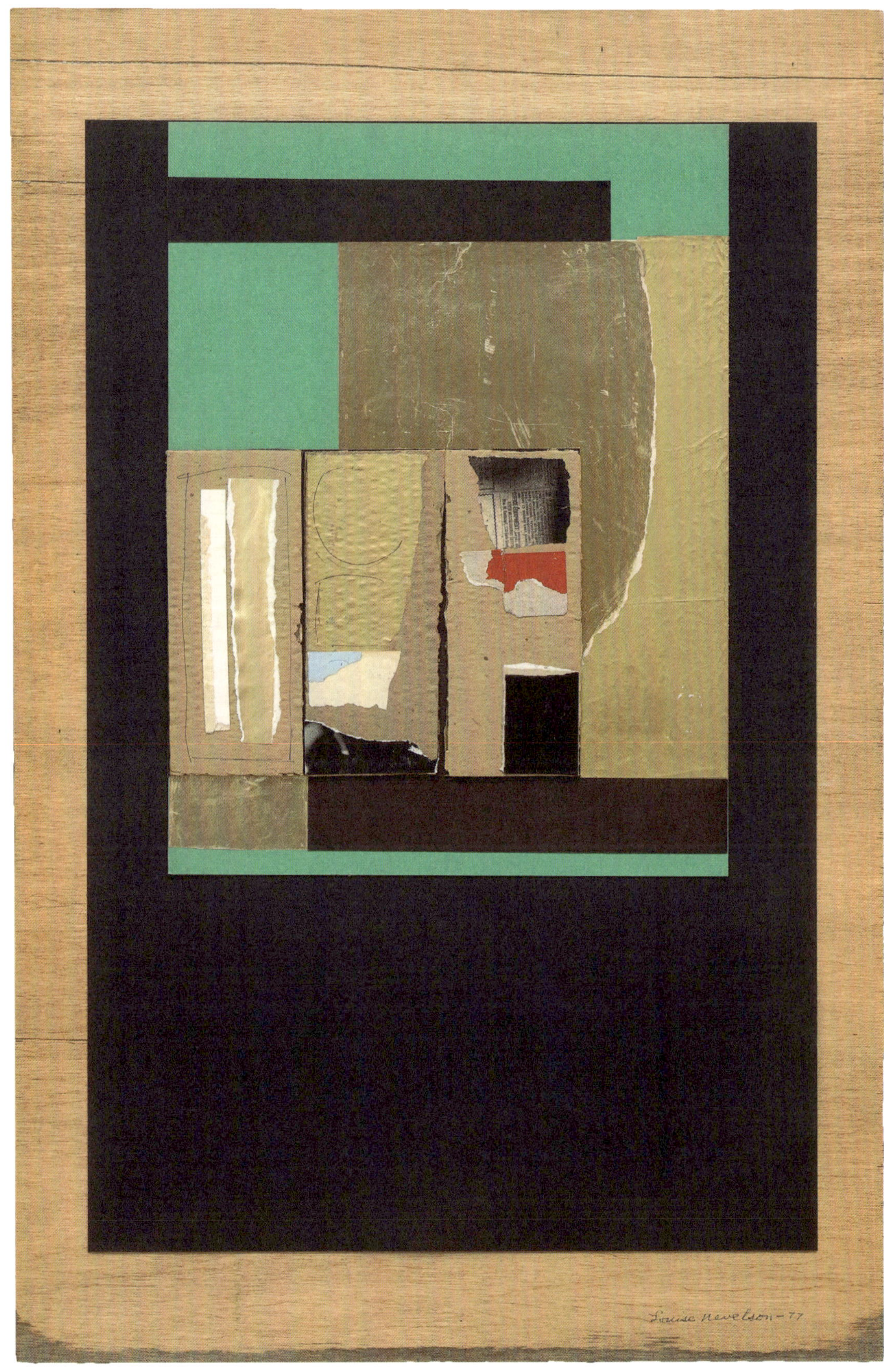

4.19 Untitled 1977, cardboard, spray paint, metal foil, newsprint, ballpoint pen and paper on board, 91.4 × 61 × 2 cm

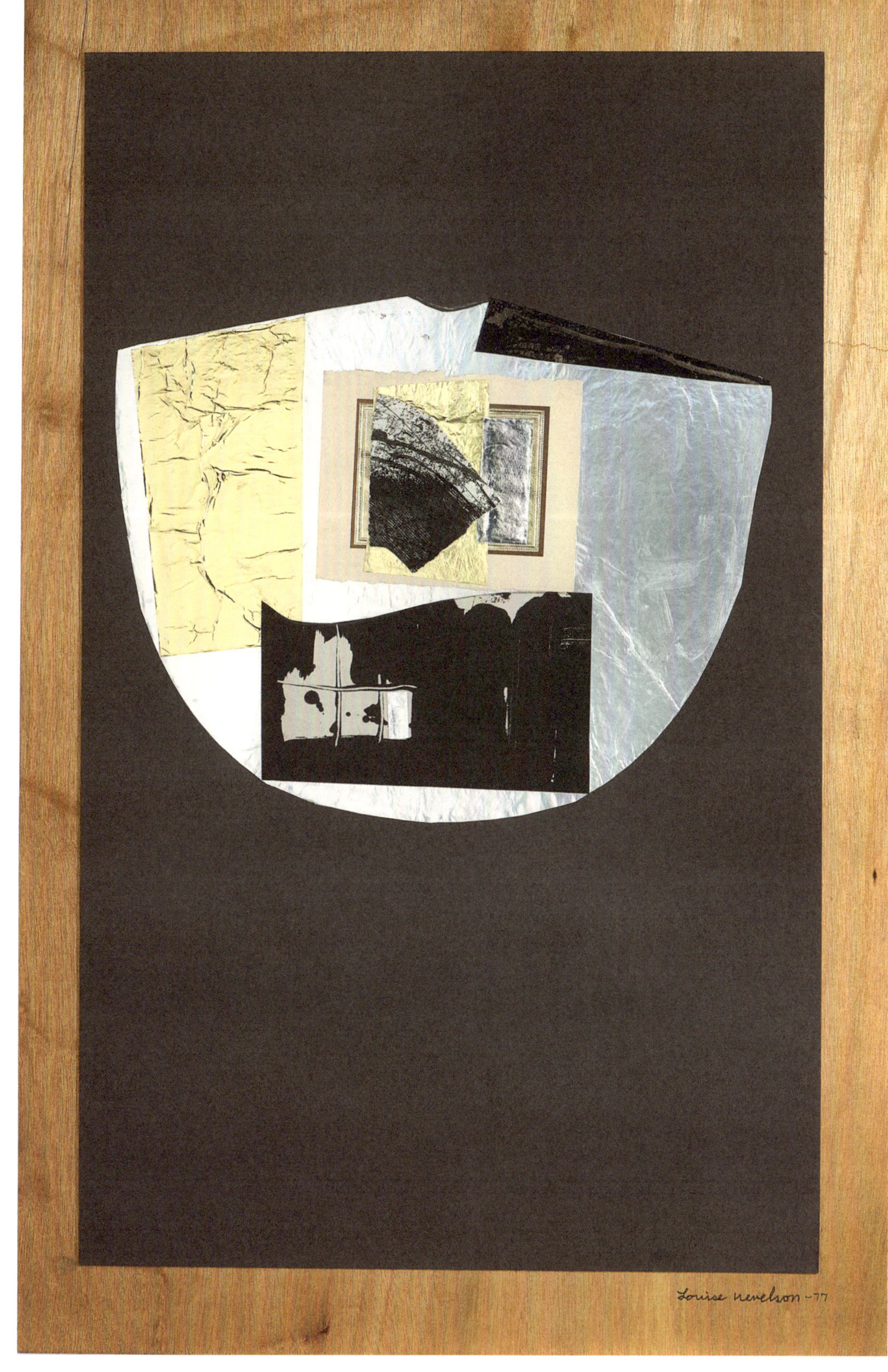

4.20 Untitled 1977, cardboard, metal foil, lithograph and paper on board, 91.5 × 61 cm

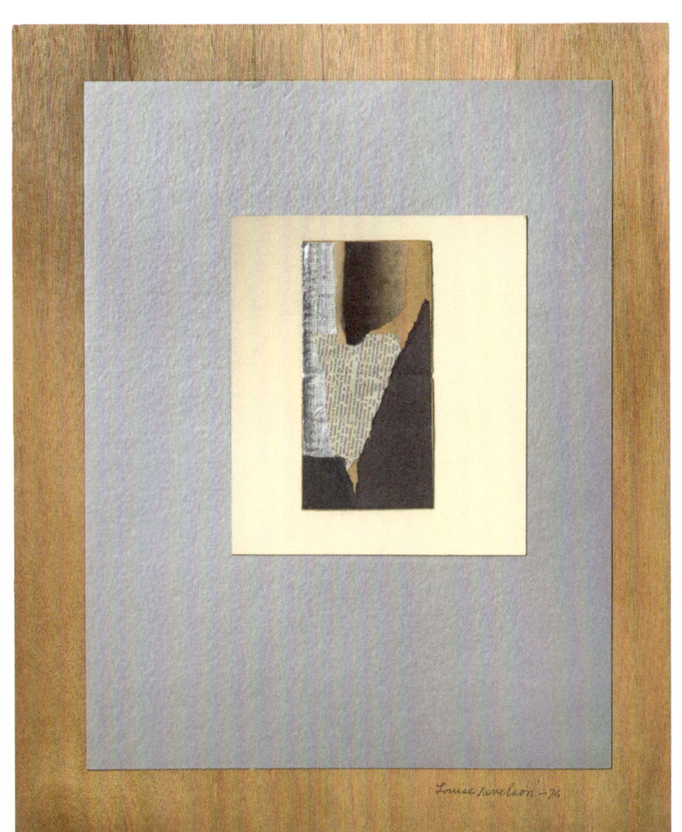

4.21 Untitled 1976, cardboard, spray paint and newsprint on board, 60.6 × 50.7 × 0.9 cm

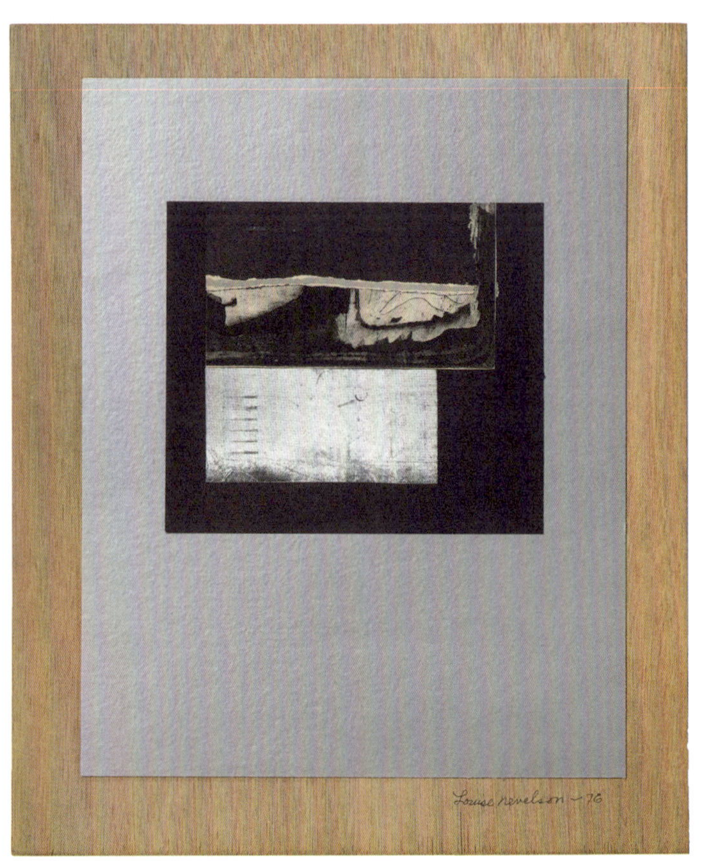

4.22 Untitled 1976, cardboard, paint, metal foil and lithograph on board, 60.5 × 50.7 × 0.9 cm

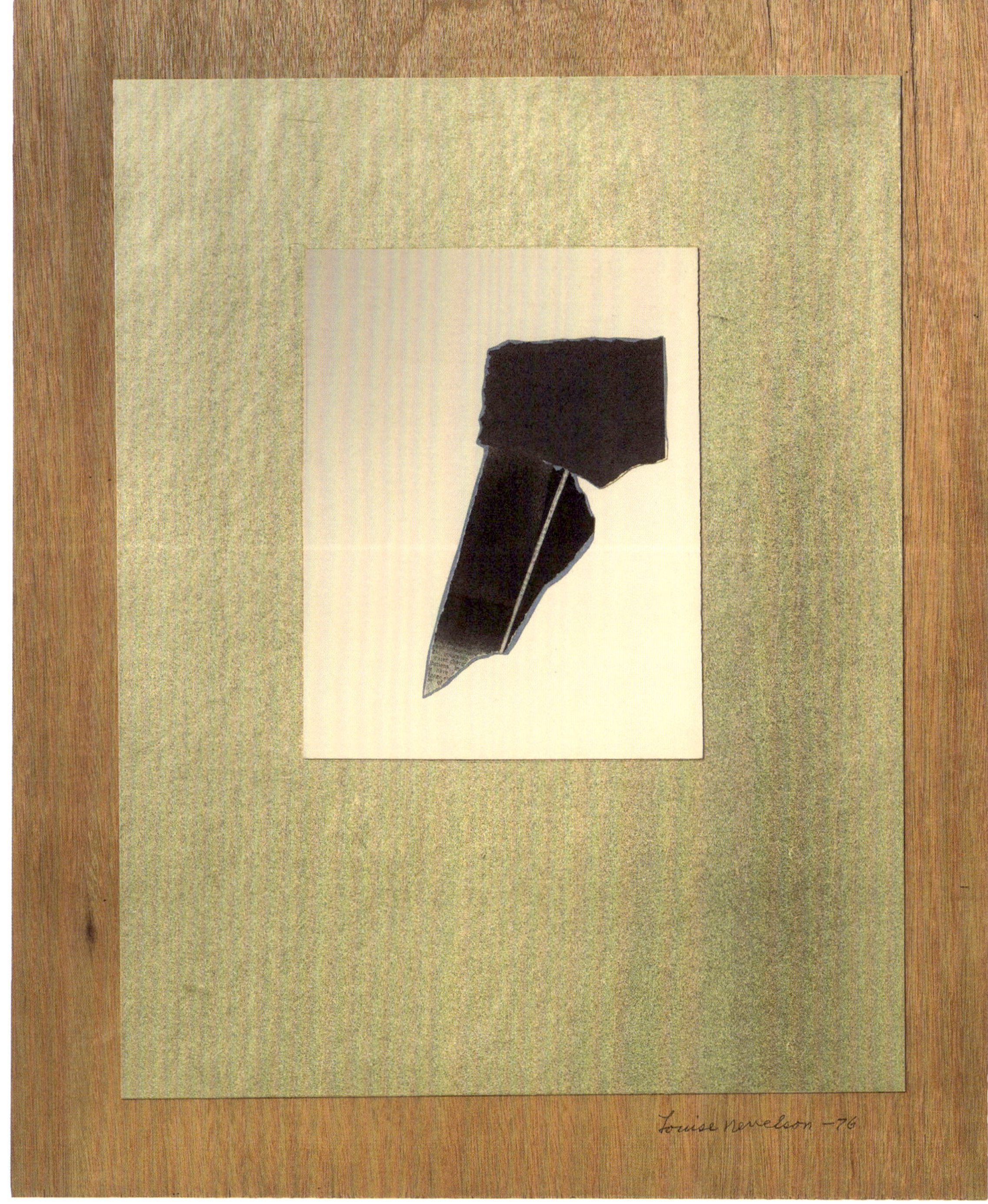

4.23 Untitled 1976, cardboard, spray paint, metal foil, newsprint and paper on board, 60.4 × 50.8 × 0.9 cm

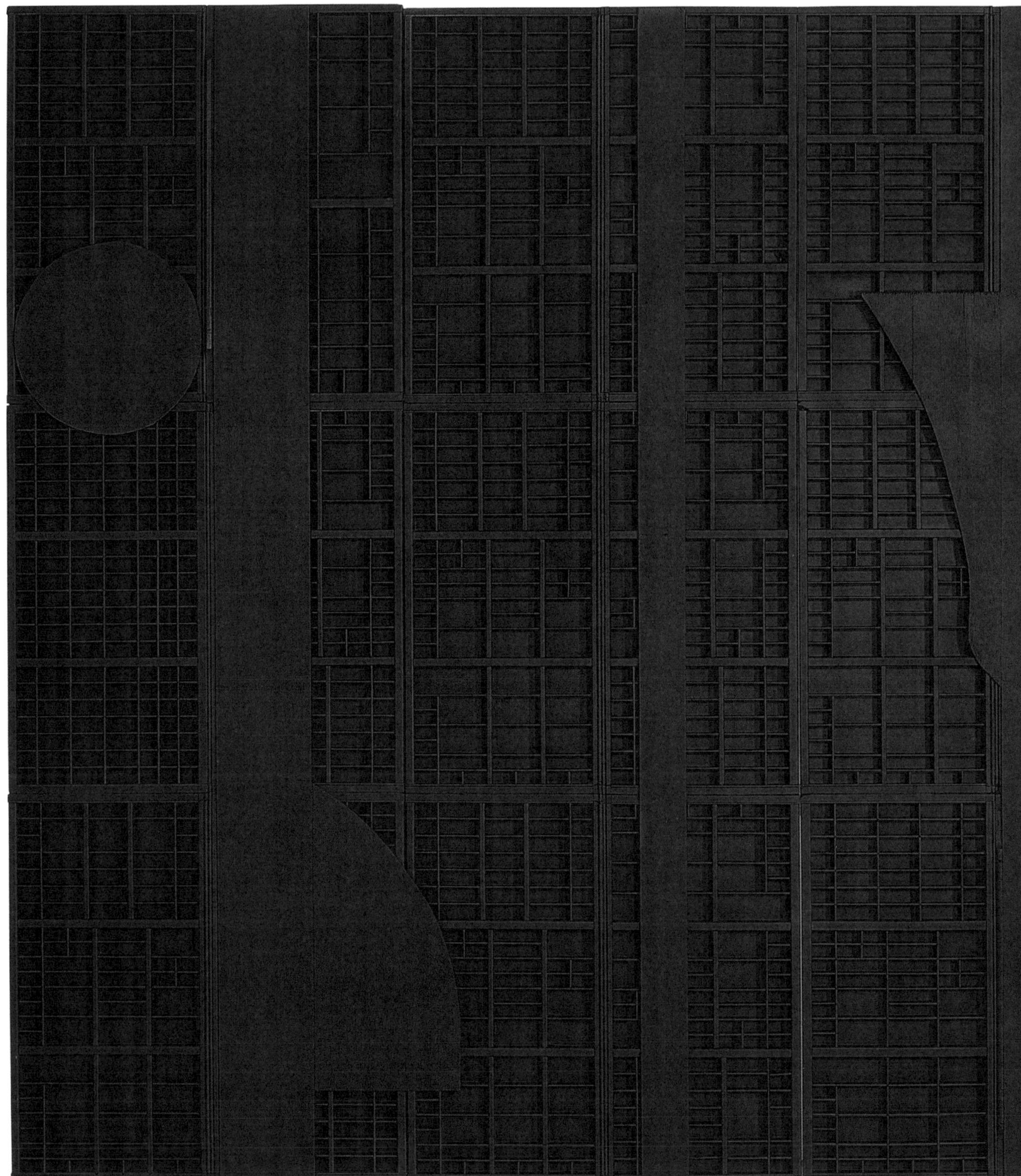

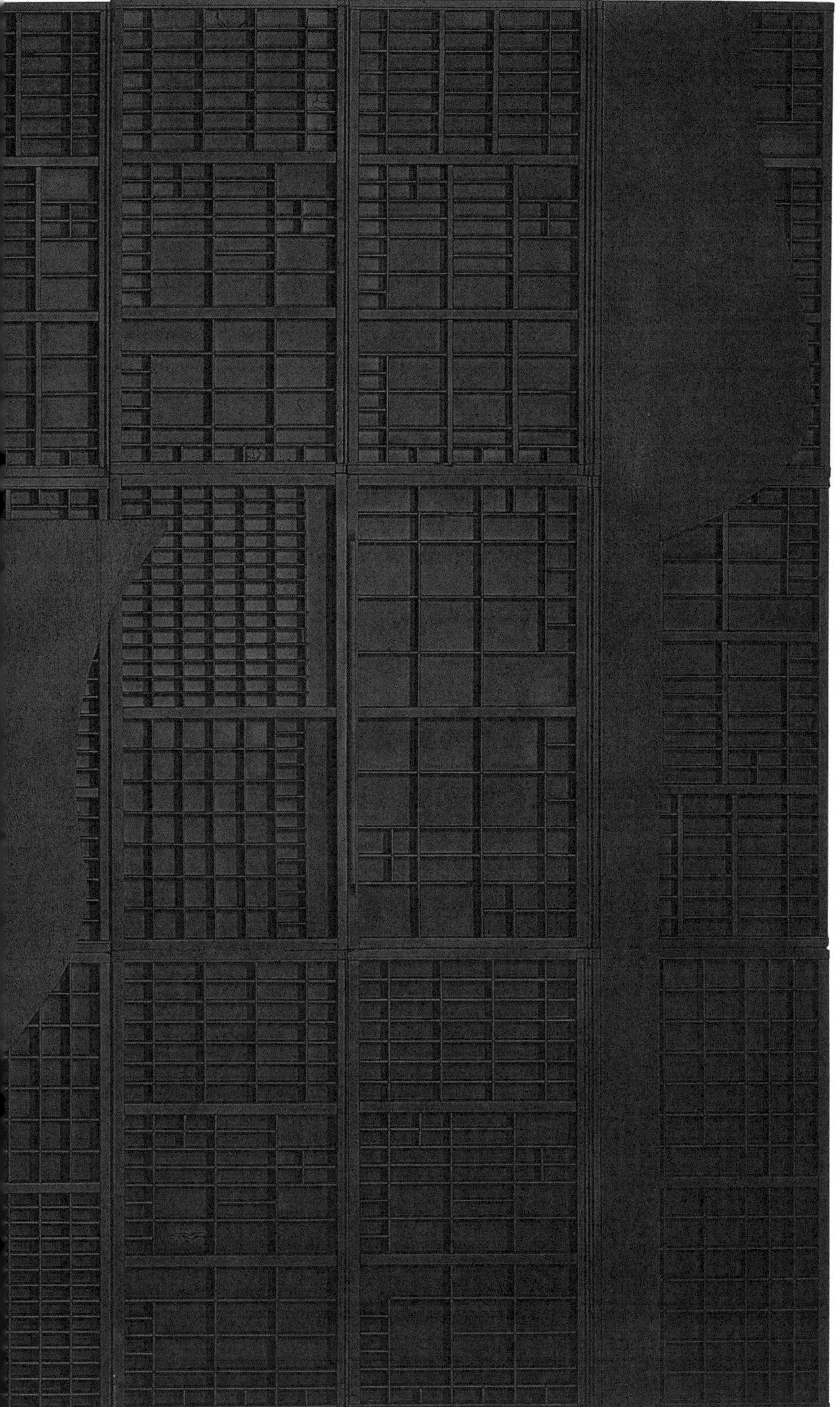

4.24 City Series 1974, wood painted black,
245 × 380 × 6 cm

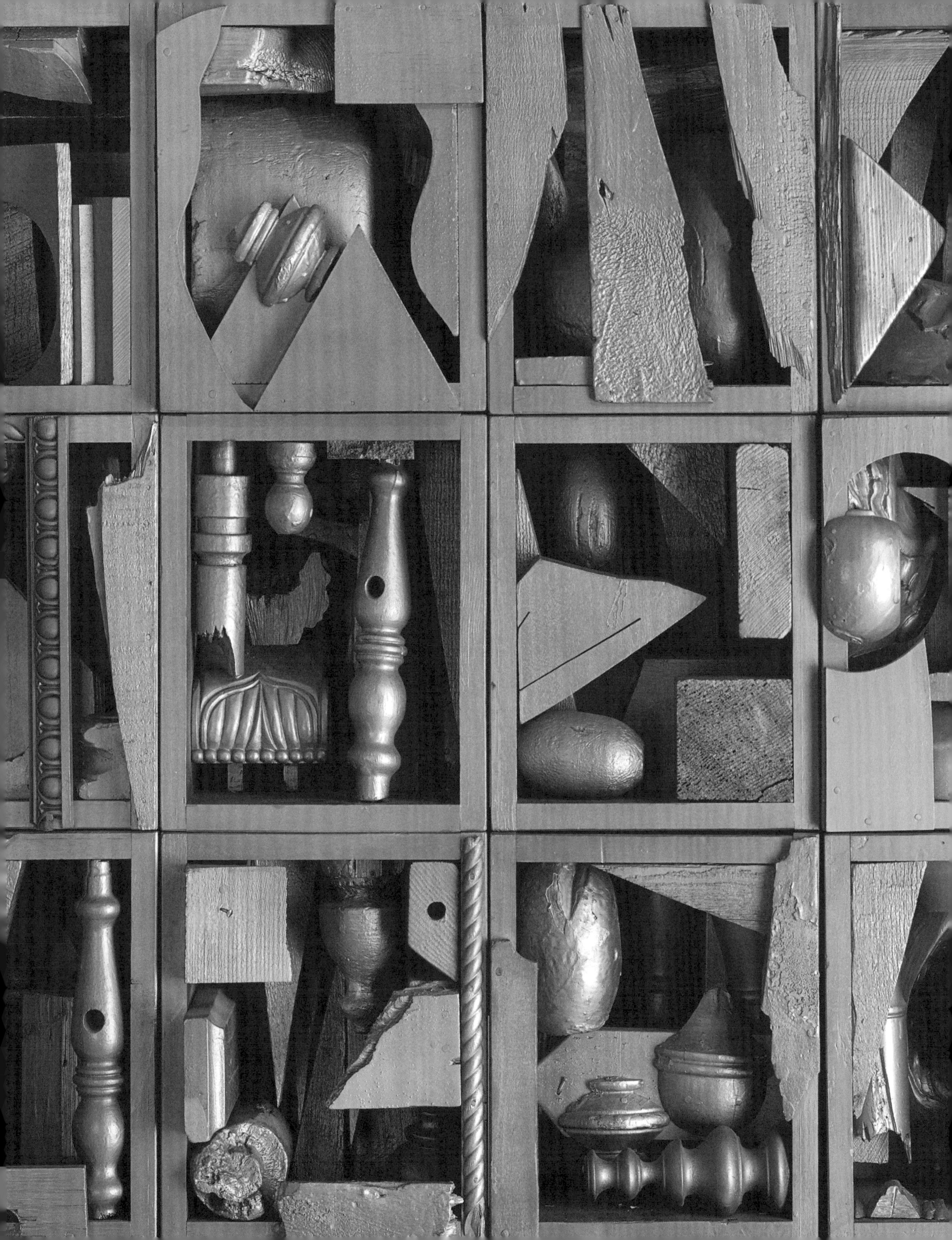

No 5

Die Suche nach Struktur und Ordnung

The Search for Structure and Order

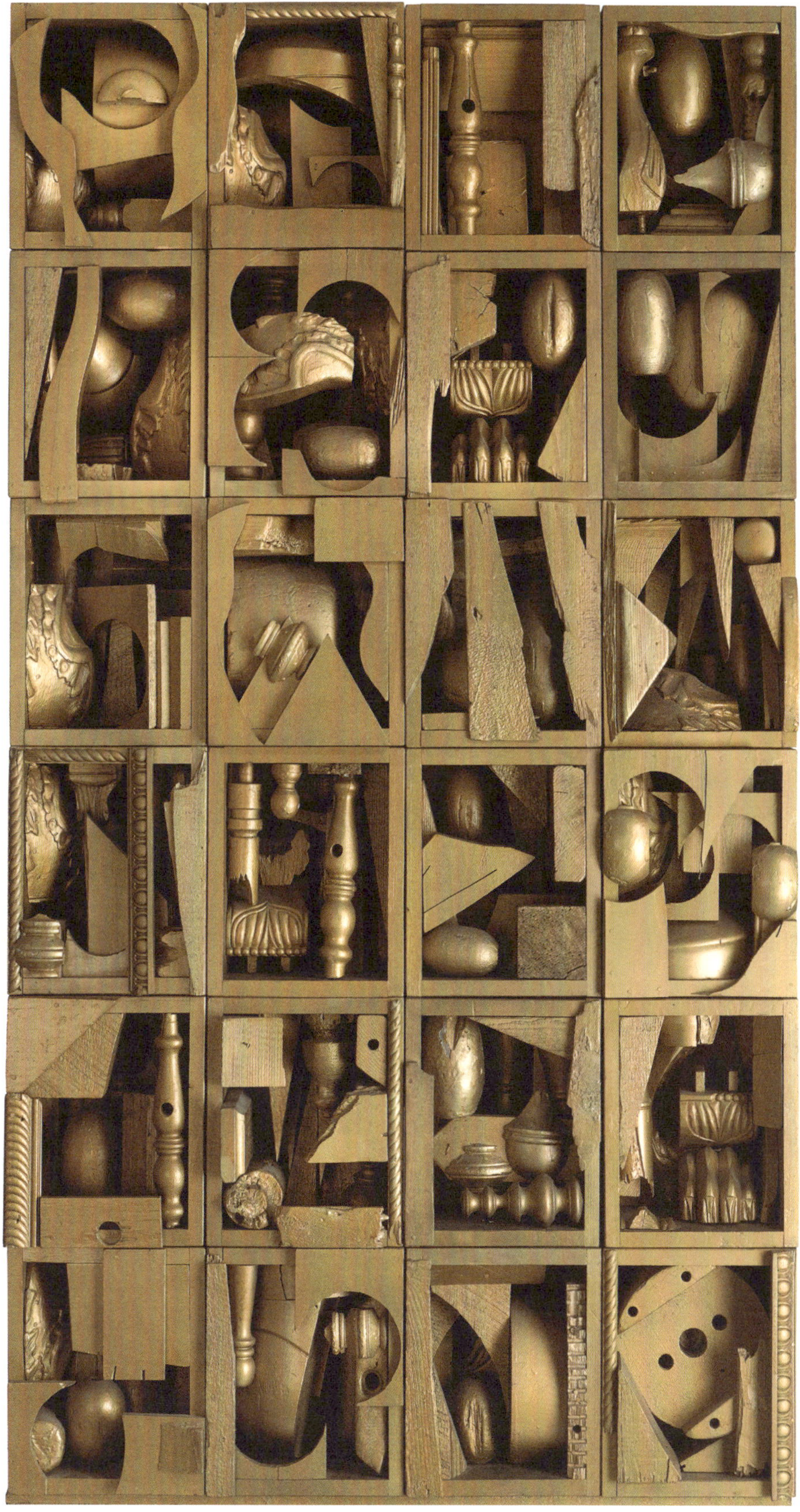

5.1 The Golden Pearl 1962, wood painted gold, 176.1 × 97.4 × 23.6 cm

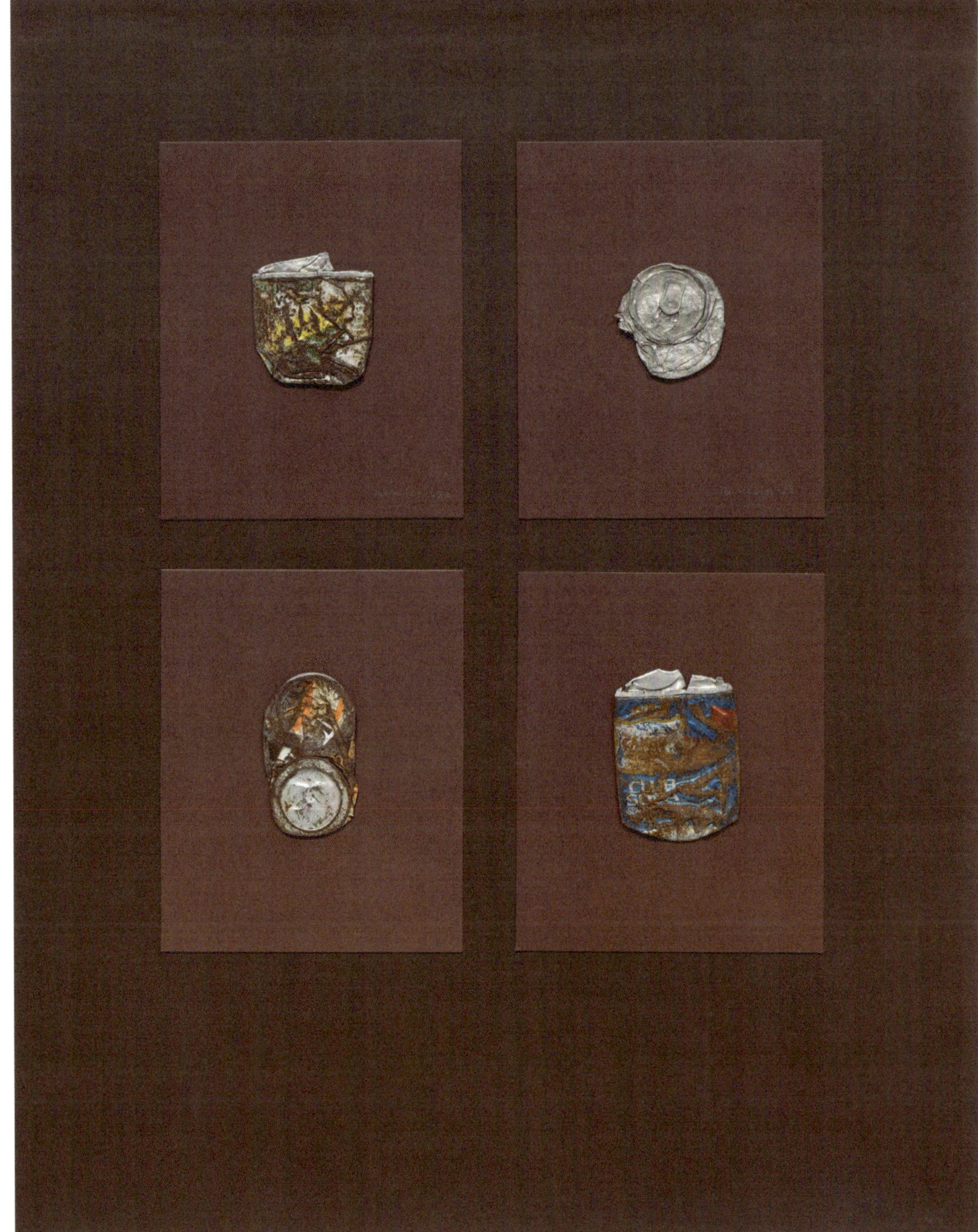

5.2 Untitled 1982, cardboard and cans on board, 101.6 × 81 × 1.7 cm

5.3 Untitled 1977–1980, cardboard and wood on board, 101.4 × 80.7 × 2.9 cm

5.4 Ancient Secrets II 1964, wood painted black,
81.1 × 133 × 12 cm

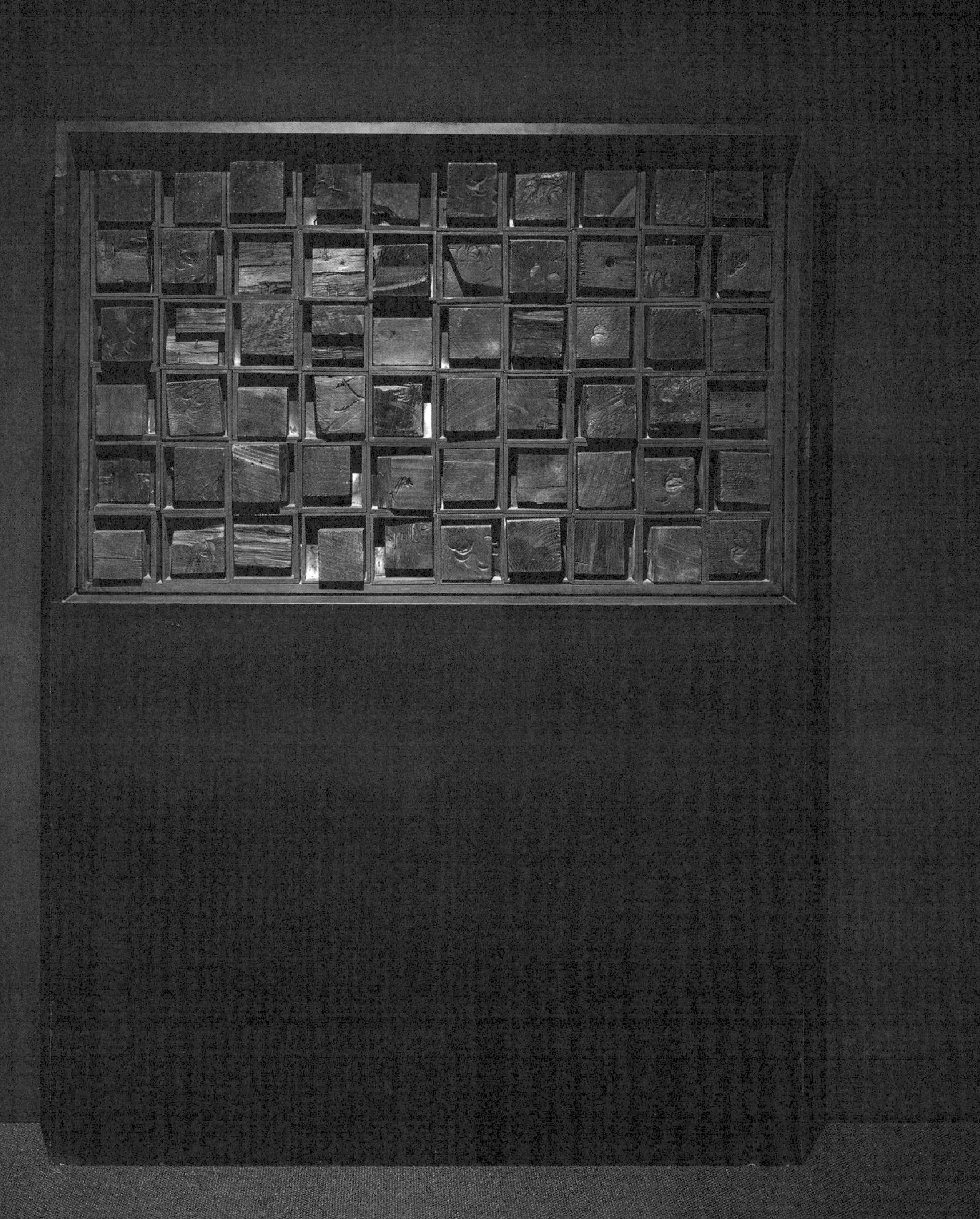

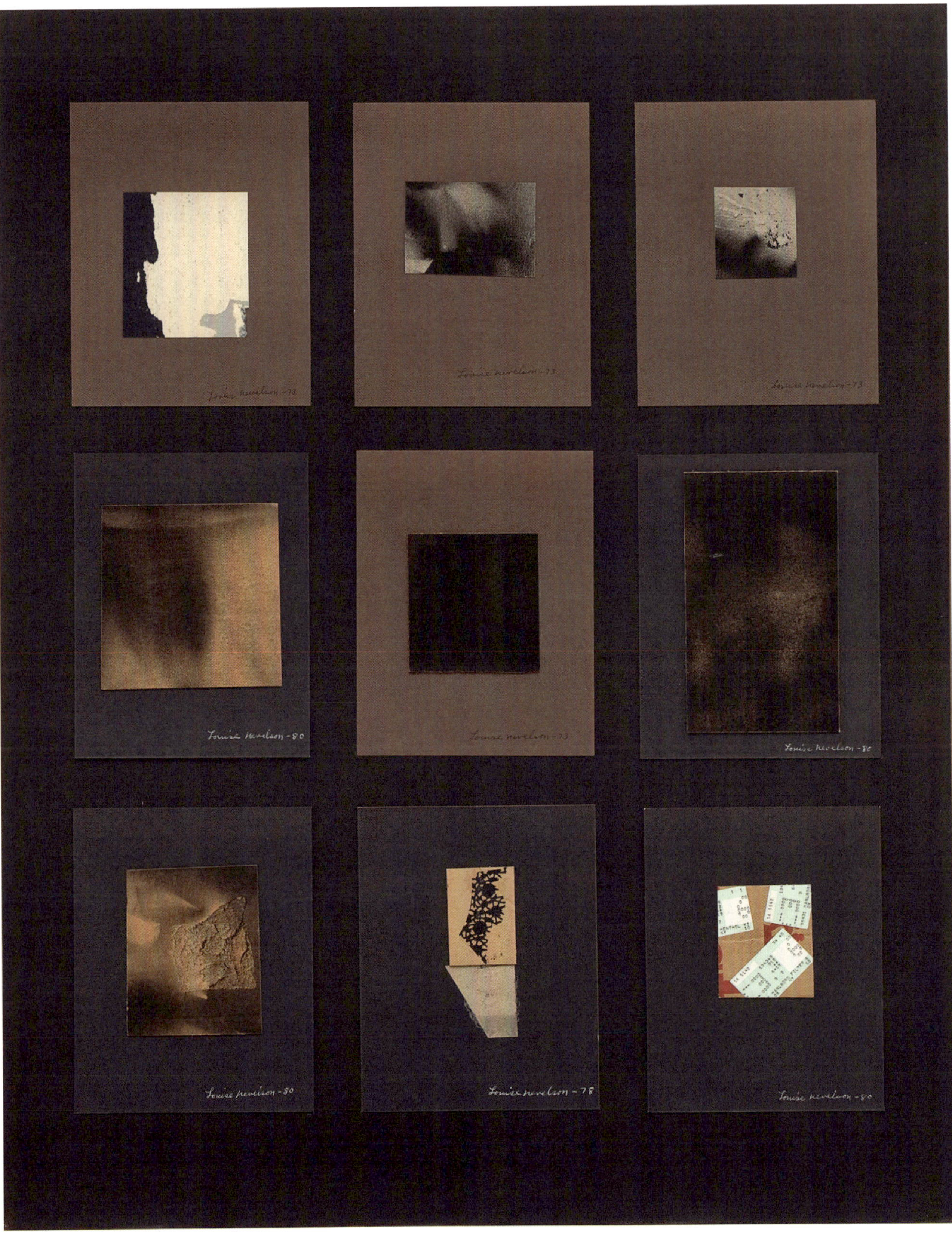

5.5 Untitled 1978–1980, cardboard, paint, paper and wood on board, 101.5 × 80.9 × 1.2 cm

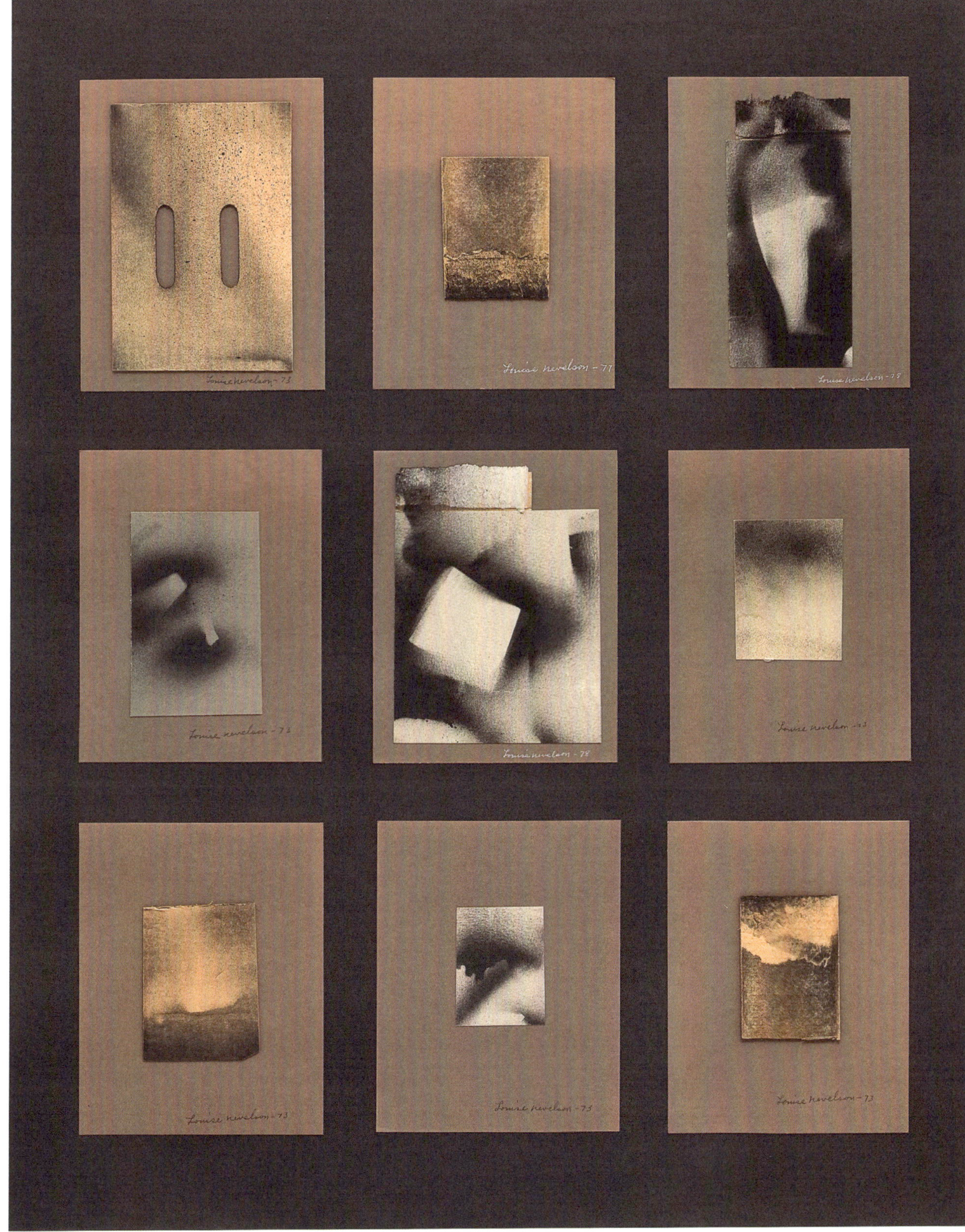

5.6 Untitled 1973–1978, cardboard, spray paint and paper on board, 100.7 × 81 × 1.3 cm

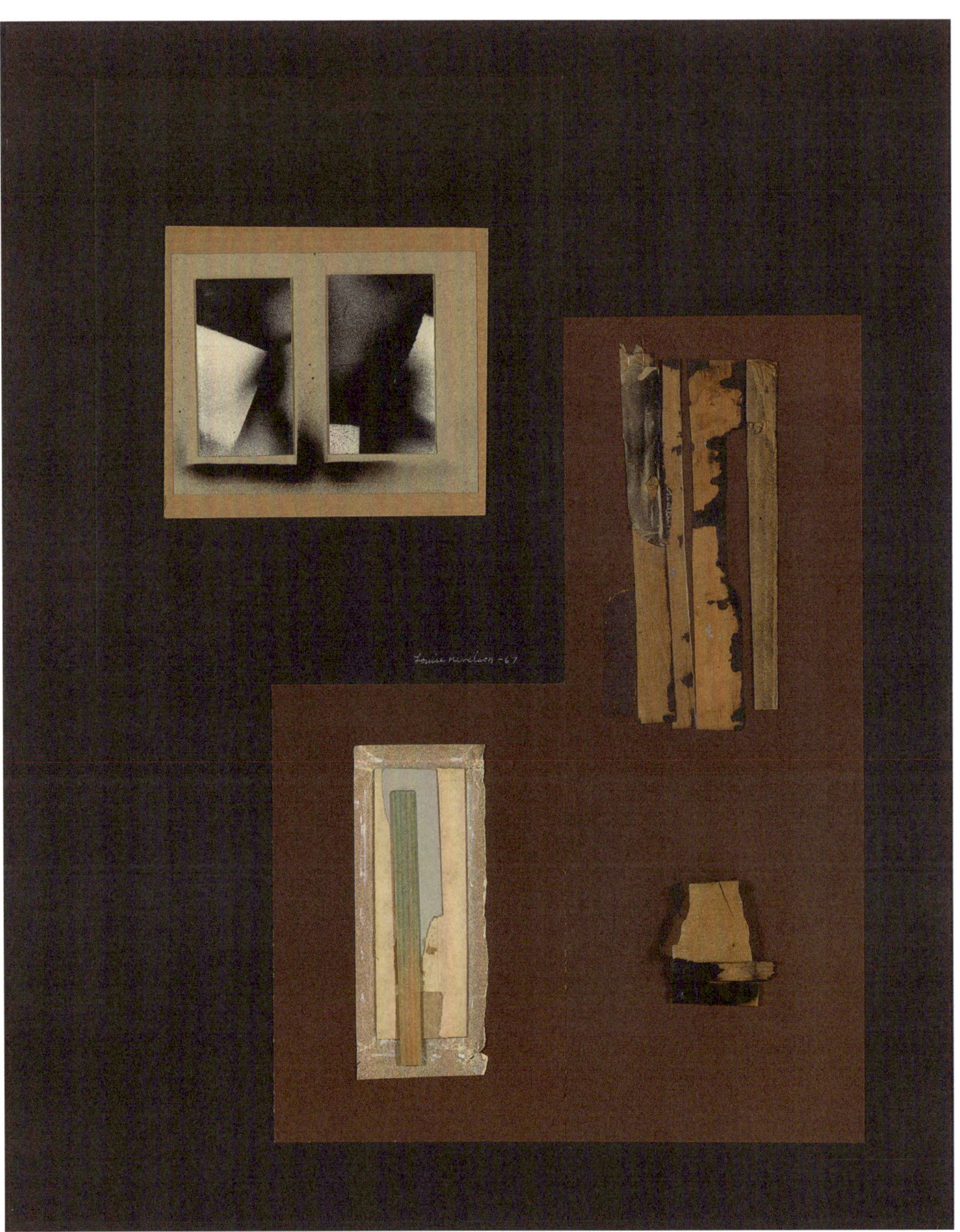

5.7 Untitled 1967, cardboard, spray paint, paint, paper and wood on board, 101.5 × 81.5 × 4.9 cm

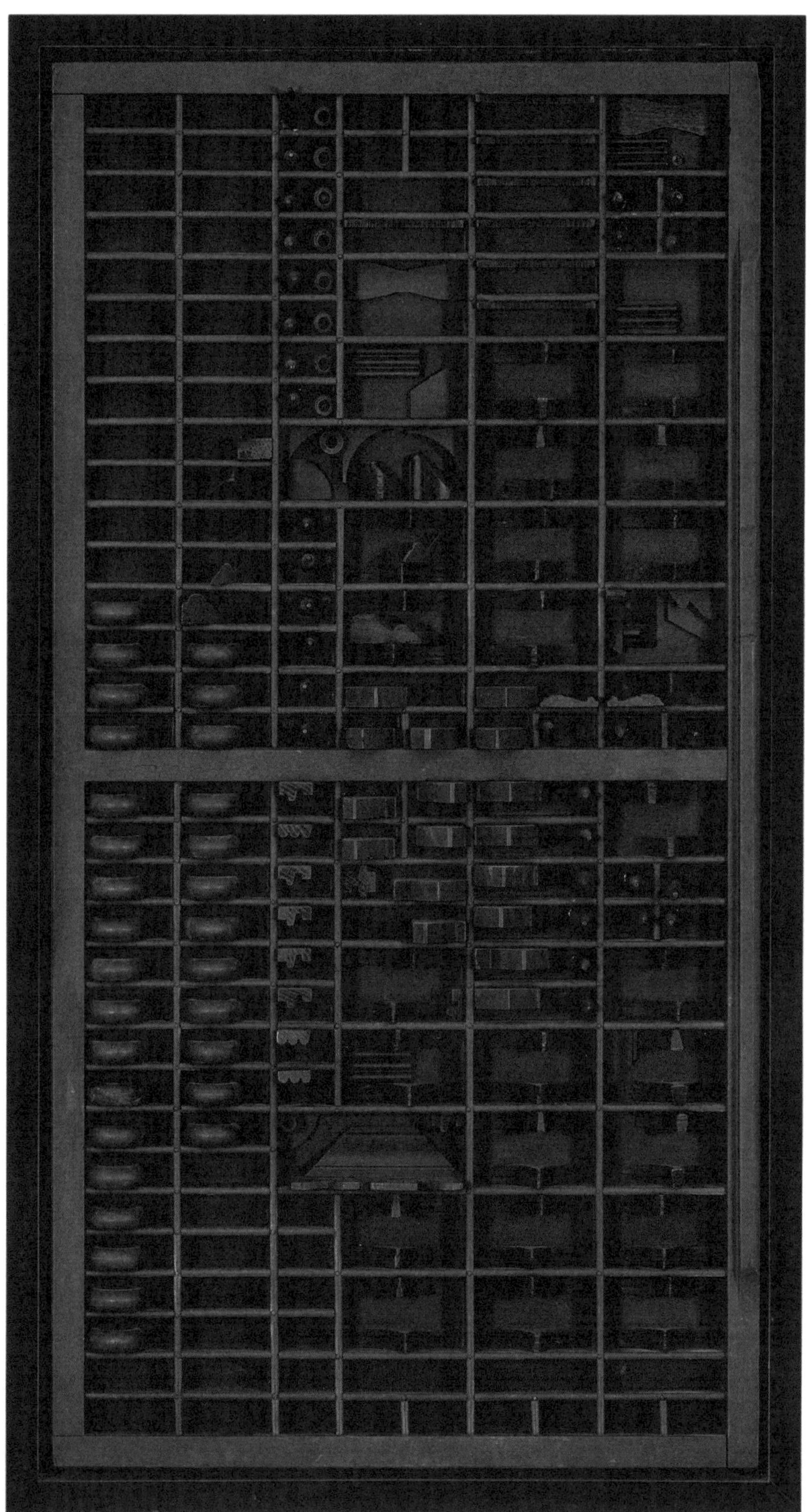

5.8 End of the Day XXII 1972, wood painted black, 87 × 47.5 × 19 cm

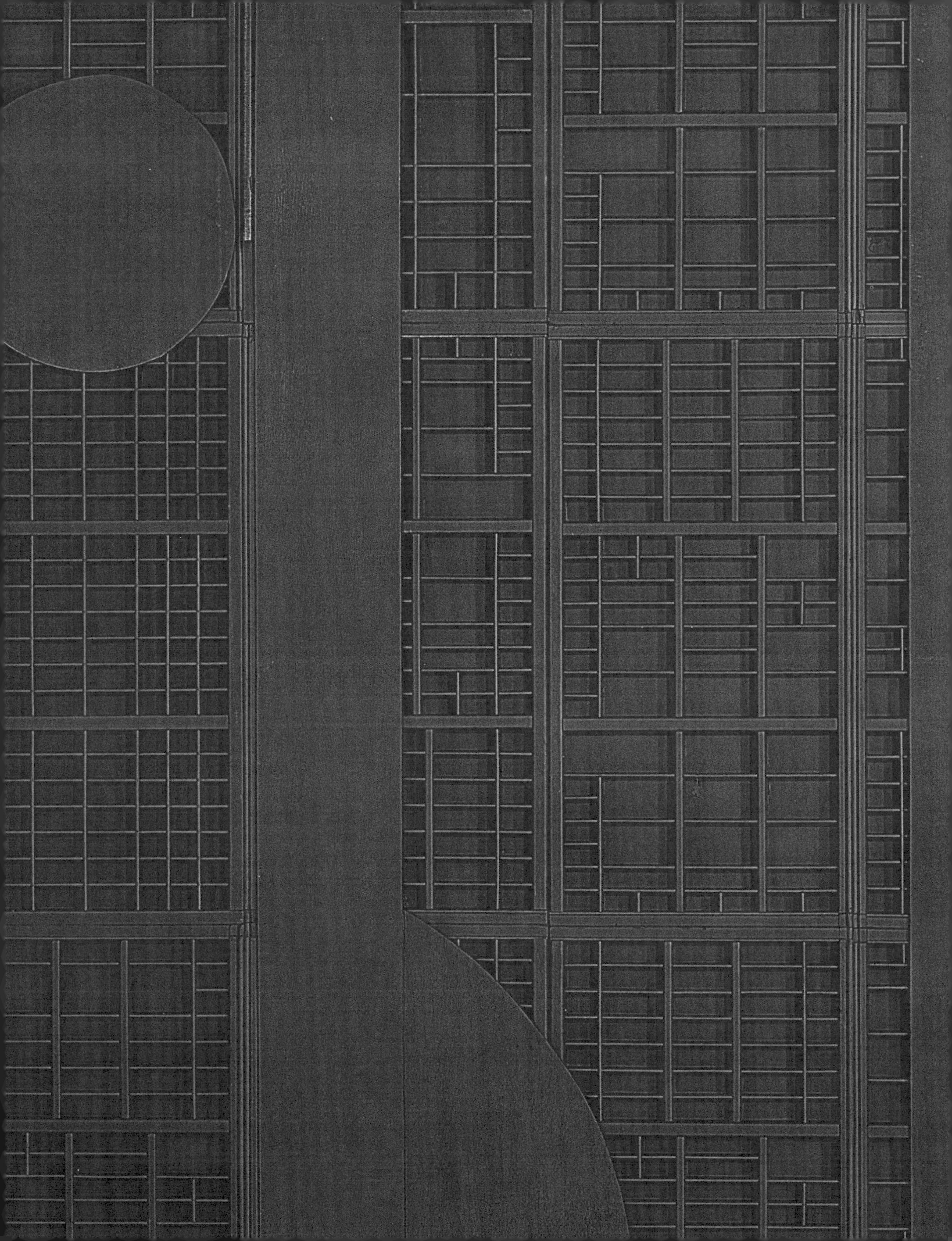

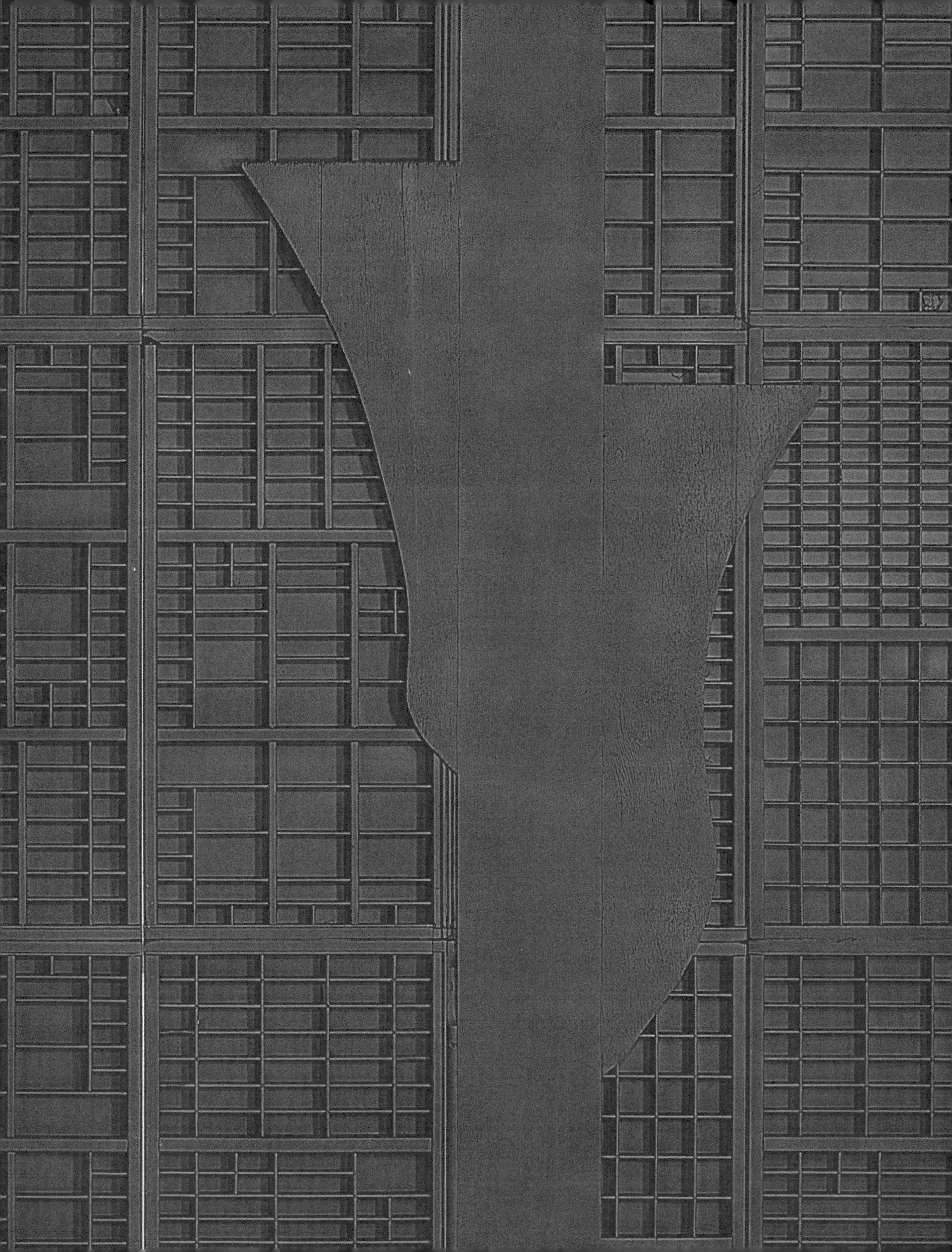

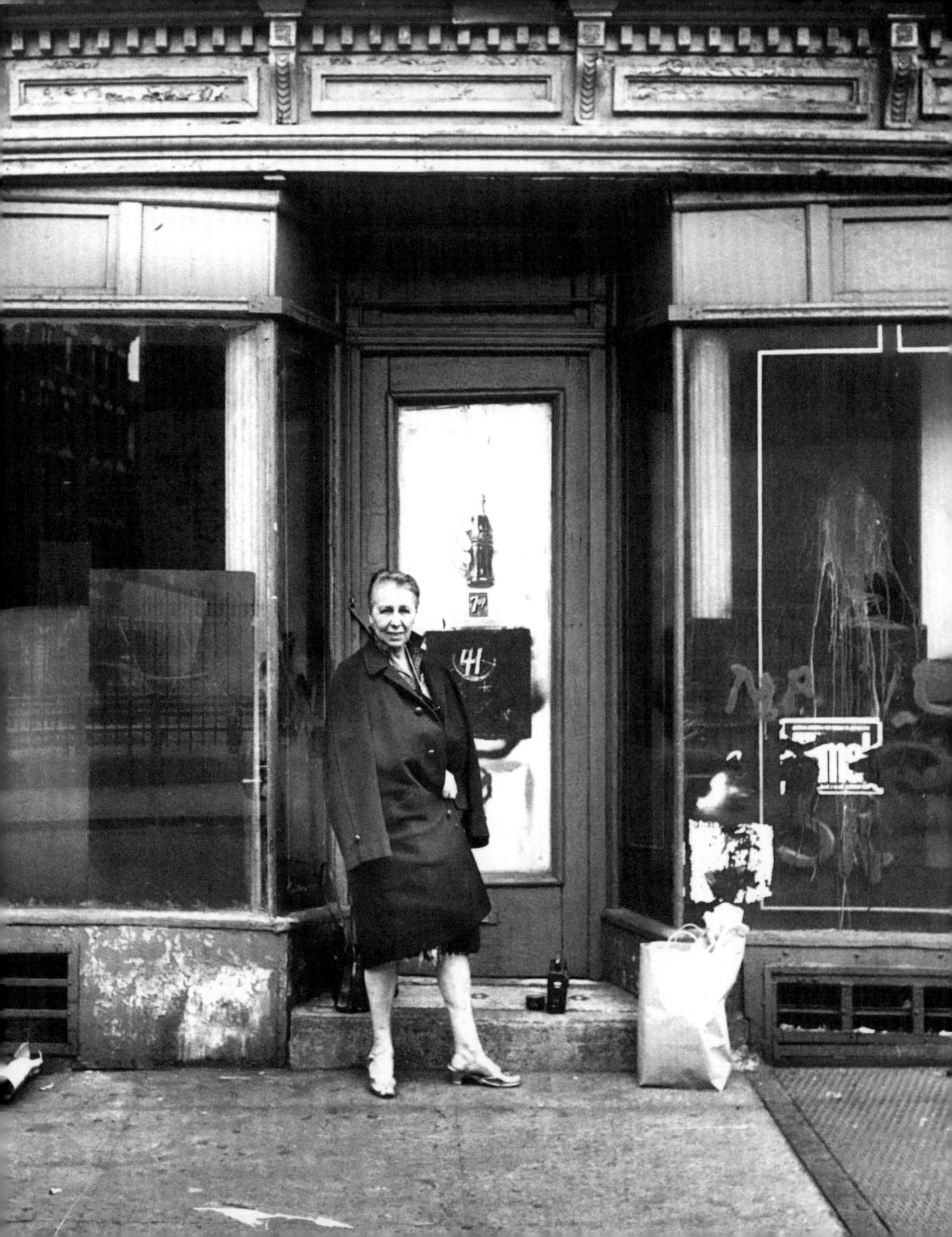
41

ICH LIEBE EIN LEERES HAUS

ANNE HORVATH

I LOVE AN EMPTY HOUSE

»I love an empty house. I love the luxury of space.«[1]

»Ich liebe ein leeres Haus. Ich liebe den Luxus des Raums.«[1]

6 Louise Nevelson in ihrer Wohnung in der Spring Street 29, New York, 1960er-Jahre
Louise Nevelson in her home at 29 Spring Street, 1960s,
Photo: Ugo Mulas, Archives of American Art, Series 9, Box 14, Folder 15 / Ugo Mulas Archives

Mrs. N's Palace

Dreizehn Jahre brauchte Louise Nevelson für die Realisierung von *Mrs. N's Palace.*[2] Die kolossale Installation bildet die Synthese ihres gesamten schöpferischen Denkens und zugleich den Höhepunkt ihrer jahrzehntelangen Reflexion über das Konzept Ausstellungsinstallation und ihre Beziehung zum Raum. Die Künstlerin erläuterte zu dem Werk 1980: »Ich denke, die Leute sind sich oft gar nicht im Klaren darüber, was Raum eigentlich ist. Sie halten ihn für leer. Dabei spielt Raum in unserem Denken und in der Projektion in die dreidimensionale Welt eine alles entscheidende Rolle. Raum entsteht durch die Dinge, mit denen man ihn füllt. Wie wenn jemand ins Zimmer tritt und den ganzen Raum beherrscht. Raum besitzt Atmosphäre, und womit man ihn füllt, färbt auf unser Denken und unsere Wahrnehmung ab.«[3]

Dieses letzte ihrer Environments,[4] das die New Yorker Pace Gallery 1977 im Rahmen der Ausstellung *Nevelson: Recent Wood Sculpture* erstmals präsentierte, zieht Betrachtende in den Strudel ihres Kosmos, ihrer mentalen Landschaft hinein. In ihnen spiegelt sich die Dichte und Energie ihrer Wahlheimat New York wider, die sie grenzenlos bewunderte und die während ihrer gesamten Laufbahn eine ihrer wichtigsten Inspirationsquellen blieb. Mit ihren Demiurgenhänden verwandelte sie den Abfall der Stadt in einen grandiosen, eines Monarchen würdigen Palast, der mythische Helden heraufbeschwört, allen voran das Seekönigspaar und den Häuptling ihrer ersten Environments *The King and The Queen of the Sea* (1956) oder *Chief* (1959).

Was aber verbirgt sich hinter *Mrs. N's Palace*? Vielleicht dachte Nevelson an Alberto Giacomettis Installation *The Palace at 4 a.m.* (1932), die sie in der Sammlung des Museum of Modern Art in New York gesehen haben mag. Ihr Verhältnis zum Raum ähnelte dem Giacomettis; für beide war er ein Ort, an dem ihre Träume und Gedanken Gestalt annehmen konnten. Doch Giacomettis zierlicher, an ein Puppenhaus erinnernder Konstruktion stellte Nevelson eine Skulptur entgegen, die wie ein Zufluchtsort wirkt. Sie versetzt uns in das Dämmerlicht der Schatten, verstärkt noch durch die Spiegel auf dem Boden der Installation, während das gedämpfte Licht die in einheitliches Schwarz getauchten Holzkonstruktionen umso plastischer hervortreten lässt. Der Dramatiker Edward Albee entdeckte darin einen Abglanz des Lebens: »Für Nevelson war es, als hätte sie begonnen, mit ihren eigenen ›Welten‹ sozusagen alternative Räume zu schaffen – eine für

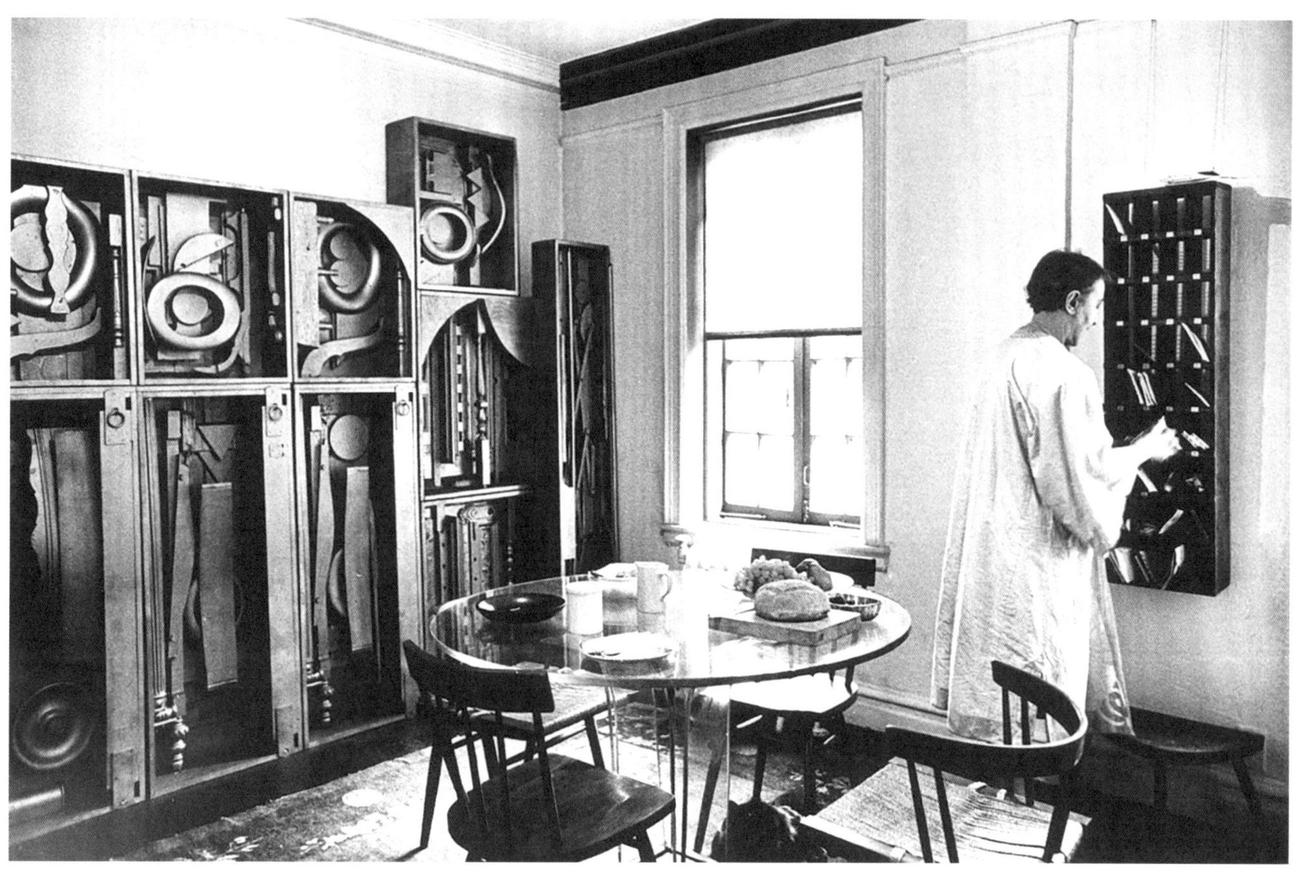

Mrs. N's Palace

Thirteen years of effort went into Louise Nevelson's *Mrs. N's Palace.*[2] The colossal piece both summarizes her creative thinking and marks the culmination of several decades reflecting on the concept of the exhibition-installation and its relationship with space. As the artist explained in 1980 concerning the work: »I think often people don't realize the meaning of space. They think space is something empty. Actually, in the mind and the projection into this three-dimensional world, space plays the most vital part in our lives. Your concept of what you put into a space will create another space. You can see a person walk into a room and dominate the space. Space has an atmosphere, and what you put into it will color your thinking and your awareness.«[3]

Unveiled to the public in 1977 at the Pace Gallery in New York at the exhibition *Nevelson: Recent Wood Sculpture,* this final environment[4] draws visitors into the maelstrom of her world, into a mental landscape that expresses the density and the energy of her adopted New York, a city Nevelson hugely admired and which remained an essential source of inspiration throughout her career. Like those of a demiurge, her hands transform the city's refuse into a palace worthy of the greatest monarchs, referencing the mythical characters – notably *The King and The Queen of the Sea* (1956) and *Chief* (1959) – who populated her early environments.

Yet what is *Mrs. N's Palace* actually concerned with? Perhaps Nevelson had in mind Alberto Giacometti's *The Palace at 4 a.m.* (1932), which she might have encountered in the collections of the Museum of Modern Art in New York. Both artists share a sense of space as a place capable of embodying dreams and spirits. In contrast to Giacometti's fragile, dollhouse-like construction, however, Nevelson's

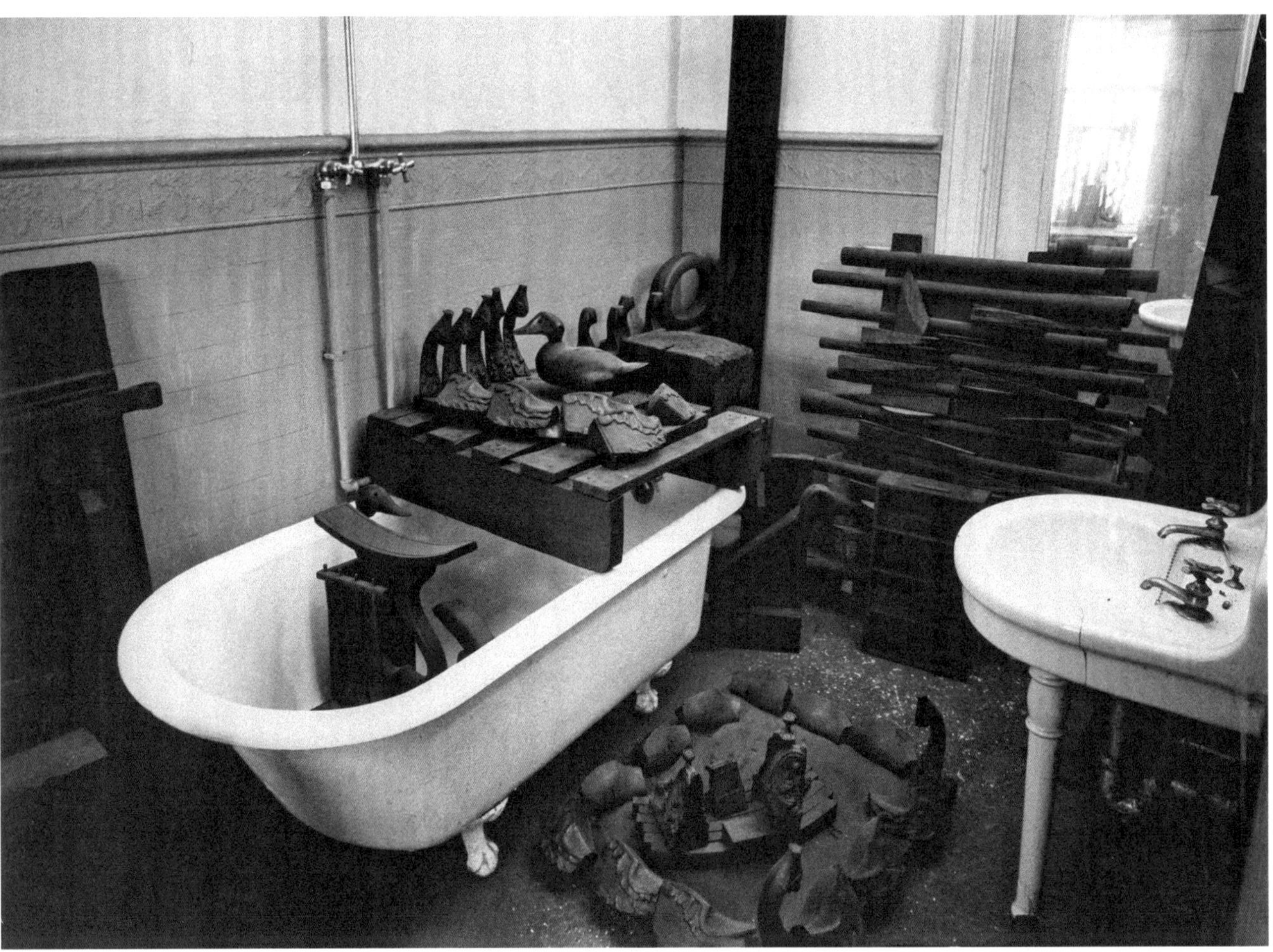

sie selbst nachvollziehbare Realität inmitten des äußeren Chaos. Es kam natürlich anders: Das Private wurde öffentlich, und ihr Zufluchtsort allen zugänglich. Wer Nevelsons Werke kennt, stellt fest, dass die Welt ihnen mehr und mehr ähnelt.«[5]

Es war ihr persönlicher Zufluchtsort. »Mrs. N« nannten sie die Kinder in der Nachbarschaft des New Yorker Quartiers, in dem sie wohnte und arbeitete. Sie sorgte dafür, dass dieses Werk sie überleben würde, indem sie es als Assemblage aus autonomen Skulpturen konzipierte, anstatt wie ihre diesem vorausgehenden Environments als Gruppe eigenständiger, durch eine Erzählung verknüpfter Werke. Von *The Circus. The Clown Is the Center of His World* ab 1944 in der Norlyst Gallery bis zu *The Royal Tides* 1961 in der Martha Jackson Gallery hatte sie mit ansehen müssen, wie eines nach dem anderen zerstückelt worden war, weil keine Institution ambitioniert genug war, sie in ihre Sammlung aufzunehmen.

30th Street

Für Nevelson verkörperte *Mrs. N's Palace* eine typisch amerikanische Erfahrung (»*American experience*«[6]), und deshalb überließ sie die Installation dem Metropolitan Museum of Art in New York; doch man kann darin auch einen Widerschein ihrer Privaträume im Herzen von Manhattan sehen. Ob das Haus von ihrer Kunst geprägt wurde oder umgekehrt, ist schwer zu sagen.

Nevelsons Haus in der 30th Street war buchstäblich untrennbar von ihrem Schaffen. In ihren Augen war es »*selbst* eine Skulptur«.[7] Sie schilderte es als einen Raum, in dem alle Gegenstände mit Rollen versehen und ständig in Bewegung seien,

7 Holzskulpturen von Louise Nevelson, 1954
Wood sculptures made by Louise Nevelson, 1954, Photo: Walter Sanders, The LIFE Magazine Collection/Shutterstock

sculpture evokes a refuge, plunging us into an immersive, shadowy twilight intensified by the mirrored floor of the installation and the subdued glow that imparts a different kind of depth to her uniformly black wooden forms. For his part, playwright Edward Albee sees them as a true reflection of life: Nevelson feels that she began making her »worlds« as an alternative space, so to speak – to create for herself a fathomable reality in the midst of the outside chaos. What has happened, of course, is that the private has become public, the refuge accessible to all, and, to those who know what a Nevelson looks like, the world is beginning to resemble her art.[5]

The refuge is for the artist herself. Mrs. N was the nickname given to Nevelson by the children in the neighborhood where she lived. Nevelson was to ensure that this work outlived her – unlike her earlier environments, which she had pictured as pieces in their own right, borne along by a narrative, rather than as a group of autonomous sculptures gathered together. Since no institution was ambitious enough to present them all in its collection, she looked on as they were dismantled one by one, from *Circus: The Clown Is the Center of the World* at the Norlyst Gallery in 1944 to *The Royal Tides* at the Martha Jackson Gallery in 1961.

30th Street

For Nevelson, *Mrs. N's Palace* embodies an »American experience«[6] – justifying her donation of the work to the Metropolitan Museum of Art, New York. The piece can also be understood as a reflection of her own home in the heart of Manhattan – though it is hard to say whether the house is an extension of her art, or vice versa.

Nevelson's home on 30th Street became inseparable from her oeuvre; the artist even declared that her »house *itself* is a sculpture.«[7] She described it as a space where everything ran on casters, constantly in motion, mirroring the back-and-forth of her ongoing investigation into the environment form. Thus, while preparing the white environment *Dawn's Wedding Feast* at the Museum of Modern Art in 1959 and the gold exhibition *The Royal Tides* at Martha Jackson Gallery in 1961, she moved into two separate studios close to her house, in which the color of the walls matched that of the sculptures she was making.

As her art gained recognition in the mid-1960s, Nevelson stripped the interior of her home of everything superfluous, so that the work might unfold in all its majesty. Visiting the house after 1967, Arnold B. Glimcher recalled the experience as »more like visiting a monastery than a garden in moonlight.«[8] *New York Times* critic Hilton Kramer recalls a visit to Nevelson: »Its interior seemed to have been stripped of everything – not only furniture and the common comforts of daily living, but of many mundane necessities – that might divert attention from the sculptures that crowded every space, occupied every wall, and at once filled and bewildered the eye wherever it turned. Divisions between the rooms seemed to dissolve in an endless sculptural environment.«[9]

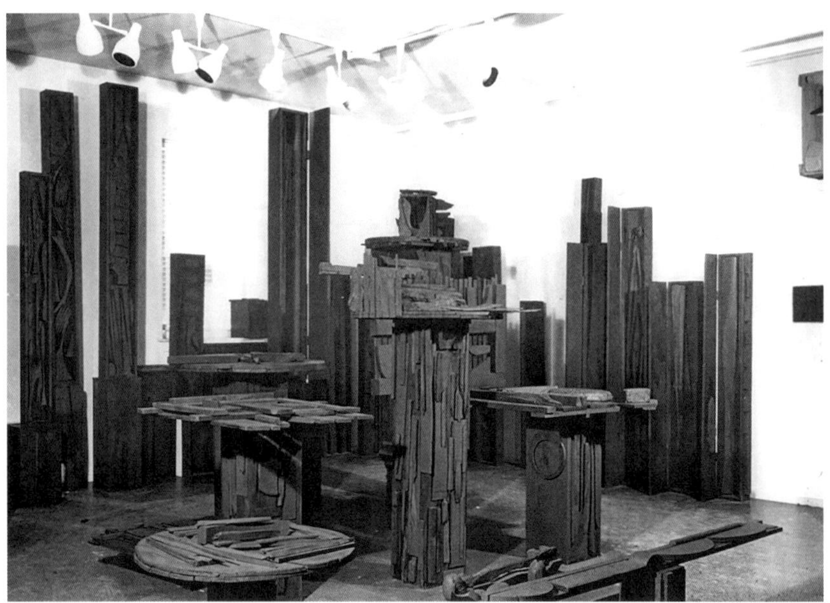

8 Installationsansicht *Moon Garden + One* (1958), Grand Central Moderns, New York, 1958
Installation view *Moon Garden + One* (1958), Grand Central Moderns, New York, 1958, Photo: unknown, Whitney Archives, Box 66, Folder 20

9 Louise Nevelsons Studio in der Spring Street 29, New York, 1974
Louise Nevelson's 29 Spring Street studio, New York, 1974, Photo: Albert L Mozel, courtesy Pace Gallery

um die sprunghaften Veränderungen im Zuge ihrer Erforschung von Environments nachvollziehen zu können. Für die Arbeit an der ganz in Weiß gehaltenen Ausstellung *Dawn's Wedding Feast* 1959 im Museum of Modern Art und an der goldverbrämten Schau *The Royal Tides* 1961 bei Martha Jackson zum Beispiel mietete sie jeweils ein zusätzliches Atelier in der Nähe an, in dem die Farbe der Wände diejenige der im Werden begriffenen Skulpturen aufgriff.

Als ihr künstlerisches Schaffen um die Mitte der 1960er-Jahre zunehmend Anerkennung fand, entschloss sich Nevelson, ihre Räume von allem Überflüssigen zu befreien, damit ihr Werk sich darin majestätisch entfalten konnte. Arnold B. Glimcher berichtet, nach 1967 habe es sich »eher angefühlt, als betrete man ein Kloster als einen Garten im Mondlicht«.[8] Hilton Kramer, Kritiker der *New York Times*, erzählte von einem seiner Besuche bei Nevelson: »Der Innenraum wirkte vollständig leer – es gab keine Möbel, keine der sonst üblichen alltäglichen Annehmlichkeiten und kaum Gebrauchsgegenstände; sie hätten womöglich die Aufmerksamkeit von den Skulpturen abgelenkt, die sich in jedem Zimmer drängten, jede Wand füllten und den Blick, wohin man auch sah, gleichermaßen fesselten und irritierten. Die verschiedenen Räume schienen zu einem einzigen endlosen skulpturalen *Environment* zu verschmelzen.«[9] Jede Fläche – bis hin zur Badewanne voller Kunstwerke – diente der Präsentation ihrer Kunst, deren Theatralität die Inszenierung ihrer Environments ergänzte. In einem 1972 genau während der Entstehungszeit von *Mrs. N's Palace* veröffentlichten Gespräch erklärte Nevelson: »Es heißt, ich hätte als erste Bildhauerin Environments geschaffen. Das ergab sich ganz von selbst. Eine Galerie ließ mich eine Ausstellung machen, und da schuf ich ein komplettes Environment. Ich ließ alles aus den Galerieräumen entfernen, auch die Möbel. Ich wollte meine Werke damit besser zur Geltung bringen, und *nichts* – nicht einmal ein Aschenbecher – sollte von ihnen ablenken. Die Galerie hatte zwei Fenster. Eines davon verkleidete ich mit einer meiner Arbeiten. Ich wollte keine Symmetrie – ich wollte ein Environment. Heute ist ständig von Environments die Rede. Der Begriff ist wirklich jedem vertraut.«[10]

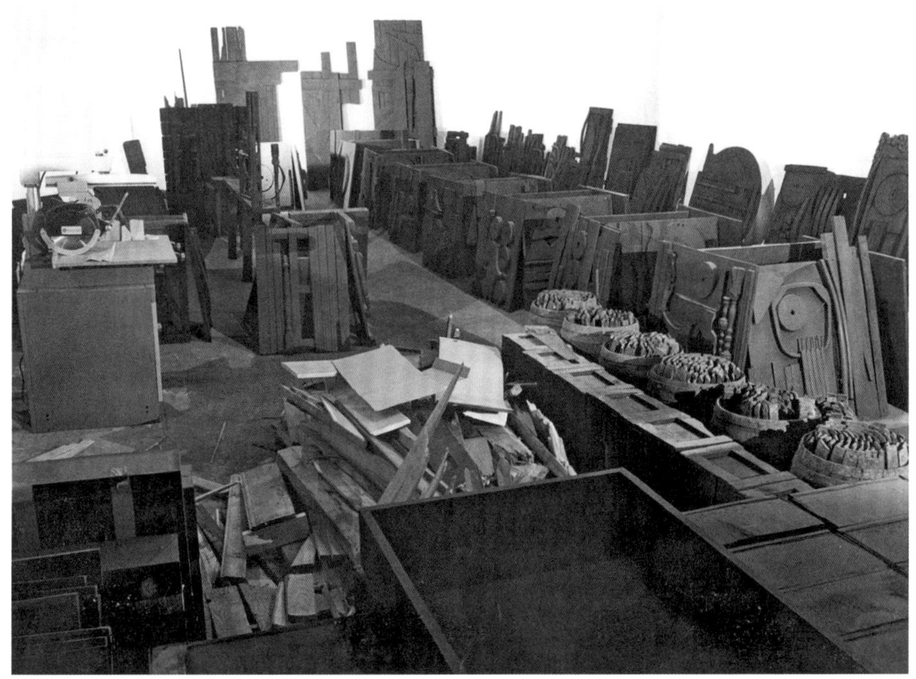

Each space, right down to a bathtub filled with works, was dedicated to unveiling an art whose theatricality extended into the staging of her environments. In an interview published in 1972, when Nevelson was working intensively on *Mrs. N's Palace,* she declared: They say I was the first environmental sculptor. It wasn't planned. A gallery let me put on my own show once and I made a whole environment. I took out the furniture and everything else in the gallery. I did this to enhance the things I had created and I didn't want *anything* superimposed on them – not even an ashtray. The gallery had two windows. One of them I enclosed with my work. I didn't want symmetry – I wanted an environment. Now, everyone talks of environment. It's become a word that's almost as close as our skin.[10]

The artist was referring to *Moon Garden + One,* her first environment, created in 1958 at Colette Roberts' Grand Central Moderns gallery in New York, for which the house at 30th Street played the role of a veritable laboratory. Its atmosphere seems to have been transposed to Grand Central Moderns, which was literally enveloped by the organic constructions of black-painted boxes. It was transformed into a stage for which the visitor's body – to which the »Plus One« of the exhibition title probably refers – became an integral part of the experience.

Likewise, the participation of the artist's own body, through a lifelong practice of eurythmy and her training in acting and singing, enabled Nevelson to constantly refocus her energies and expand the scale of her art from sculpture to installation – a phenomenon then emerging on the New York scene under her aegis.

Beyond questions of gravity, balance and rhythm – preoccupations that converge in Nevelson's sculpture and in the choreographic innovations of modern dance, particularly those of Martha Graham, whose performances Nevelson enthusiastically attended in New York – theatricality also plays out on a psychological level. The re-creation of private space in terms of sculptural space becomes a metaphor for the inner landscape of the psyche.

»Wenn ich das Haus putze oder die Straße vor dem Haus fege, putze ich in Wahrheit nicht, sondern erschaffe Architektur«

Gemeint ist *Moon Garden + One*, Nevelsons erstes *Environment*, das sie 1958 in Colette Roberts New Yorker Galerie Grand Central Moderns präsentierte. Ihr Haus in der 30th Street diente ihr dabei in jeder Hinsicht als Versuchslabor. Es wirkt, als habe sie die Atmosphäre des Hauses auf die Galerie übertragen, wo ihre organischen Konstruktionen aus schwarz bemalten Kisten buchstäblich den Raum ummantelten. Die Installation wurde quasi zur Bühne, auf der auch dem Körper des/der jeweiligen Besuchers/Besucherin – auf die das »+ One« im Ausstellungstitel verweisen dürfte – eine aktive Rolle im Dialog mit dem Werk zukommt.

Auch ihre eigene Körperlichkeit nutzte Nevelson, die sich eingehend mit Eurythmie beschäftigte, Schauspiel- und Gesangsunterricht genommen hatte, um ihre Energie zu fokussieren und die Bandbreite ihrer bildhauerischen Arbeit um Installationen zu erweitern, die von ihr inspiriert in der damaligen New Yorker Kunstszene rasch Nachahmer fanden.

Jenseits von Schwerkraft, Balance und Rhythmus – zentralen Themen der Skulpturen Nevelsons ebenso wie der experimentellen Choreografien des modernen Balletts, allen voran von Martha Graham, deren Vorstellungen Nevelson in New York begeistert besuchte, – wirkt die Theatralität ihrer Werke auch auf psychischer Ebene: Die Neuschöpfung des intimen Raums als skulpturaler Raum wird dabei zur Metapher für den Innenraum der Psyche.

Dream Houses

Zeitgleich mit *Mrs. N's Palace* beschäftigte sich Nevelson 1972 mit *Dream Houses*, einer Reihe von Skulpturen in Form einzelner menschengroßer Kästen mit zahlreichen Türen und Fenstern, die auf der formalen Ebene mit der Ambiguität zwischen Voyeurismus und erwünschten Einblicken in die Privatsphäre spielen. Während ihr Atelierhaus ihr ohnehin als Nährboden für ihr Schaffen diente und es immer ihr Wunsch war, im engen Kontakt mit den Werkstoffen zu leben, die sie in Skulpturen verwandelte, rückte nun das Motiv des häuslichen Raums an sich erstmals in den Fokus.

1972[11] war dieses Umfeld, der Haushalt, natürlich auch ein Politikum, und Nevelson griff mit ihren *Dream Houses* Silvia Federicis Manifest *Wages against Housework*[12] auf, das »Lohn für Hausarbeit« als ersten Schritt zu deren Verweigerung forderte, oder auch das Konzept der Gemeinschaftsausstellung *Womanhouse*, das aus einem feministischen Ermächtigungsprojekt unter Leitung von Judy Chicago und Miriam Schapiro am California Institute of Art hervorgegangen war.

Nevelsons unkonventioneller Ansatz war ein Ausdruck ihrer persönlichen Wahrnehmung und Umdeutung der geschlechtsspezifischen Aufgabenteilung im häuslichen ebenso wie im künstlerischen Bereich. Sie erklärte dazu: »Wenn ich das Haus putze oder die Straße vor dem Haus fege, putze ich in Wahrheit nicht, sondern erschaffe Architektur«[13], wobei mit »Architektur« sowohl physische als auch psychische Räume gemeint sind. Das Haus kann sich wie eine Krypta anfühlen, wie eine geschlossene

»When I clean house or sweep the street in front of the house, I am not really cleaning house. I am building architecture.«

Dream Houses

Coinciding with the creation of *Mrs. N's Palace*, in 1972, Nevelson began the *Dream Houses* series, sculptures in the form of a single, human-sized box with a number of doors and windows, whose form plays on the ambiguity between voyeurism and the deliberate unveiling of private space. While Nevelson's home-cum-workshop served as a generative matrix for her practice, and she often expressed her desire to live immersed in the materials she transformed into sculptures, this moment marked a shift in focus toward the subject of the domestic interior.

In 1972,[11] the domestic sphere was also patently political: Nevelson's series resonated with the publication of the manifesto *Wages Against Work*,[12] in which Silvia Federici advocated for the remuneration of domestic tasks as a first step towards their abolition, as well as with the group exhibition *Womanhouse*, the outcome of a feminist education project led by Judy Chicago and Miriam Schapiro at CalArts.

Nevelson's sinuous path reflects her own sense and redefinition of the gendered demarcation of tasks in both the domestic and artistic spheres. As she put it: »When I clean house or sweep the street in front of the house, I am not really cleaning house. I am building architecture.«[13] Architecture is meant here as a psychological as much as a physical space. A house can conjure a crypt, a hideaway, or a place where the richness of a private world can blossom. As seen in Marvin W. Schwartz's photograph ↪ **fig. 10** of Nevelson on the doorstep of one of her *Dream Houses*, the artist consciously presented these quasi-inhabitable sculptures as straddling the line between protection and self-disclosure in the public sphere. Just like *Mrs. N's Palace*, Nevelson's *Dream Houses* offer an alternative view of the space of the home, at odds with every norm and thus conducive to art, where dreams and the power of the imagination can be expressed to the full.

The spaces Nevelson creates blend together into a collage of the psyche, in which the house at 30th Street, the galleries showing her environments, and the *Dream Houses* are interwoven with an imaginary landscape, which itself reflects back onto her entire corpus: »The essence of living is in doing, and in doing, I have made my world and it's a much better world than I ever saw outside.«[14]

Höhle oder wie ein Ort, an dem sich eine Privatsphäre in all ihrem Reichtum entfalten kann. Wie das Foto von Marvin W. Schwartz ↳Abb. 10 belegt, das sie vor einem ihrer *Dream Houses* zeigt, versteht Nevelson diese quasi bewohnbaren Skulpturen als Orte auf der Grenze zwischen Rückzugsort und Entschleierung des Ich im öffentlichen Raum. Genau wie *Mrs. N's Palace* bieten die *Dream Houses* eine alternative Vision von einem Wohnraum an, der unter Missachtung jeglicher Normen die Kreativität fördert und in dem sich Träume und die Kraft der Fantasie frei entfalten können.

Die von Nevelson geschaffenen Räume verschwimmen zu einer psychischen Collage. Darin verschmelzen ihr Haus in der 30th Street, die Galerien, in denen sie ihre Environments ausstellte, und die *Dream Houses* mit ihrer Fantasielandschaft, die sich wiederum in all ihren Werken wiederfindet: »Im Leben dreht sich alles um das Tun, und durch mein Tun habe ich mir meine Welt erschaffen. Und sie ist viel besser als alles, was ich jemals außerhalb gesehen habe.«[14]

10 Louise Nevelson vor einem ihrer *Dream Houses*, 1972
Louise Nevelson in front of one of her *Dream Houses*, 1972, Photo: Marvin W. Schwartz Photograph Collection, Special Collections, Frances Mulhall Achilles Library and Archives, Digital image Whitney Museum of American Art / Licensed by Scala

---

1 Louise Nevelson, zit. in: Jean Lipman, *Nevelson's World*, New York 1983, S. 39.

2 *Mrs. N's Palace* lautet der Titel einer Ausstellung von Arbeiten Louise Nevelsons vom 24.1. bis 31.8.2026 im Centre Pompidou-Metz, für die ihre Environments rekonstruiert werden (vgl. den begleitenden Katalog der Editions du Centre Pompidou-Metz).

3 Louise Nevelson, zit. in: *Louise Nevelson. Atmospheres and Environments*, hg. von Clarkson N. Potter (Ausst.-Kat. Whitney Museum of American Art, New York), New York 1980, S. 161.

4 Mit *environment* und *atmosphere* beschrieb Louise Nevelson ab den 1950er-Jahren selbst die von ihr konzipierten Ausstellungen / Installationen.

5 Edward Albee, zit. in: Ausst.-Kat. New York 1980 (wie Anm. 3), S. 30.

6 Brief Nevelson an William S. Lieberman, 13.12.1984, Metropolitan Museum Archives.

7 Louise Nevelson im Gespräch mit Louis Botto, »Work in Progress/Louise Nevelson«, in: *Intellectual Digest*, April 1972, S. 8.

8 Arnold B. Glimcher, *Louise Nevelson*, New York 1976, S. 141.

9 Hilton Kramer, »Nevelson. Her sculpture changed the way we look at things«, in: *The New York Times Magazine*, 30.10.1983, S. 28.

10 Louise Nevelson in: Botto 1972 (wie Anm. 7), S. 8.

11 Zur Erschaffung der *Dream Houses* siehe Julia Bryan-Wilson, »Louise Nevelson's Modernism«, in: Zhang Jian und Bruce Robertson (Hg.), *Complementary Modernisms in China and the United States*, New York 2020, S. 462–481.

12 Silvia Federici, *Wages Against Housework*, Bristol 1975.

13 Louise Nevelson, zit. in: *Dawns + Dusks. Taped Conversations with Diana MacKown*, New York 1976, S. 184.

14 Ebd., S. 70.

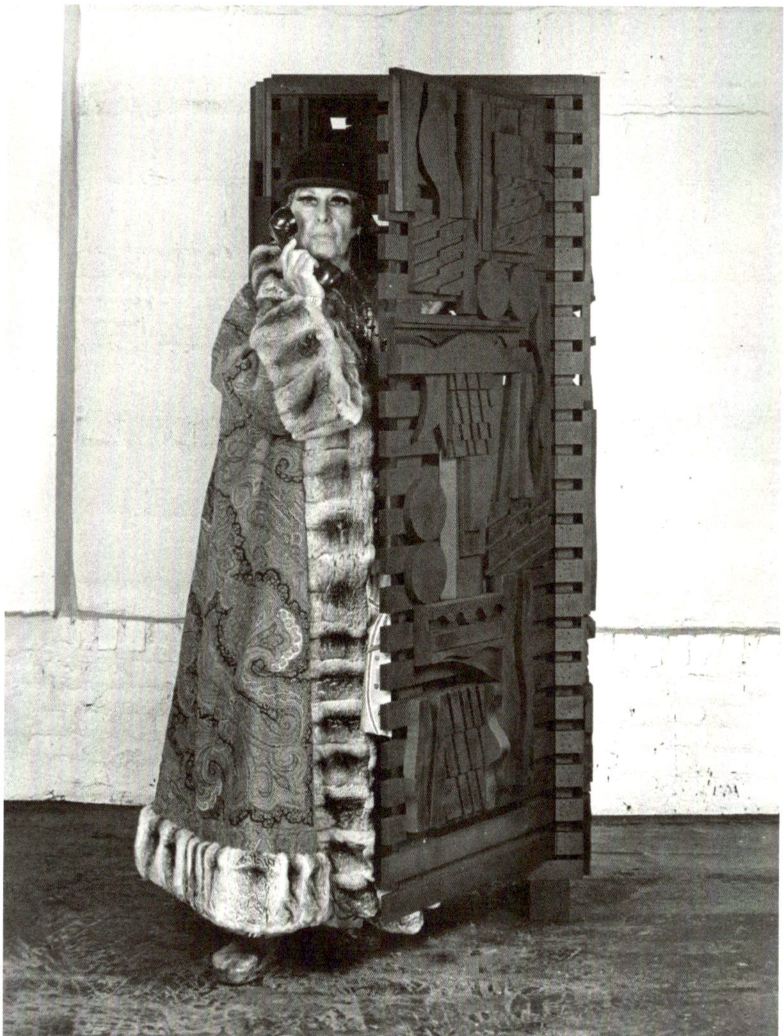

1 Louise Nevelson quoted in Jean Lipman, *Nevelson's World* (New York: Hudson Hills Press, 1983), p. 39.

2 *Mrs. N's Palace* is the title of the exhibition devoted to Louise Nevelson at the Centre Pompidou-Metz from January 24 to August 31, 2026, for which some of her environments have been reconstructed (see the catalogue published by the Editions du Centre Pompidou-Metz).

3 Louise Nevelson quoted in *Louise Nevelson: Atmospheres and Environments* (exh. cat. Whitney Museum of American Art, New York), New York 1980, p. 161.

4 Louise Nevelson used this term, along with *»atmosphere«*, to describe her exhibition-installations from the 1950s onwards.

5 Edward Albee, quoted in *Atmospheres and Environments* (see note 3), p. 30.

6 Letter from Louise Nevelson to William S. Lieberman, December 13, 1984, Metropolitan Museum Archives.

7 Louise Nevelson, interview with Louis Botto, »Work in Progress/Louise Nevelson«, *Intellectual Digest*, April 1972, p. 8.

8 Arnold B. Glimcher, *Louise Nevelson* (New York: Dutton, 1976), p. 141.

9 Hilton Kramer, »Nevelson: Her Sculpture Changed the Way We Look at Things«, *The New York Times Magazine*, October 30, 1983, p. 28.

10 Nevelson 1972 (see note 7), p. 8.

11 On the context in which the *Dream Houses* were created, see the article by Julia Bryan-Wilson, »Louise Nevelson's Modernism«, in Zhang Jian and Robertson Bruce, *Complementary Modernisms in China and the United States* (New York: Punctum Books, 2020), pp. 462–481.

12 Silvia Federici, *Wages Against Work* (Bristol: Power of Women Collective and the Falling Wall Press, 1975).

13 Louise Nevelson quoted in *Dawns + Dusks. Taped Conversations With Diana MacKown* (New York: Charles Scribner's Sons, 1976), p. 184.

14 Ibid., p. 70.

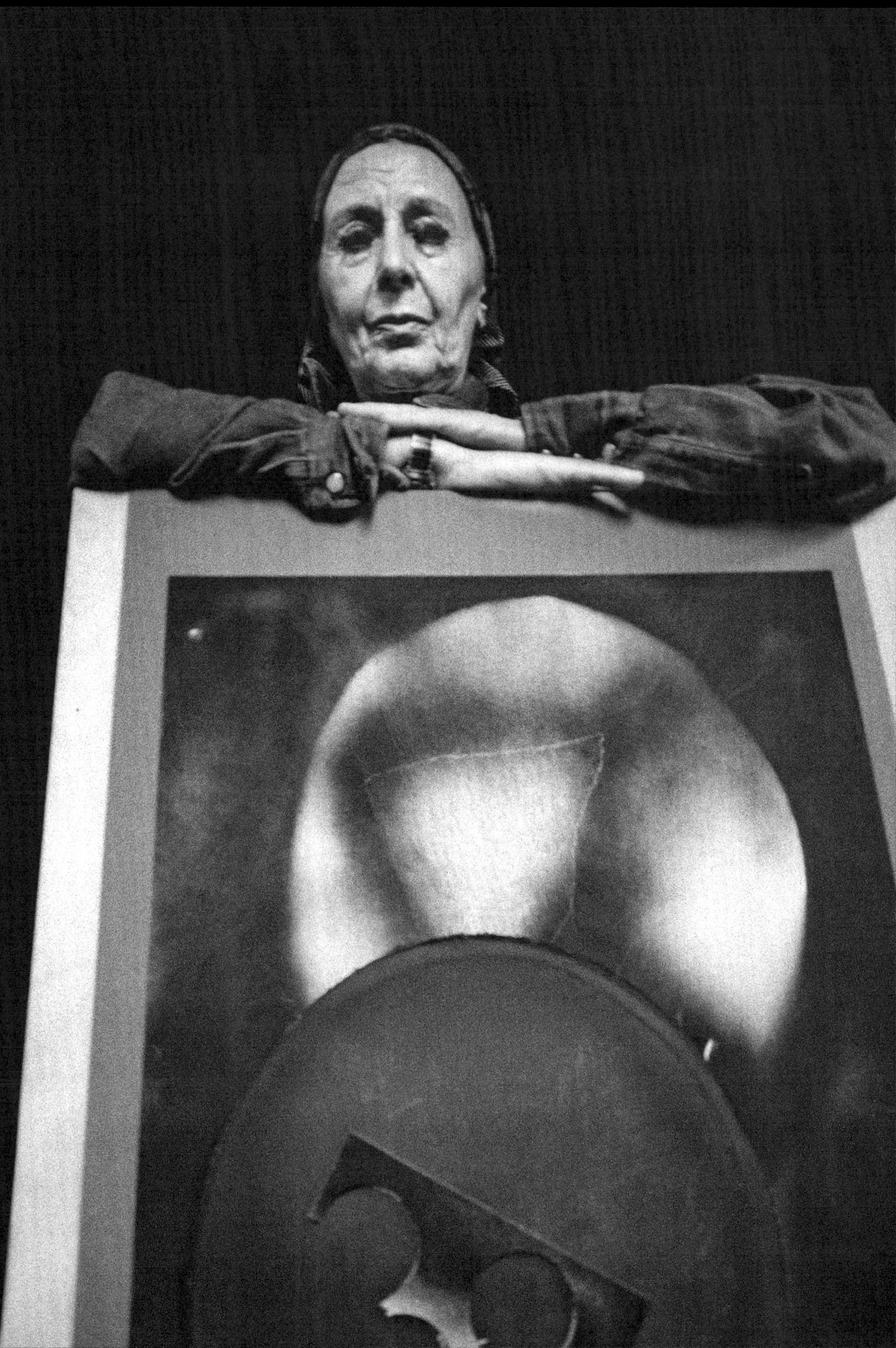

GEORDNET CLASSIFIED

YUVAL ETGAR

»Meine Art zu denken ist eine Collage.«

Geordnet. Materialien und Funktion in Louise Nevelsons Collagen

Die Collagen stellen einen bedeutenden Teil von Louise Nevelsons Schaffen dar, sie sind aber in der Kunstwissenschaft und von Kurator:innen kaum beachtet worden, weshalb zu diesem Werkkomplex nur wenige Publikationen und Essays vorliegen.[1] Dass die Collagen zu Lebzeiten der Künstlerin selten ausgestellt wurden – und wenn, dann stets in Verbindung mit Skulpturen –, hat eine tiefergehende Forschung dazu zweifellos verzögert. Dabei hat Nevelson selbst immer wieder beteuert: »Meine Art zu denken ist eine Collage.«

Nevelsons Collagen waren inspiriert von und eng verbunden mit ihrem bildhauerischen Werk. Einer eingehenden Untersuchung dieser beiden Gattungen ihrer künstlerischen Praxis und der Bezüge zwischen ihnen sollte eine Klärung wichtiger Unterschiede vorausgehen. Zunächst einmal waren die Collagen nie als Entwurfs- oder Vorarbeiten für die größeren, frei stehenden Konstruktionen gedacht. So wurden sie zum Beispiel wegen ihrer relativen Flachheit und den mit einer Präsentation an der Wand verbundenen Bedingungen oft aus leichteren Materialien als Holz gefertigt – etwa aus Kartonagen, gefundenem Papier, Folie und Schleifpapier –, die sich leichter in Form bringen ließen als die Holzkästen, die als strukturelle Basis für die Skulpturen dienten. Der kleinere Maßstab wiederum motivierte Nevelson zur Erkundung eines völlig anderen Spektrums von Objekten in ihrem umfangreichen Arsenal von Überresten aus dem Haushalt: keine schweren Holzelemente von Treppengeländern oder große Schrankfüße, sondern geformte Schubladengriffe, Wäscheklammern und Zuschnitte aus gebrochenem, dünnem Sperrholz. Damit einhergehend scheint sich der Fokus bei den Collagen auf eine intimere Größenordnung häuslicher Kleinteile verschoben zu haben – von den Assoziationen mit architektonischen Strukturen zur Sphäre der Alltags- und Gebrauchsgegenstände. An die Stelle des monochromen Schwarz, das zum Inbegriff für Nevelsons Skulpturen wurde, trat in ihren Collagen nun ein deutlich freierer Umgang mit unbearbeiteten Materialien. Sie weisen vielfältige Oberflächen, Farbgebungen und Texturen auf, es dominieren Holzsichtflächen, außerdem zerrissenes und geklebtes Papier, Gold- und Silberfolie, bunte Textilien, Metalle sowie stärkerer Karton in dunklen Farben, die häufig als Untergrund für kleinere Kompositionen dienen. Auch schwarze Sprühfarbe taucht regelmäßig in Nevelsons Collagearbeiten auf, aber nur selten als einheitliche, geschlossene Oberfläche. Vielmehr benutzte die Künstlerin Schablonen zur Gestaltung von Formkompositionen oder Farbverläufen, lackierte einige Elemente allerdings auch von Hand.

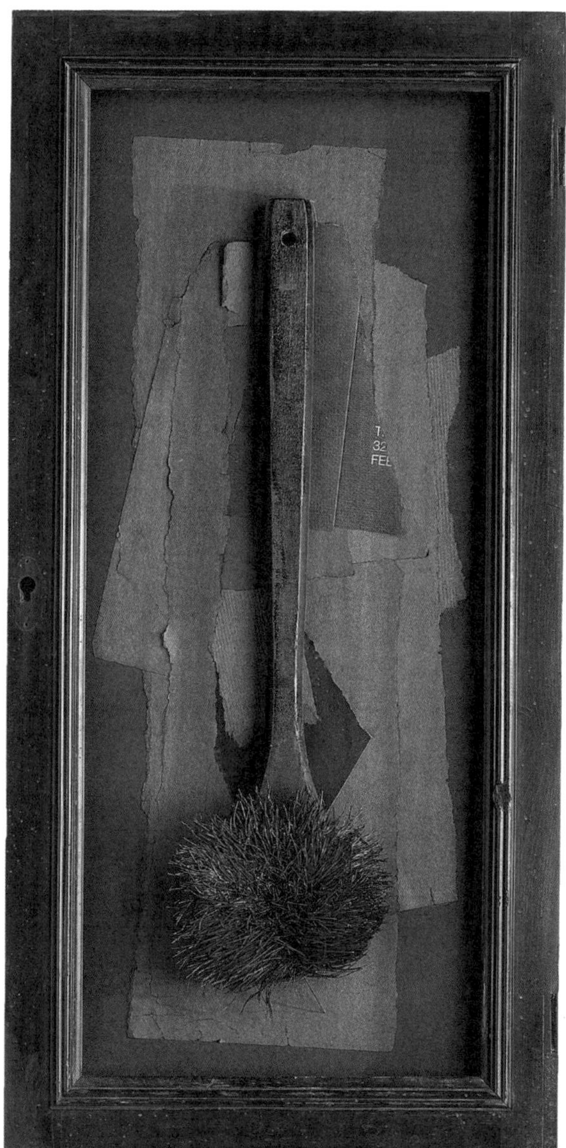

11 Untitled ca. 1984, cardboard, paint, paper, scrub brush and wood on board, 76 × 81.5 × 51 cm, Photo: Gianni Ummarino, Fondazione Marconi, Milan

»The way I think is collage.«

Classified. Materials and Function in Louise Nevelson's Collages

Despite occupying a significant portion of the artist's creative output, Louise Nevelson's collages have been largely neglected by scholars and curators, with only few publications and essays dedicated to this body of work.[1] The fact that Nevelson's collages were exhibited only on rare occasions during her lifetime, and always alongside sculpture, has undoubtedly delayed the emergence of sustained or established scholarship on the subject. At the same time, Nevelson herself frequently asserted that fundamentally, »the way I think is collage.«

Nevelson's collages were inspired by and closely linked to her sculptural work, yet important distinctions must be made between these categories in her practice before they can be related and analyzed in depth. To begin with, the collages were never executed as sketches or preparatory works towards the larger, free-standing constructions. Their relative flatness, and the constraints of wall-mounted display, for example, meant that these works were often composed from lighter materials than wood, such as cardboard packaging, found paper, foil, and sandpaper, all of which were easier to model than the wooden crates that otherwise served as the structural foundations of her sculptures. Their smaller

Bis in jüngste Zeit wurde diese Werkgruppe im Rahmen theoretischer Studien als Einheit behandelt, ohne jede Differenzierung von Untergruppen oder Beachtung ihrer Unterschiede. Es folgt hier eine gekürzte Fassung einer Forschungsarbeit, die ich 2022 mit Unterstützung der Fondazione Marconi in Mailand zu Nevelsons Collagen erstellt habe. Anhand der verwendeten Ausgangsmaterialien habe ich die Arbeiten in sechs große Kategorien unterteilt: »Container«, »Sprühfarbe«, »zerschnittenes und zerrissenes Papier«, »Gebrauchsgegenstände«, »Reststücke und Abfälle« sowie eine formale Kategorie, die eine Zusammenstellung mehrerer Kompositionen in Form von »Mustertafeln« umfasst.[2] Zwar bestehen in der Praxis große Überschneidungen zwischen den einzelnen Kategorien, doch sie erweisen sich als nützlich für eine Betrachtung technischer und materieller Gesten, die diesen Werkkorpus auszeichnen, und erlauben eine tiefere Einsicht in Nevelsons bildhauerische und künstlerische Zielsetzungen. Zwei weitere, kleinere Werkgruppen bilden die »Holzfliesenwände« und die »Textilcollagen«. Eine solche Kategorisierung von Nevelsons Collagen gestattet es, die große Ansammlung einzelner Komponenten und Bestandteile, die meist als unterschiedslos angesehen werden, in separate Gesten, Materialien und kompositorische Strategien auszudifferenzieren und sie somit für Analysen und Deutungen zugänglich zu machen. Auch wenn eine konsequente Einteilung der Arbeiten in Kategorien letztlich unmöglich ist, erweist sie sich doch als sinnvoller Ausgangspunkt für jede Annäherung an Fragestellungen, die Nevelsons Praxis zugrunde lagen.[3]

Container

Der Akt der Verschachtelung faszinierte Nevelson mehr als jede andere bildhauerische Tätigkeit. Dies gilt für ihre frei stehenden Skulpturen gleichermaßen wie für ihre Collagen, wobei Holzkästen oder Pappkartons als kompositorisches Hauptelement immer wiederkehren. Dieser Akt konnte sich in dreidimensionaler Form oder auch in referenzieller Weise vollziehen. Die hieraus resultierenden Arbeiten entstanden überwiegend in der ersten Dekade von Nevelsons Beschäftigung mit Collage, also zwischen 1952 und 1963, einige davon aber auch noch in den folgenden Jahrzehnten. Nachdem Nevelson Ende der 1940er-Jahre zu einer eigenen Handschrift als Bildhauerin gefunden hatte, besann sie sich zunehmend auf das Prinzip der Verschachtelung und seine Bedeutung im Kontext ihrer Arbeit – als eine Klammer, die Kunst, Architektur und häusliches Leben umschließt. Dabei war sie entschlossen, den Original-Maßstab der von ihr erkundeten Objekte beizubehalten. Bei den Collagen kam sie jedoch oft nicht umhin, die verwendeten Verpackungsmaterialien – hauptsächlich verschiedene Arten von Kartonagen – flachzudrücken und auf Holztafeln zu kleben, als komprimierte oder abstrahierte Versionen ihrer ursprünglichen Form. Der grundlegende Unterschied zwischen den Container-Collagen und ihren Entsprechungen in der Skulptur besteht demnach in der Differenzierung von Erscheinung und Funktionalität. Viele Skulpturen Nevelsons bestehen aus Konstellationen kleiner Holzkästen, die bis zum Rand mit Möbelteilen und Holzfragmenten gefüllt, sodann auf die Seite gedreht und zur Präsentation des akkumulierten Inhalts gestapelt wurden. Die Collagen hingegen setzen sich mit dem Prinzip der Verschachtelung weitgehend in einem bildhaften Format auseinander, bedingt vor allem durch die relative Flachheit der Arbeiten und ihre eindeutige Bestimmung als Wandobjekte. Zumeist sind die Container auch sofort als solche erkennbar, doch bleibt ihre ursprüngliche Funktion – trotz ihres konzeptuellen Schwerpunkts – nur selten erhalten.

scale, in turn, meant that Nevelson was encouraged to explore an entirely different range of objects from her expansive arsenal of household refuse; no longer heavy wood sections from staircase railings or large armoire legs, but rather shaped drawer handles, clothes pins, and thin sections of torn plywood. As a result, the collages appear to shift focus toward a more intimate scale of domestic detail – less associated with architectural structures and more attuned to everyday objects and items of use. Finally, the monochromatic black that became synonymous with Nevelson's sculptures is replaced in her collages by a far more liberal approach to bare materials, including varied surfaces of different colors and textures, dominated by the appearance of wood surfaces and including also torn and pasted paper, foils in gold and silver, colorful textiles, metals, as well as thicker card surfaces in dark colors, which often function as backgrounds for the smaller pasted compositions. Black spray paint does indeed appear regularly in Nevelson's collage work, but rarely as a unified, consistent surface. In her collages, Nevelson primarily employed spray paint through stencils to produce formal compositions or gradients, though she also painted some elements free-hand.

Until recently, theoretical analysis of this group of works has treated them as a unified entity, with little distinction between subgroupings or attention to difference. What follows is a shortened version of the research I undertook in 2022 with the support of Fondazione Marconi, Milan, into Nevelson's collages, in which I divided these collages into six main categories based on the nature of their primary material: »containers«, »spray paint«, »cut and torn papers«, »objects-of-use«, »offcuts and debris«, as well as one formal category based on the presentation of multiple compositions in the form of »specimen charts«.[2] Despite much overlap between these categories in practice, they prove useful for the exploration of technical and material gestures that characterize this body of work, as well as for a deeper understanding of Nevelson's aims as a sculptor and artist. Two additional, smaller groups of work include »woodblock walls« and »textile collages«. By dividing Nevelson's collages into categories, the large accumulation of details and elements that is typically regarded as indistinguishable can be dismantled into discrete gestures, materials, and compositional strategies, rendering them available to analysis and interpretation. While such categorization is bound to fail when applied as a strict rule, it is nonetheless essential for any understanding of the questions that motivated Nevelson's practice at large.[3]

Containers

Above all, it was the act of containment that fascinated Nevelson more than any other sculptural action. This is true of her free-standing sculptures as much as her collages, where wooden crates or cardboard boxes function as the main compositional element on numerous occasions. This can take place either in three-dimensional form or in a referential manner. Such works were predominantly executed during the first decade of Nevelson's engagement with collage, between 1952–63, with some examples recurring in the following decades. Having established a coherent voice as a sculptor towards the end of the 1940s, Nevelson began to reflect on what the notion of containment might mean within the context of her work, as a link that binds art, architecture, and domestic life. She was determined, however, to do so without diminishing the one-to-one scale of the objects she explored. In collage, however,

Sprühfarbe

Der Gebrauch von Sprühfarbe in Nevelsons Collagen ist allzu vielfältig, um eine eigene Kategorie zu bilden, ohne dass sich erhebliche Überschneidungen mit weiteren Ausgangsmaterialien ergäben. Zum Lackieren von Möbelteilen und anderen Objekten für ihre Skulpturen setzte Nevelson diese häufig auf Holztafeln, die sie anschließend – ganz im Sinne der Abfallvermeidung – als Untergrund für ihre Collagen nutzte. Häufig wurden diese Basen dann mit großen Stücken Pappe abgedeckt oder mit einer einheitlicheren Oberfläche versehen, manche Collagen fertigte sie aber auch ausschließlich und bewusst mit Sprühfarbe. Zur Gestaltung von Mustern und Formen improvisierte Nevelson Schablonen aus Holzresten oder Fundstücken, oder aber sie sprühte frei aus der Hand mit unterschiedlichem Abstand und wechselnder Intensität. Bei den Skulpturen wurde jedes Element vor seiner Befestigung in der Gesamtkonstruktion sorgfältig mit einer schwarzen, weißen oder goldenen Farbschicht überzogen, und nach der Zusammenfügung aller Teile folgte ein weiterer Farbauftrag. Im Unterschied dazu sind die Collagen mit einer Vielzahl von Methoden und fast ausschließlich in Schwarz lackiert. Gold und Weiß hingegen wurden zumeist durch die Verwendung von gefundenem Papier oder Folie erzielt.

Gebrauchsgegenstände

Für ihre Collagearbeiten verwendete Nevelson zwar zahlreiche Materialien und Objekte, die zuvor einen praktischen Nutzen erfüllt hatten, darunter Möbel, Behälter und Maschinenteile, doch behielten diese nur selten ihr funktionales Aussehen oder ihre ursprüngliche Form. So zeigt *Untitled*, um 1984 ↪ **Abb. 11**, eine Komposition in verschiedenen Schwarzschattierungen, eine große, mit dem Stiel nach oben befestigte Bürste mit fast unmerklichen Spuren roter Farbe an den Borsten. Umgeben ist sie von mehreren aufeinandergeklebten Stücken zerschnittenem und zerrissenem schwarzen Papier, der hölzerne Rahmen war anscheinend eine Schranktüreinfassung mit Schlüsselloch. Was zunächst wie ein einfacher Gebrauchsgegenstand (Bürste) wirkt, angeordnet in einem rechteckigen Rahmen (Schranktür), ruft sogleich alle möglichen Assoziationen auf – ob nun abstrakter, surrealer oder auch bio- oder anthropomorpher Art. Allgemein enthalten die Collagen aus der Kategorie der Gebrauchsgegenstände oftmals vertraute Dinge, die sich im kompositorischen Spiel zu abstrakten oder unkenntlichen Formen und Gebilden wandeln. Typische Bestandteile sind hölzerne Zahnräder, Bolzen und Ringe, Getränkedosen, Wäscheklammern, Papierrollen, Bilderrahmen, Bürstengriffe und Türklinken sowie intakte Holzbehälter.

In Nevelsons Collagen einbezogene Werkzeuge zeichnen sich häufig durch eine auffällige Dreidimensionalität aus und unterwandern insofern die Ausrichtung der Arbeit oder ihren Schwerpunkt. Die meisten Werke aus diesem Zyklus entstanden in den 1950er-Jahren, also in der Frühzeit von Nevelsons Beschäftigung mit der Collage, und erneut zu einem späteren Zeitpunkt in den 1980er-Jahren. Diese zeitliche Zuordnung ist nicht überraschend, zumindest nicht im Hinblick auf die erste Periode, verweist diese doch auf eine Phase des Übergangs in Nevelsons Praxis von der Anfertigung frei stehender Skulpturen zu Wandinstallationen. Auch wenn die mithilfe von Alltagsobjekten gefertigten Collagen nur einen vergleichsweise kleinen Teil ausmachen, sind sie insofern von Bedeutung, als sie unsere Vorstellung von Nevelsons Identität als einer *bricoleuse* prägen.

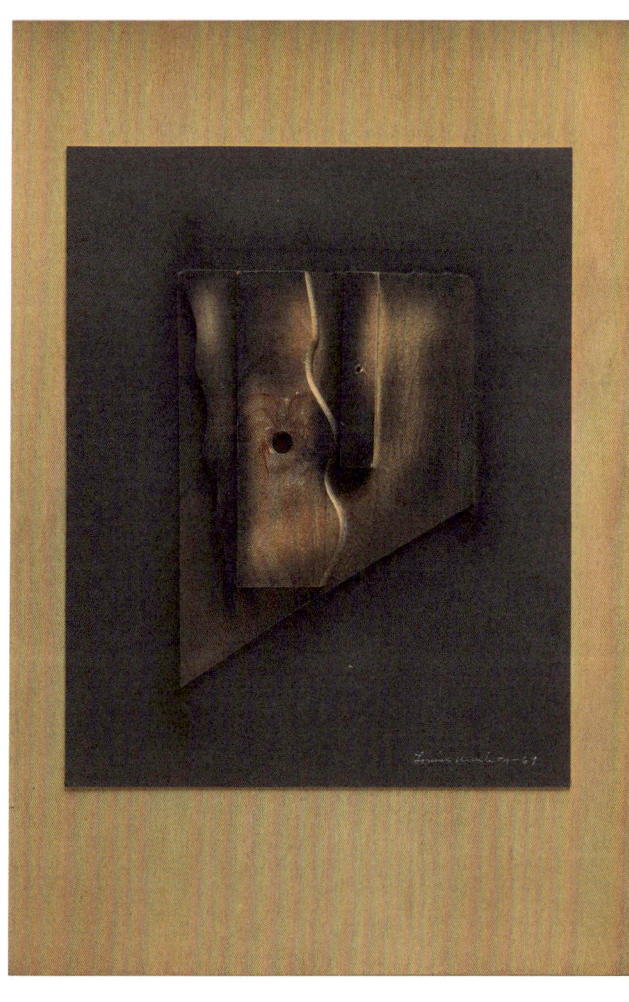

12 Untitled ca. 1984, cardboard, paint, paper, scrub brush and wood on board, 76 × 81.5 × 51 cm, Photo: Moderna Museet, Stockholm

Nevelson was often forced to flatten the packaging materials she used, chiefly various kinds of cardboard boxes, pasting them onto wooden panels as compressed or abstracted versions of their original forms. The most fundamental difference between the container collages and their counterparts in sculpture, therefore, lies in the question of appearance versus functionality. Many of Nevelson's sculptures were built as constellations of smaller wooden box units filled to the brim with furniture parts and wooden elements, then stacked on their sides to display their content in accumulation. The exploration of containment in the collages, on the other hand, is largely representational by nature, much thanks to the relative flatness of these works and their clear designation as wall-mounted. Containers are for the most part immediately recognizable for what they are, but their previous function is only rarely maintained even if conceptually emphasized.

Spray Paint

The use of spray paint in Nevelson's collages is far too extensive to represent a distinct category without substantial overlap with other source material. When painting furniture parts and other objects in preparation for sculptures, Nevelson often placed them on top of wooden panels, which she then used as backdrops for her collages in a manner consistent with her waste-not ideology. But while many of the panels were then concealed by large pieces of card, or transformed into more consistent surfaces, some collages were executed exclusively and intentionally in spray paint. In these Nevelson employed improvised stencils made from wooden offcuts or found objects to create patterns, shapes, or alternatively to engage in freehand compositions executed from different distances and at various intensities. In opposition to the painting process of her sculptures – in which each element was thoroughly coated in a layer of black, white, or gold in advance of its attachment to the overall construction, before the application of a second coat to the final work – the collages are painted in a broad range of methods and almost exclusively in black. Gold and white, on the other hand, are achieved through the use of found paper or foil in most works.

Objects-of-Use

While Nevelson appropriated into her collage work many materials and objects that were previously used for pragmatic purposes, including furniture, containers, and machinery parts, only in certain cases do these maintain their functional appearance or their intact shape. For example, in *Untitled*, ca. 1984 ↪ **fig. 11**, a composition in several shades of black presents a large brush hanging upside down with almost imperceptible traces of red residue in its hairs. The brush is surrounded by several pieces of cut and

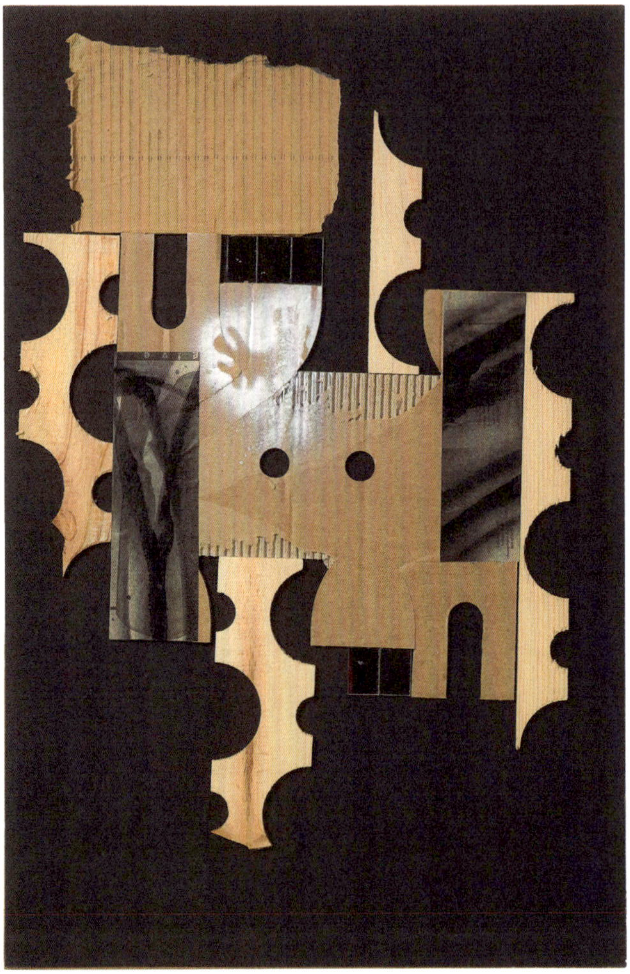

13 Untitled 1983, cardboard, mirror, paint and wood on board, 76 × 51 cm, Photo: Sammlung Goetz, Munich

Reststücke und Abfälle

Von allen Collage-Kategorien Nevelsons bezeugt die der »Reststücke« wohl am deutlichsten die ökologischen Anschauungen der Künstlerin: Diese Gruppe umfasst fast ausschließlich Holzreste aus Schreinereien oder von Baustellen, Möbelteile sowie skulpturale Elemente, die im Atelier der Künstlerin zugeschnitten wurden. Gegenüber den Collagen aus Gebrauchsgegenständen büßen die kombinierten Elemente und zerlegten Möbel etwas von ihrer funktionalen Erscheinung ein oder aber geben zu erkennen, dass sie nie eine Funktion besaßen. Einige von Nevelsons Collagen bestehen vollständig aus solchen Materialien, so etwa *Untitled* (1969) aus der Sammlung des Moderna Museet in Stockholm ↳ **Abb. 12.** Typischerweise aber enthalten die aus Reststücken und Abfällen gefertigten Collagen außerdem Materialien wie Papier, Sprühfarbe, Gebrauchsobjekte und vorgefertigte Holzfliesen. Ihre ungewöhnlichen Formen gestatten die Gestaltung einer großen Bandbreite von Mustern, die spielerisch, humorvoll, rhythmisch sind. Beispiele hierfür finden sich vor allem gegen Ende der 1970er- und Anfang der 1980er-Jahre, wie etwa in *Untitled*, 1983 ↳ **Abb. 13.**[4] Interessanterweise verknüpfen die Arbeiten dieser Kategorie mehrere übergreifende Merkmale der Kunst Nevelsons – vor allem die Wiederverwendung jedes Elements aus ihrem Arsenal in mehreren Stadien: als skulpturale Komponente, als Schablone für gesprayte Formen, als Modell für Kompositionen aus zerschnittenem oder zerrissenem Papier und als Ausgangsmaterial.

Zerschnittenes und zerrissenes Papier

In der Verwendung von zerrissenem Papier für die Collagen klingt die vor allem europäisch beeinflusste Praxis der *décollage affichiste* aus den frühen 1950er-Jahren an. Es ist ungewiss, inwieweit Nevelson mit Künstlern wie Mimmo Rotella, Jacques Villeglé, Raymond Hains und Wolf Vostell vertraut war. Diese rissen in ihren jeweiligen Städten systematisch Papier von Plakatwänden und legten damit faszinierende Kompositionen offen, die sich aus dem Nebeneinander der Schichtungen von Werbung ergaben. Ein Vergleich ist insofern aufschlussreich, als er das gemeinsame Streben in der Nachkriegszeit verdeutlicht, die Collage aus ihrem überschaubaren Maßstab zu lösen (auch wenn Nevelson dem Haushalt in der Wahl ihrer Werkmaterialen treu blieb). Typisch für ihre Collagen aus gerissenem Papier in den späten 1950er- und frühen 1960er-Jahren sind die großformatigen Bogen, von denen die Holztafeln fast vollständig bedeckt sind. Allmählich scheint sich die Künstlerin aber wieder dem haushaltsüblichen Papierformat zugewandt zu haben. Bald schon erschienen kleinere, intimere Kompositionen, montiert auf größere Holzträger, unter Einbeziehung von Packpapier, Gold- und Silberfolie, Wellpappe und einlagigem Karton, komplexen abstrakten Strichzeichnungen und Lithografien, Zeitungsausschnitten sowie Stücken von Schleifpapier, Fotos und Zierdeckchen aus Papier.

torn black paper pasted one on top of the other and framed by what appears to be a wooden cabinet door frame with a keyhole. What initially communicates itself as a simple utilitarian object (the brush) displayed through a rectangular frame (the cabinet door) soon lends itself to all manner of associations, whether abstract, surreal or even bio- or anthropomorphic. Indeed, the objects-of-use collages frequently present familiar objects that, through compositional play, shift into abstract or unrecognizable shapes and figures. Typical objects in this group include wooden cogs, bolts and rings, soda cans, clothes pegs, paper rolls, picture frames, brush and door handles, as well intact wooden containers.

Collages including tools in Nevelson's work are often characterized by their obtrusive three-dimensionality, frequently challenging the very orientation of the work or its center of gravity. Most of the works belonging to this cycle were executed early in Nevelson's engagement with collage, during the 1950s, and then again later in her life during the 1980s. This historic division is not surprising, at least with regards to the first period, as it indicates a transitional phase in Nevelson's practice from making free-standing sculptures to wall-mounted works. While the objects-of-use collages are a relatively small group within Nevelson's collage practice, their importance lies above all in the way they inform our reading of her identity as a *bricoleur*.

Offcuts And Debris

Of all Nevelson's collage categories, the offcuts are perhaps most indicative of her ecological ideology, relying almost entirely on leftover wood sections from carpentry workshops, building sites, and dismantled furniture, as well as sculptural elements that were cut in the artist's studio. In opposition to the objects-of-use collages, here the composite elements and out-of-use furniture items lose something of their functional appearance or otherwise indicate that they never possessed a function at all. While certain of Nevelson's collages are entirely composed of these elements, such as *Untitled*, 1969, from the collection of the Moderna Museet, Stockholm ↪ **fig. 12**, off-cut and debris collages typically incorporate additional materials, such as paper, spray paint, functional objects, and readymade wooden tiles. Owing to their odd shapes, the offcuts enabled Nevelson to achieve a broad range of patterns that were playful, humorous, and rhythmic. Examples of such compositions are most common towards the end of the 1970s and the early 1980s, such as *Untitled*, 1983 ↪ **fig. 13**.[4] In effect, the offcut and debris collages tie together several characteristics of Nevelson's practice in general – above all, how each element in her arsenal was used in multiple stages: as a sculptural component, a stencil for spray-painted shapes, a model for cut or torn paper compositions, and as source material.

Cut And Torn Papers

The use of torn papers in Nevelson's collages inevitably echoes the predominantly European practice of *décollage affichiste* from the beginning of the 1950s. It is uncertain to what extent Nevelson was aware of artists such as Mimmo Rotella, Jacques Villeglé, Raymond Hains, and Wolf Vostell, who systematically appropriated public noticeboards in their cities, tearing their layered surfaces to reveal exciting compositions made from the accumulation of advertising materials. The comparison remains instructive insofar as it demonstrates a shared post-war impulse take the practice of collage out of its domestic scale (even if Nevelson kept her allegiance to

Mustercollagen

Nevelsons Praxis, kleine Kompositionen oder interessante formale Elemente in einem größeren, rasterartigen Format zusammenzufügen, wird oft in Bezug gesetzt zu ihrem bildhauerischen Werk ab den 1950er-Jahren. Wo ihre Skulpturen jedoch auf dem Ansammeln und Verbinden von Bestandteilen zu einem kohärenten Arrangement beruhen, da erkunden ihre Collagen der 1960er-Jahre Konzepte der Unterteilung und Taxonomie als Möglichkeit, verschiedenartige Bilder in einem gemeinsamen Werk zusammenzuführen. Eines der ersten Experimente dieser Art, *Untitled* von 1967 ↪ **Abb. 14**, besteht aus einer Holztafel mit vier einzelnen Kompositionen, die jeweils auf einem eigenen Trägermaterial montiert sind. Drei der Collagen sind so nebeneinander angeordnet, als sollten sie eine Einheit bilden. Die vierte hingegen ist größer, stilistisch anders gestaltet und trägt in der rechten unteren Ecke ihres sich abhebenden Untergrunds die Signatur und Datierung der Künstlerin – wie zur Bezeugung ihrer eigenständigen Existenz als Kunstwerk. In solchen Mustercollagen verband Nevelson mitunter auch mehrere separate Kompositionen auf einem gemeinsamen Holzträger, wobei sich die Ausführung über einen Zeitraum von einem Jahrzehnt oder auch länger erstrecken konnte. Auch diese erhielten jeweils eine eigene Signatur. Um 1980 erinnerten solche komparativen Kompositionen zunehmend an eine Art visuelles Lexikon zu Nevelsons technischen Experimenten. Die Künstlerin richtete ihr Augenmerk nun vermehrt auf das Kollationieren einander ähnlicher technischer Verfahren, vergleichbar mit einem Katalog oder einer taxonomischen Studie zu biologischen, botanischen oder geologischen Arten oder Gruppen. Insofern bietet der Begriff der »Mustercollagen« eine wichtige, aber auch ungewöhnliche Sicht auf diesen Werkkomplex, der Nevelson nicht nur als Künstlerin, sondern auch als Sammlerin, Forscherin und als Enzyklopädistin ausweist.

Bei den sogenannten Musterkompositionen erweist sich die Einteilung der Collagen in Kategorien als wesentlich für ein Verständnis von Nevelsons Praxis, und zwar im Hinblick auf ihre ausgiebige Beschäftigung mit vielfältigen Produktionsweisen wie auch mit stilistischen Fragestellungen. Dass die Künstlerin kontinuierlich mit der Neubewertung und Analyse ihres ästhetischen Vokabulars befasst war, unterstreicht, dass das Sortieren nicht nur ein Grundzug ihrer künstlerischen Methodik ist, sondern auch als Verfahren unabdingbar ist für jeden Versuch der Deutung ihres Werkes. Dennoch wäre es falsch, in ihr eine Sammlerin zu sehen, jedenfalls im üblichen Wortsinn. Nevelsons Art der Beschaffung von Werkstoffen erinnert eher an die Methoden eines Schrotthändlers als die eines passionierten Sammlers. In welchem Zustand oder wie kostbar etwas auch war, sie nahm alles an sich, von hochwertigen Möbeln über Latten oder gebrochenes Sperrholz bis hin zu Gebrauchsgegenständen, Schreinereiabfällen und Holzverschnitt. Nichts wurde weggeworfen. Die größeren, dreidimensionalen Elemente wurden für die Skulpturen verwertet, die flacheren ebenso wie die kleineren in Skulpturen oder aber Collagen. Die für die bildhauerischen Arbeiten bestimmten Werkstoffe zeichnen sich durch ihre Langlebigkeit aus, wohingegen für die Collagen Karton,

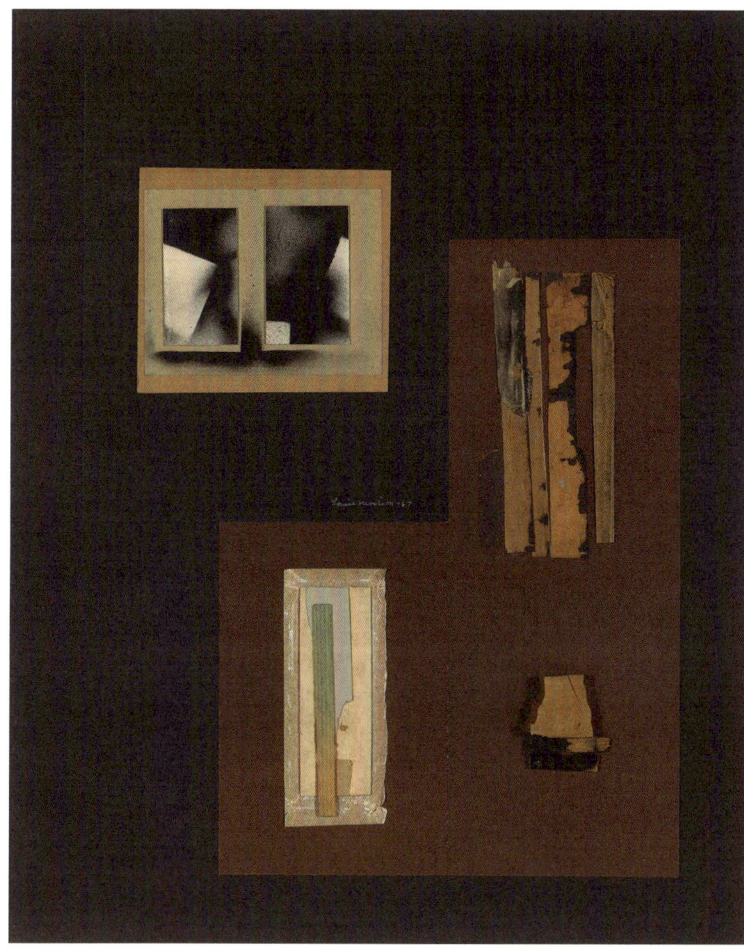

14 Untitled 1967, cardboard, paint, paper, sandpaper and wood on board, 101.5 × 81.5 cm, Photo: Fabio Mantegna, Fondazione Marconi, Milan

the home in her choice of materials). Indeed, during the late 1950s and early 1960s, Nevelson's torn paper collages are characterized by the use of large sheets of paper that cover her wood panel supports almost entirely. Over time, however, her collages appear to gravitate back toward the scale of paper as encountered in the domestic environment of her home. Smaller, more intimate compositions soon began to populate larger wooden supports, in which wrapping paper, foil (in gold and silver), corrugated and single-layer cardboard, intricate abstract line drawings and lithographs, pieces of sandpaper photographic materials, newspapers, and paper doilies were included.

Specimen Collages

The practice of combining small compositions or intriguing formal elements into a larger, grid-like format is often associated with Nevelson's sculptural work from the 1950s onwards. While her sculptures relied on fusion and the cohesive assembly of elements, her collages from the 1960s on began to explore concepts of division and taxonomy as ways to include distinct pictures within a single work. One of the first experiments of this kind, *Untitled*, 1967 ↪ **fig. 14**, presents four individual compositions on a wooden panel, each pasted on its own background. Three of the collages are laid side by side as if to merge into a unity, while the fourth is larger and stylistically different, bearing the artist's signature and date at the bottom right-hand corner of its distinct background, as if to testify to its independent existence as an artwork. Indeed, in such specimen

Papier und weitere empfindlichere Materialien zum Einsatz kamen, die eine behutsamere Behandlung erforderlich machten. Als Ausgangspunkt für ihre Collagen dienten Nevelson Abfälle und Überreste ihrer bildhauerischen Arbeit, Archiv- und Lagerbehälter ebenso wie für ihren persönlichen Gebrauch und für den Konsum bestimmte Alltagsgegenstände. Die Wahl dieser Materialien war klarer Ausdruck eines persönlichen Bekenntnisses der Künstlerin gegen Verschwendung, beginnend bei den Häusern, deren Inventar sie erwarb, über dessen Wiederverwendung in den Skulpturen bis hin zur Anfertigung von Collagen aus Alltagsresten und Abfallprodukten des eigenen Haushalts.

---

1 *Louise Nevelson: I Collages*, hg. von Bruno Corà (Ausst.-Kat. Fondazione Marconi, Mailand), Mailand 2016; *Louise Nevelson: The Way I Think is Collage*, hg. von Krystyna Gmurzynska und Mathias Rastorfer (Ausst.-Kat. Galerie Gmurzynska, Zürich), Zürich 2012; *Louise Nevelson: Collages, 1959–1986*, hg. von Andrea Alibrandi (Ausst.-Kat. Mara Coccia Arte Contemporanea, Rom/Galleria Il Ponte, Florenz), Florenz 2009.

2 In anderen Beiträgen habe ich die Kategorie der »Gebrauchsgegenstände« *(objects-of-use)* als »Nutzgegenstände« *(utilities)* bezeichnet.

3 Der vorliegende Text besteht aus überarbeiteten Exzerpten aus: *Out of Order: The Collages of Louise Nevelson*, hg. von Yuval Etgar (Ausst.-Kat. Galleria Marconi, Mailand), Mailand 2022. Die umfassende Originalpublikation enthält zudem einen erhellenden Essay von Pia Gottschaller mit ausführlichen Untersuchungen zu Techniken und Materialien in den Collagen Nevelsons.

4 Dieses Werk gehört zu den wenigen Beispielen im Œuvre Nevelsons, für die sie weiße Sprühfarbe verwendete.

collages, Nevelson would sometimes join several independent compositions onto a single wooden support, even though they were often executed over a period of a decade or longer. Again, each would be marked by a separate signature. By 1980, such comparative compositions began to resemble a kind of visual lexicon of her technical experiments. Now, focusing more often on collating similar types of technical procedures, as if in a catalogue or indeed a taxonomical study of a biological, botanical or geological species or group. Thus, the term »specimen collages« offers an important, albeit unusual, lens through which to view this body of work, revealing Nevelson not only as an artist, but also as a collector, researcher, and indeed an encyclopaedist.

It is through these so-called specimen compositions that the classification of Nevelson's collages into distinct categories emerges as essential to understanding her practice and the breadth of her engagement with various modes of production and stylistic questions. Her own interest in the constant re-evaluation and analysis of her aesthetic vocabulary confirms sorting not only as a intrinsic to her artistic method, but also renders it a necessary part of any attempt to continue and interpret her work. Despite the nature of Nevelson's practice, it would be wrong to suggest that she was a collector, certainly not in the conventional sense of the word. Nevelson's sourcing process resembled the work of a commercial junkyard merchant rather than a dedicated collector, operating an indiscriminate process of admitting items of varying condition and degrees of desirability – from quality furniture to laths or broken plywood, to utilitarian objects and carpenters' rejects and offcuts – into her custody. Nothing went to waste. The larger, three-dimensional elements went into making her sculptures; the flatter as well as smaller items could be used for either sculpture or collage. While the material designated for the sculptures was characterized by its durability, the collages incorporated cardboard, paper, and other perishable materials that required more careful treatment. As such, Nevelson's starting point for working on collages ranged from rejects and offcuts left over from her sculptural work, to archival and storage containers, to everyday items meant for her personal use and consumption. The choice of these materials was a clear expression of the artist's »waste not« ideology, which began with the homes whose contents she purchased, continued with its recycling in the form of sculpture, and ended with the making of collages using leftovers and waste from her own household.

---

1 *Louise Nevelson: I Collages*, ed. Bruno Corà (exh. cat. Fondazione Marconi, Milan), Milan 2016; *Louise Nevelson: The Way I Think Is Collage*, eds. Krystyna Gmurzynska, Robert Indiana, Bill Katz et al. (exh. cat. Galerie Gmurzynska, Zurich), Zurich 2012; *Louise Nevelson: Collages, 1959–1986*, ed. Andrea Alibrandi (exh. cat. Mara Coccia Arte Contemporanea, Rome and Galleria Il Ponte, Florence), Florence 2009.

2 On previous occasions I have referred to the category »objects-of-use« as »utilities«.

3 The present text is composed of edited excerpts from *Out of Order: The Collages of Louise Nevelson*, ed. Yugal Etgar (exh. cat. Galleria Marconi, Milan), Milan 2022. The original, comprehensive publication also includes an eye-opening essay by Pia Gottschaller, offering extensive technical and material analysis of Nevelson's collages.

4 This work is also a rare occasion in which Nevelson used white spray paint.

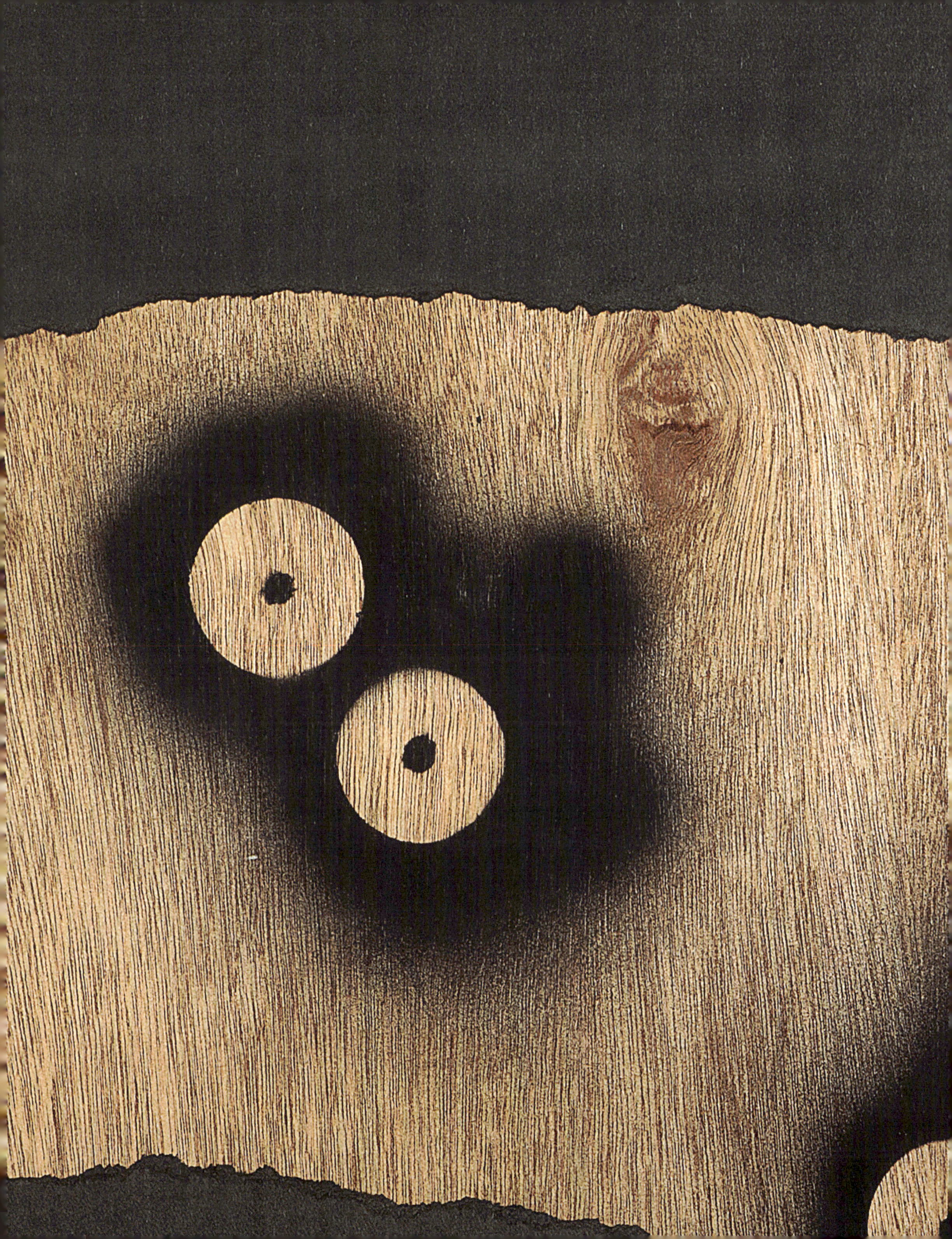

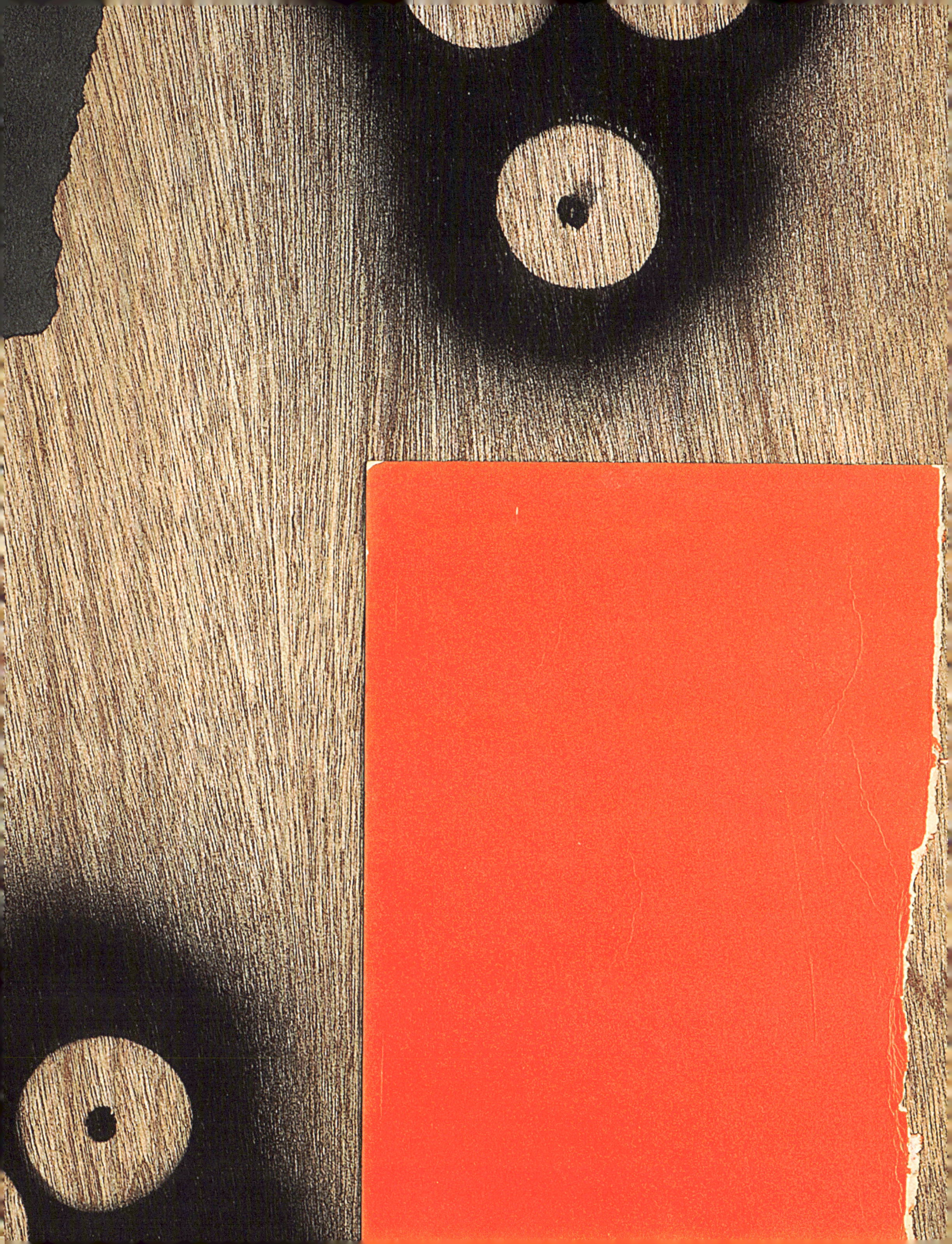

BIOGRAFIE

15 Louise Nevelson umgeben von ihren Collagen, New York 1974
Louise Nevelson among her collages, New York 1974, Photo: Ara Güler / Ara Güler Museum

Louise Nevelson wurde am 23. September 1899 als Leah Berliawsky in Pereislav-Khmelnytskyi, Russland (heute Ukraine), geboren. 1905 wanderte sie mit ihrer Familie in die Vereinigten Staaten aus; sie ließen sich in Rockland, Maine, nieder.

1920 heiratete sie Charles Nevelson und das Paar zog nach New York City, wo Louise Nevelson Schauspiel studierte und sich später an der Art Students League einschrieb. Auch nach der Geburt ihres Sohnes Myron (genannt Mike) 1922 versuchte sie, ihre künstlerische Laufbahn zu verfolgen.

1931 trennte sich Louise von Charles und gab Mike in die Obhut ihrer Eltern in Rockland, um nach München zu gehen. Hier studierte sie an der Kunstschule von Hans Hofmann und arbeitete als Filmstatistin in Wien und Berlin. Im Anschluss reiste sie nach Italien und Paris, wo sie insbesondere vom Kubismus begeistert war.

Sie kehrte 1932 nach New York zurück, um ihr Studium an der Art Students League fortzusetzen. In den folgenden Jahren nahm sie erneut Unterricht bei dem inzwischen emigrierten Hans Hofmann sowie bei George Grosz und Chaim Gross und arbeitete als Assistentin von Diego Rivera an der New Workers School, wo sie auch mit Frida Kahlo Bekanntschaft machte.

Nevelson begann 1941, mit gefundenen Objekten zu arbeiten. Ihre erste Einzelausstellung fand im selben Jahr in der Nierendorf Gallery in New York statt; es war die erste von mehreren Ausstellungen in dieser Galerie in einem Jahrzehnt, das für sie von Reisen nach Europa, der Beschäftigung mit Druckgrafik und der Arbeit am Sculpture Center in New York geprägt war. 1943 nahm sie an der von Peggy Guggenheim kuratierten Gruppenschau *Thirty-One Women* im Museum Art of This Century in New York teil. Noch geschwächt von einer Tumor-Operation und depressiven Phasen, bereiste Nevelson 1948 mit ihrer Schwester Anita Europa. Nach dieser schwierigen Zeit schöpfte sie neue Energie und es begann eine produktive Phase.

Anfang der 1950er-Jahre unternahm Louise Nevelson eine Reise nach Mexiko und Guatemala, außerdem fanden in diesen Jahren zahlreiche Ausstellungen ihrer Werke statt. Sie wurde in die National Association of American Woman Artists gewählt. Gleichzeitig entstanden die ersten Collagen, und 1955 verwendete sie erstmals Holzkästen als Container für ihre Assemblagen. Das Whitney Museum of American Art und das Museum of Modern Art New York kauften 1956 und 1958 erste Arbeiten an.

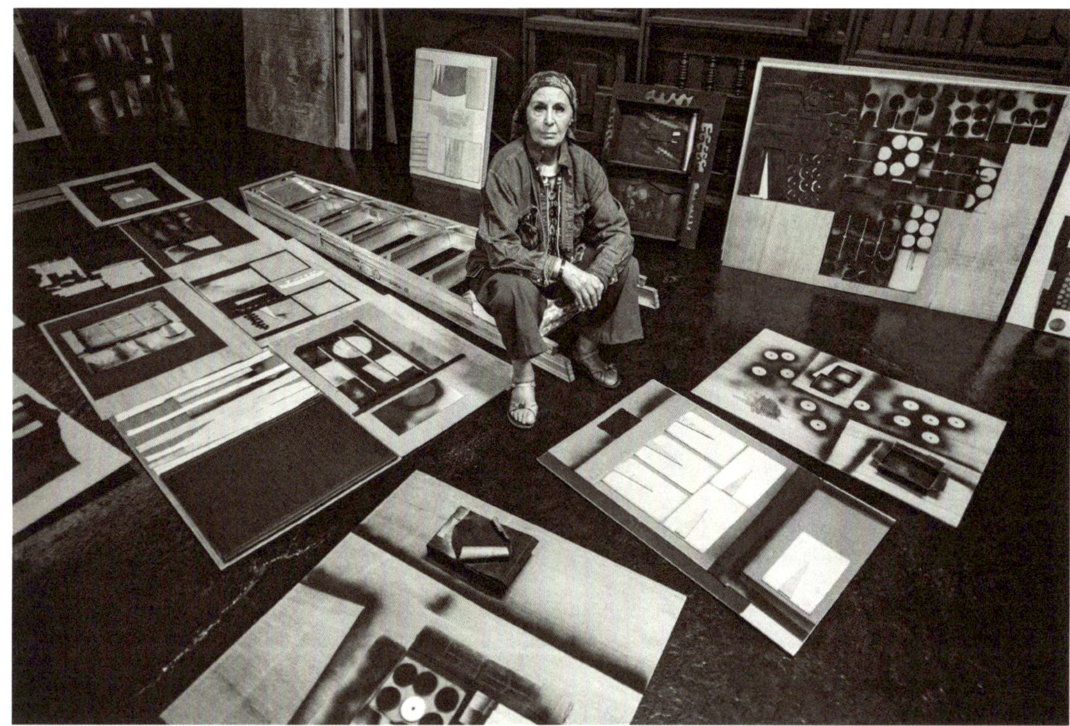

BIOGRAPHY

Louise Nevelson was born Leah Berliawsky in Pereislav-Khmelnytskyi, Russia (now Ukraine). She emigrated in 1905 with her family from czarist Russia to the United States in 1905, settling in Rockland, Maine.

In 1920, she married Charles Nevelson and the couple moved to New York City, where she studied drama and later enrolled at the Art Students League. Even after the birth of their son Myron (called Mike) in 1922, she continued to pursue her artistic career.

In 1931 Louise separated from Charles and left Mike in the care of her parents in Rockland to travel to Munich. Here she studied at Hans Hofmann's art school and worked as a film extra in Vienna and Berlin. She then traveled to Italy and Paris, where she was particularly enthusiastic about Cubism.

She returned to New York in 1932 to continue her studies at the Art Students League. In the following years, she again took lessons again with Hans Hofmann (who had since emigrated), as well as with George Grosz and Chaim Gross, and worked as an assistant to Diego Riviera at the New Workers' School, where she met Frida Kahlo.

Nevelson began working with found objects in 1941. Her first solo exhibition took place that same year at the Nierendorf Gallery, New York – the first of several with the gallery throughout a decade punctuated by travels to Europe, explorations in printmaking, and work at the Sculpture Center in New York. In 1943, she participated in the group exhibition *Thirty-One Women,* curated by Peggy Guggenheim, at the Museum of Art of This Century in New York.

In den 1960er-Jahren festigte sich ihr Ruf auch international, u. a. mit der Teilnahme an der Biennale in Venedig 1962 sowie an der Documenta III und IV in Kassel. Nach der ersten musealen Retrospektive ihres Werkes 1967 im Whitney Museum of American Art erhielt sie zwei Jahre später den ersten Auftrag für eine monumentale Skulptur im öffentlichen Raum von der Princeton University.

In den folgenden Jahren realisierte Nevelson zahlreiche weitere großformatige Skulpturen aus Cortenstahl für zentrale Plätze in US-amerikanischen Städten und arbeitete weiter intensiv an den Assemblagen und Collagen. 1983 erhielt sie als eine von mehreren Auszeichnungen die Goldmedaille für Skulptur von der American Academy of Arts and Letters sowie 1985 die National Medal of the Arts von Präsident Ronald Reagan.

Louise Nevelson starb am 17. April 1988 in New York.

Ausführliche Auflistungen aller Ausstellungen, Auszeichnungen sowie weitere biografische Stationen finden sich in folgender Publikation: *Louise Nevelson*, hg. von Germano Celant, Mailand 2012.

In the early 1950s, Nevelson traveled to to Mexico and Guatemala, and her work was exhibited widely. Among other honors, she was elected to the National Association of American Woman Artists. In the early years of the decade, she created her first collages, and in 1955 she used wooden crates as containers for her assemblages for the first time. The Whitney Museum of American Art and the Museum of Modern Art New York purchased works in 1956 and 1958.

In the 1960s, her international success was consolidated by her participation in the 1962 Venice Biennale and in documenta III and IV in Kassel. Following the first museum retrospective of her work at the Whitney Museum of American Art in 1967, she received her first commission for a monumental sculpture in a public space from Princeton University two years later.

Over the following years, Nevelson realized numerous other large-scale sculptures in Cor-Ten steel for public spaces in US cities and continued to work intensively on assemblages and collages. In 1983, she received the Gold Medal for Sculpture from the American Academy of Arts and Letters, and the National Medal of the Arts from President Ronald Reagan in 1985.

Louise Nevelson died on April 17, 1988, in New York City.

Detailed listings of all exhibitions, awards and other biographical milestones can be found in: *Louise Nevelson*, ed. by Germano Celant, Skira editore S.p.A., Milan 2012.

BILDNACHWEIS IMAGE CREDITS

Nº1
Gesprühte Poesie
Sprayed Poetry

1.1 o. T. Untitled 1956, Karton, Sprühfarbe auf Holzplatte, Cardboard and spray paint on board, 56 × 46 cm, Privatsammlung, Private Collection, Courtesy Fondazione Marconi and Gió Marconi, Milan, Photo: Gianni Ummarino

1.2 o. T. Untitled 1966, Karton, Sprühfarbe, Holz auf Holzplatte, Cardboard, spray paint and wood on board, 90 × 60 × 9 cm, Privatsammlung, Private Collection, Courtesy Fondazione Marconi and Gió Marconi, Milan, Photo: Alessandro Zambianchi

1.3 o. T. Untitled 1956, Karton, Sprühfarbe, Farbe, Holz auf Holzplatte, Cardboard, spray paint, paint and wood on board, 76 × 61 cm, Privatsammlung, Private Collection, Courtesy Fondazione Marconi and Gió Marconi, Milan, Photo: Gianni Ummarino

1.4 o. T. Untitled 1978, Karton, Sprühfarbe auf Holzplatte, Cardboard and spray paint on board, 88.8 × 60.8 × 0.9 cm, Privatsammlung, Private Collection, Courtesy Fondazione Marconi and Gió Marconi, Milan, Photo: Alessandro Zambianchi

1.5 o. T. Untitled 1977, Karton, Sprühfarbe, Metallfolie, Zeitungspapier, Papier auf Holzplatte, Cardboard, spray paint, metal foil, newsprint, lithograph and paper on board, 91.5 × 61 cm, Privatsammlung, Private Collection, Courtesy Fondazione Marconi and Gió Marconi, Milan, Photo: Gianni Ummarino

1.6 Night Sun I 1959, Holz, schwarze Farbe, Wood painted black, 293 × 164 × 27.5 cm, Privatsammlung, Private Collection, Courtesy Fondazione Marconi and Gió Marconi, Milan, Photo: Fabio Mantegna

1.7 o. T. Untitled 1957, Karton, Sprühfarbe, Papier, Holz auf Holzplatte, Cardboard, spray paint, paper and wood on board, 102 × 76 cm, Privatsammlung, Private Collection, Courtesy Fondazione Marconi and Gió Marconi, Milan, Photo: Gianni Ummarino

1.8 o. T. Untitled 1956, Karton, Sprühfarbe, Plastik, Holz auf Holzplatte, Cardboard, spray paint, plastic and wood on board, 76 × 61 cm, Privatsammlung, Private Collection, Courtesy Fondazione Marconi and Gió Marconi, Milan, Photo: Gianni Ummarino

1.9 o. T. Untitled 1972, Karton, Sprühfarbe auf Holzplatte, Cardboard and spray paint on board, 76.1 × 50.1 × 0.9 cm, Privatsammlung, Private Collection, Courtesy Fondazione Marconi and Gió Marconi, Milan, Photo: Alessandro Zambianchi

1.10 o. T. Untitled 1958, Karton, Sprühfarbe, Farbe, Papier, Holz auf Holzplatte, Cardboard, spray paint, paint, paper and wood on board, 102 × 76 cm, Privatsammlung, Private Collection, Courtesy Fondazione Marconi and Gió Marconi, Milan, Photo: Gianni Ummarino

1.11 o. T. Untitled 1957, Karton, Sprühfarbe, Lithografie, Holz auf Holzplatte, Cardboard, spray paint, lithograph and wood on board, 102 × 76 cm, Privatsammlung, Private Collection, Courtesy Fondazione Marconi and Gió Marconi, Milan, Photo: Gianni Ummarino

1.12 o. T. Untitled 1976, Karton, Sprühfarbe auf Holzplatte, Cardboard and spray paint on board, 88.8 × 60.6 × 1 cm, Privatsammlung, Private Collection, Courtesy Fondazione Marconi and Gió Marconi, Milan, Photo: Alessandro Zambianchi

1.13 o. T. Untitled ca. 1976, Holz, schwarze Farbe, Wood painted black, 203 × 111.5 cm, Privatsammlung, Private Collection, Courtesy Fondazione Marconi and Gió Marconi, Milan, Photo: Alessandro Zambianchi

1.14 o. T. Untitled 1976-1978-1980 (datiert dated), Karton, Sprühfarbe auf Holzplatte, Cardboard and spray paint on board, 60.7 × 48.5 × 1 cm, Privatsammlung, Private Collection, Courtesy Fondazione Marconi and Gió Marconi, Milan, Photo: Filippo Armellin

1.15 o. T. Untitled 1972, Karton, Sprühfarbe auf Holzplatte, Cardboard and spray paint on board, 76 × 50 × 0.9 cm, Privatsammlung, Private Collection, Courtesy Fondazione Marconi and Gió Marconi, Milan, Photo: Alessandro Zambianchi

1.16 o. T. Untitled 1956, Karton, Sprühfarbe, Holz auf Holzplatte, Cardboard, spray paint and wood on board, 90.6 × 90.7 × 3.8 cm, Privatsammlung, Private Collection, Courtesy Fondazione Marconi and Gió Marconi, Milan, Photo: Gianni Ummarino

1.17 o. T. Untitled 1974, Karton, Sprühfarbe, Farbe, Holz auf Holzplatte, Cardboard, spray paint, paint and wood on board, 91.5 × 61 cm, Privatsammlung, Private Collection, Courtesy Fondazione Marconi and Gió Marconi, Milan, Photo: Gianni Ummarino

1.18 World Garden IV 1959, Holz, Metall, schwarz bemalt, Wood and metal painted black, 152 × 40 × 28 cm, Museum Ludwig, Inv.-Nr. ML 76/SK 0266, Wallraf-Richartz-Museum 1976, Photo: © Rheinisches Bildarchiv Köln

Nº2
Die Suche nach dem Alltäglichen
The Search for the Everyday

2.1 Volcanic Magic XIII 1985, Karton, Sprühfarbe, Farbe, Holz auf Holzplatte, Cardboard, spray paint, paint and wood on board, 101 × 80.7 × 8 cm, Privatsammlung, Private Collection, Courtesy Fondazione Marconi and Gió Marconi, Milan, Photo: Alessandro Zambianchi

2.2 o. T. Untitled 1976, Schwarz bemaltes Holz, Wood painted black, 203.2 × 122 × 15.5 cm, Privatsammlung, Private Collection, Courtesy Fondazione Marconi and Gió Marconi, Milan, Photo: Alessandro Zambianchi

2.3 o. T. Untitled 1976–1978, Holz, schwarze Farbe, Wood painted black, 203.2 × 122 × 24.5 cm, Privatsammlung, Private Collection, Courtesy Fondazione Marconi and Gió Marconi, Milan, Photo: Alessandro Zambianchi

2.4 o. T. Untitled 1986, Karton, Farbe, Metall, Holz, Holzlöffel, Faserplatte, Holz auf Holzplatte, Cardboard, paint, metal, wood, wooden spoon, fiber building board and wood on board, 122 × 81.7 x 15 cm, Privatsammlung Private Collection, Courtesy Fondazione Marconi and Gió Marconi, Milan, Photo: Alessandro Zambianchi

2.5 Volcanic Magic XXXII 1985, Karton, Farbe, Holz auf Holzplatte, Cardboard, paint and wood on board, 129 × 100.5 × 9.5 cm, Privatsammlung, Private Collection, Courtesy Fondazione Marconi and Gió Marconi, Milan, Photo: Alessandro Zambianchi

2.6 o. T. Untitled 1982, Karton, Farbe, Holz auf Holzplatte, Cardboard, paint and wood on board, 76 × 51 cm, Privatsammlung, Private Collection, Courtesy Fondazione Marconi and Gió Marconi, Milan, Photo: Gianni Ummarino

2.7 o. T. Untitled 1981, Stoff, Farbe, Papier, Holz auf Holzplatte, Fabric, paint, paper and wood on board, 81 × 51 cm, Privatsammlung, Private Collection, Courtesy Fondazione Marconi and Gió Marconi, Milan, Photo: Gianni Ummarino

2.8 o. T. Untitled 1980, Collage auf bemaltem Holz, Collage on painted wood, 202.7 × 122 × 14 cm, Privatsammlung, Private Collection, Courtesy Fondazione Marconi and Gió Marconi, Milan, Photo: Alessandro Zambianchi

NO3
Vom Suchen und Finden
Searching and Finding

3.1 o. T. Untitled 1985, Farbe, Holz auf Holzplatte, Paint and wood on board, 136.9 × 91.3 × 2.5 cm, Privatsammlung, Private Collection, Courtesy Fondazione Marconi and Gió Marconi, Milan, Photo: Alessandro Zambianchi

3.2 o. T. Untitled 1982, Holz, Farbe auf Holzplatte, Wood and paint on board, 101.5 × 81.2 × 3 cm, Privatsammlung, Private Collection, Courtesy Fondazione Marconi and Gió Marconi, Milan, Photo: Alessandro Zambianchi

3.3 o. T. Untitled 1970, Karton, Farbe, Holz auf Holzplatte, Cardboard, paint and wood on board, 76 × 51 cm, Privatsammlung, Private Collection, Courtesy Fondazione Marconi and Gió Marconi, Milan, Photo: Gianni Ummarino

3.4 o. T. Untitled 1980, Karton, Holz auf Holzplatte, Cardboard and wood on board, 88.8 × 60.6 × 3.8 cm, Privatsammlung, Private Collection, Courtesy Fondazione Marconi and Gió Marconi, Milan, Photo: Alessandro Zambianchi

3.5 o. T. Untitled 1969, Karton, Holz auf Holzplatte, Cardboard and wood on board, 76.2 × 51.3 × 2.8 cm, Privatsammlung, Private Collection, Courtesy Fondazione Marconi and Gió Marconi, Milan, Photo: Alessandro Zambianchi

3.6 o. T. Untitled 1980, Holz, schwarze Farbe, Wood painted black, ca. 212 × 85 × 68 cm, Privatsammlung, Private Collection, Courtesy Fondazione Marconi and Gió Marconi, Milan, Photo: Fabio Mantegna

3.7 o. T. Untitled 1959, Karton, Holz auf Holzplatte, Cardboard and wood on board, 112 × 91.5 cm, Privatsammlung, Private Collection, Courtesy Fondazione Marconi and Gió Marconi, Milan, Photo: Gianni Ummarino

3.8 o. T. Untitled 1956, Karton, Sprühfarbe, Holz auf Holzplatte, Cardboard, spray paint and wood on board, 122 × 91 cm, Privatsammlung, Private Collection, Courtesy Fondazione Marconi and Gió Marconi, Milan, Photo: Gianni Ummarino

3.9 o. T. Untitled 1981, Karton, Sprühfarbe, Farbe, Holz auf Holzplatte, Cardboard, spray paint, paint and wood on board, 76 × 50.5 × 1.4 cm, Privatsammlung, Private Collection, Courtesy Fondazione Marconi and Gió Marconi, Milan, Photo: Alessandro Zambianchi

3.10 o. T. Untitled 1980, Karton, Holz auf Holzplatte, Cardboard and wood on board, 60.6 × 48.5 × 1.4 cm, Privatsammlung, Private Collection, Courtesy Fondazione Marconi and Gió Marconi, Milan, Photo: Alessandro Zambianchi

3.11 o. T. Untitled 1980, Karton, Farbe, Papier, Holz auf Holzplatte, Cardboard, paint, paper and wood on board, 88.8 × 60.6 × 2.2 cm, Privatsammlung, Private Collection, Courtesy Fondazione Marconi and Gió Marconi, Milan, Photo: Alessandro Zambianchi

NO4
Das fortwährende Entdecken
The Ongoing Discovery

4.1 o. T. Untitled 1968, Karton, Sprühfarbe, Zeitungspapier auf Holzplatte, Cardboard, spray paint, newsprint on board, 91.5 × 91.5 cm, Privatsammlung, Private Collection, Courtesy Fondazione Marconi and Gió Marconi, Milan, Photo: Gianni Ummarino

4.2 o. T. Untitled 1967, Karton, Farbe auf Holzplatte, Cardboard and paint on board, 91.4 × 91.2 × 0.8 cm, Privatsammlung, Private Collection, Courtesy Fondazione Marconi and Gió Marconi, Milan, Photo: Alessandro Zambianchi

4.3 o. T. Untitled 1959, Karton, Sprühfarbe, Zeitungspapier, Holz auf Holzplatte, Cardboard, spray paint, newsprint and wood on board, 122 × 91.5 cm, Privatsammlung, Private Collection, Courtesy Fondazione Marconi and Gió Marconi, Milan, Photo: Gianni Ummarino

4.4 Moon Spikes IV 1955, Holz, schwarze Farbe, Wood painted black, 93.5 × 108.3 × 25.5 cm, Privatsammlung, Private Collection, Courtesy Fondazione Marconi and Gió Marconi, Milan, Photo: Fabio Mantegna

4.6 o. T. Untitled 1963, Karton, Metallfolie auf Holzplatte, Cardboard and metal foil on board, 91.5 × 61 cm, Privatsammlung, Private Collection, Courtesy Fondazione Marconi and Gió Marconi, Milan, Photo: Gianni Ummarino

4.7 o. T. Untitled 1958, Karton, Metallfolie, Papier auf Holzplatte Cardboard, metal foil and paper on board, 102 × 75.8 × 1.3 cm, Privatsammlung, Private Collection, Courtesy Fondazione Marconi and Gió Marconi, Milan, Photo: Alessandro Zambianchi

4.8 o. T. Untitled 1959, Karton, Sprühfarbe, Metallfolie, Papier, Holz auf Holzplatte, Cardboard, spray paint, metal foil, paper and wood on board, 117 × 91.5 cm, Privatsammlung, Private Collection, Courtesy Fondazione Marconi and Gió Marconi, Milan, Photo: Gianni Ummarino

4.9 o. T. Untitled 1961, Karton, Papier auf Holzplatte, Cardboard and paper on board, 91.5 × 61 cm, Privatsammlung, Private Collection, Courtesy Fondazione Marconi and Gió Marconi, Milan, Photo: Gianni Ummarino

4.10 o. T. Untitled 1963, Karton, Sprühfarbe, Metallfolie, Papier, Holz auf Holzplatte, Cardboard, spray paint, metal foil, paper and wood on board, 91.4 × 60.3 × 0.8 cm, Privatsammlung, Private Collection, Courtesy Fondazione Marconi and Gió Marconi, Milan, Photo: Alessandro Zambianchi

4.11 o. T. Untitled 1963, Karton, Papier, Holz auf Holzplatte, Cardboard, paper and wood on board, 91.2 × 60.6 × 2.2 cm, Privatsammlung, Private Collection, Courtesy Fondazione Marconi and Gió Marconi, Milan, Photo: Alessandro Zambianchi

4.12 o. T. Untitled 1960, Karton, Metallfolie, Papier auf Holzplatte, Cardboard, metal foil and paper on board, 91.2 × 91.6 × 1 cm, Privatsammlung, Private Collection, Courtesy Fondazione Marconi and Gió Marconi, Milan, Photo: Alessandro Zambianchi

4.13 o. T. Untitled 1956, Karton, Metallfolie, Papier auf Holzplatte, Cardboard, paint, metal foil, printed paper and wood on board, 122 × 91 cm, Privatsammlung, Private Collection, Courtesy Fondazione Marconi and Gió Marconi, Milan, Photo: Gianni Ummarino

4.14 o. T. Untitled 1957, Karton, Metallfolie, Papier, Holz auf Holzplatte, Cardboard, metal foil, paper and wood on board, 102 × 76 cm, Privatsammlung Private Collection, Courtesy Fondazione Marconi and Gió Marconi, Milan, Photo: Gianni Ummarino

4.15 o. T. Untitled 1963, Karton, Metallfolie, Papier, Bleistift auf Holzplatte, Cardboard, metal foil, paper and pencil on board, 91.5 × 61 cm, Privatsammlung Private Collection, Courtesy Fondazione Marconi and Gió Marconi, Milan, Photo: Gianni Ummarino

4.16 o. T. Untitled 1958, Karton, Papier auf Holzplatte, Cardboard and paper on board, 122 × 91.5 cm, Privatsammlung, Private Collection, Courtesy Fondazione Marconi and Gió Marconi, Milan, Photo: Gianni Ummarino

4.17 o. T. Untitled 1981, Karton, Sprühfarbe auf Holzplatte, Cardboard and spray paint on board, 89 × 61 cm, Privatsammlung, Private Collection, Courtesy Fondazione Marconi and Gió Marconi, Milan, Photo: Gianni Ummarino

4.18 o. T. Untitled 1961, Karton, Metallfolie, Papier auf Holzplatte, Cardboard, metal foil and paper on board, 91.5 × 61 cm, Privatsammlung, Private Collection, Courtesy Fondazione Marconi and Gió Marconi, Milan, Photo: Gianni Ummarino

4.19 o. T. Untitled 1977, Karton, Sprühfarbe, Metallfolie, Zeitungspapier, Kugelschreiber, Papier auf Holzplatte, Cardboard, spray paint, metal foil, newsprint, ballpoint pen and paper on board, 91.4 × 61 × 2 cm, Privatsammlung, Private Collection, Courtesy Fondazione Marconi and Gió Marconi, Milan, Photo: Gianni Ummarino

4.20 o. T. Untitled 1977, Karton, Metallfolie, Lithografie, Papier auf Holzplatte, Cardboard, metal foil, lithograph and paper on board, 91.5 × 61 cm, Privatsammlung, Private Collection, Courtesy Fondazione Marconi and Gió Marconi, Milan, Photo: Gianni Ummarino

4.21 o. T. Untitled 1976, Karton, Sprühfarbe, Zeitungspapier auf Holzplatte, Cardboard, spray paint and newsprint on board, 60.6 × 50. 7 × 0.9 cm, Privatsammlung, Private Collection, Courtesy Fondazione Marconi and Gió Marconi, Milan, Photo: Alessandro Zambianchi

4.22 o. T. Untitled 1976, Karton, Farbe, Metallfolie, Lithografie auf Holzplatte, Cardboard, paint, metal foil and lithograph on board, 60.5 × 50. 7 × 0.9 cm, Privatsammlung, Private Collection, Courtesy Fondazione Marconi and Gió Marconi, Milan, Photo: Alessandro Zambianchi

4.23 o. T. Untitled 1976, Karton, Sprühfarbe, Metallfolie, Zeitungspapier, Papier auf Holzplatte, Cardboard, spray paint, metal foil, newsprint and paper on board, 60.4 × 50.8 × 0.9 cm, Privatsammlung, Private Collection, Courtesy Fondazione Marconi and Gió Marconi, Milan, Photo: Alessandro Zambianchi

4.24 City Series 1974, Holz, schwarze Farbe, Wood painted black, 245 × 380 × 6 cm, Privatsammlung, Private Collection, Courtesy Fondazione Marconi and Gió Marconi, Milan, Photo: Gianni Ummarino

№5
Die Suche nach Struktur und Ordnung
The Search for Structure and Order

5.1 The Golden Pearl 1962, Holz, goldene Farbe, Wood painted gold, 176.1 × 97.4 × 23.6 cm, Privatsammlung, Private Collection, Courtesy Fondazione Marconi and Gió Marconi, Milan, Photo: Gianni Ummarino

5.2 o. T. Untitled 1982, Karton, Dosen auf Holzplatte, Cardboard and cans on board, 101.6 × 81 × 1.7 cm, Privatsammlung, Private Collection, Courtesy Fondazione Marconi and Gió Marconi, Milan, Photo: Filippo Armellin

5.3 o. T. Untitled 1977–1980, Karton, Holz auf Holzplatte, Cardboard and wood on board, 101.4 × 80.7 × 2.9 cm, Privatsammlung, Private Collection, Courtesy Fondazione Marconi and Gió Marconi, Milan, Photo: Alessandro Zambianchi

5.4 Ancient Secrets II 1964, Holz, schwarze Farbe, Wood painted black, 81.1 × 133 × 12 cm, Privatsammlung, Private Collection, Courtesy Fondazione Marconi and Gió Marconi, Milan, Photo: Niels Fabæk

5.5 o. T. Untitled 1978–1980, Karton, Farbe, Papier, Holz auf Holzplatte, Cardboard, paint, paper and wood on board, 101.5 × 80.9 × 1.2 cm, Privatsammlung, Private Collection, Courtesy Fondazione Marconi and Gió Marconi, Milan, Photo: Filippo Armellin

5.6 o. T. Untitled 1973–1978, Karton, Sprühfarbe, Papier auf Holzplatte, Cardboard, spray paint and paper on board, 100.7 × 81 × 1.3 cm, Privatsammlung, Private Collection, Courtesy Fondazione Marconi and Gió Marconi, Milan, Photo: Filippo Armellin

5.7 o. T. Untitled 1967, Karton, Sprühfarbe, Farbe, Papier, Holz auf Holzplatte, Cardboard, spray paint, paint, paper and wood on board, 101.5 × 81.5 × 4.9 cm, Privatsammlung, Private Collection, Courtesy Fondazione Marconi and Gió Marconi, Milan, Photo: Fabio Mantegna

5.8 End of the Day XXII 1972, Holz, schwarze Farbe, Wood painted black, 87 × 47.5 × 19 cm, Privatsammlung, Private Collection, Courtesy Fondazione Marconi and Gió Marconi, Milan, Photo: Fabio Mantegna

Weitere Bildseiten
Further image pages

12/13 o. T. (Ausschnitt) Untitled (Detail) 1957, Karton, Sprühfarbe, Papier und Holz auf Holzplatte, Cardboard, spray paint, paper and wood on board, 102 × 76 cm, Privatsammlung, Private Collection, Courtesy Fondazione Marconi and Gió Marconi, Milan, Photo: Gianni Ummarino

14 Louise Nevelson umgeben von ihren Collagen, New York 1974 Louise Nevelson among her collages, New York 1974, Photo: Ara Güler/ Ara Güler Museum

26/27 o. T. (Ausschnitt) Untitled (Detail) 1977, Karton, Metallfolie, Lithografie, Papier auf Holzplatte, Cardboard, metal foil, lithograph and paper on board, 91.5 × 61 cm, Privatsammlung, Private Collection, Courtesy Fondazione Marconi and Gió Marconi, Milan, Photo: Gianni Ummarino

122 Louise Nevelson, ca. 1965, Photo: Ugo Mulas, Archives of American Art, Series 9, Box 14, Folder 15/Ugo Mulas Archives

134 Louise Nevelson, New York 1974, Photo: Ara Güler/ Ara Güler Museum

148/149 o. T. (Ausschnitt) Untitled (Detail) 1958, Karton, Sprühfarbe, Farbe, Papier und Holz auf Holzplatte, Cardboard, spray paint, paint, paper and wood on board, 102 × 76 cm, Privatsammlung, Private Collection, Courtesy Fondazione Marconi and Gió Marconi, Milan, Photo: Gianni Ummarino

---

IMPRESSUM
IMPRINT

Dieser Katalog erscheint anlässlich der Ausstellung This catalogue is published on the occasion of the exhibition

Louise Nevelson
Die Poesie des Suchens
The Poetry of Searching

Museum Wiesbaden
31. Oktober October 2025 – 15. März March 2026

Ausstellung Exhibition

Kuratorin Curator
Valerie Ucke
Museum Wiesbaden
Kunstsammlungen Art collections

Ausstellungsassistenz Exhibition assistance
Bettina Löwen

Direktor Director
Andreas Henning

Verwaltungsleitung Administrative management
Patricia Becker-Matthews

Kustoden Custodians
Jörg Daur, Peter Forster, Roman Zieglgänsberger

Presse- und Öffentlichkeitsarbeit
Press and public relations
Martina Brand, Susanne Hirschmann, Sarah Schach, Sarah Schadt

Registrarin Registrar
Caren Jones

Digital Unit und and IT
Thessa Brenner, Helene Kokenbrink, Marc Lieser, Alexander Rücker

Fotografie und Bildarchiv
Photography and picture archive
Bernd Fickert

Mediengestaltung Media design
Theresa Duck

Restaurierung Restoration
Anne-Sophie Bennke, Jana Merseburg, Pascale Regnault, Ines Unger

Bildung und Vermittlung Education and mediation
Daniel Altzweig, Ann-Katrin Spieß

Haustechnik und Werkstatt
Building services and workshop
Renato Coraggioso, Michael Edler, Johanna Faupel, Michael Krag, Christian Rücker

FSJ Kultur Cultural service volunteer
Elias Bittner, Marei Löffler

Publikation Catalogue

Herausgeberin Editor
Valerie Ucke, Museum Wiesbaden

Redaktion Editorial lead
Valerie Ucke, Museum Wiesbaden

Bildredaktion Picture editing
Elias Bittner, Museum Wiesbaden

Projektmanagement Hirmer Verlag
Project management Hirmer Publishers
Judith Kárpáty

Übersetzungen aus dem Französischen ins Deutsche
Translations from the French into German
Birgit Lamerz-Beckschäfer (Essay Horvath)

Übersetzungen aus dem Französischen ins Englische
Translations from the French into English
David Radzinowicz (Essay Horvath)

Übersetzungen aus dem Englischen ins Deutsche
Translations from the English into German
Ursula Fethke (Essay Etgar)

Übersetzungen aus dem Deutschen ins Englische
Translations from the German into English
Gérard Goodrow (Essay Ucke, Vorwort Foreword)

Deutsches Lektorat German Copy-editing
Barbara Delius

Englisches Lektorat English Copy-editing
Olivia Parkes

Buchgestaltung Book design
Uta Kopp, Eva-Maria Bolz

Herstellung Manufacturing
Studio Uta Kopp

Produktion Hirmer Verlag
Production Hirmer Publishers
Hannes Halder

Lithografie Prepress
Tilman Lothspeich

Papier Paper
140g/qm Arena Smooth Natural

Schriften Typefaces
Gimlet, Twinczyk

Druck und Bindung Printing and binding
Beltz Grafische Betriebe, Bad Langensalza

Printed in Germany

Bibliografische Information der Deutschen Nationalbibliothek
Die Deutsche Nationalbibliothek verzeichnet diese Publikation in der Deutschen Nationalbibliografie; detaillierte bibliografische Daten sind im Internet über https://www.dnb.de abrufbar.

Bibliographic information published by the Deutsche Nationalbibliothek
The Deutsche Nationalbibliothek lists this publication in the Deutsche Nationalbibliografie; detailed bibliographic data are available online at https://www.dnb.de.

ISBN 978-3-7774-4647-9

Museum Wiesbaden
Hessisches Landesmuseum für Kunst und Natur
Friedrich-Ebert-Allee 2
65185 Wiesbaden
www.museum-wiesbaden.de

HIRMER VERLAG
Geschäftsführerin Managing Director
Kerstin Ludolph
Bayerstraße 57–59
80335 München Munich

hirmerverlag.de
hirmerpublishers.com
hirmerpublishers.co.uk

Cover Vorderseite Cover image
o. T. Untitled 1956 Karton, Sprühfarbe, Holz auf Holzplatte, Cardboard, spray paint and wood on board, 122 × 91 cm, Privatsammlung, Private Collection, Courtesy Fondazione Marconi and Gió Marconi, Milan, Photo: Gianni Ummarino